Praise for:

What Smart Teenagers Kn
Relationships and Sex®

MW00909826

"I can't believe an adult figured this out and put it in a book. This is the best teenage dating book I've ever seen."
– **Janet Krupin**, age 15, Kennewick, WA

"Every once in a while a door to your teen's world is opened. This book is a key that will take you to the heart of what's on a teenager's mind."
– **Jack Canfield**, Co-Author *Chicken Soup for the Teenage Soul®*

"When I was given a copy of *What Smart Teenagers Know*... I didn't think my 13-year old daughter would be interested because she's so young. When she saw it she said, "Oh, what's this?" I couldn't get her to put it down. What amazed me the most were the great things we talked about afterwards. I had no idea this would strike such a chord with her."
– **Dina Castillo**, Professor and parent of a teen daughter

"From breaking the ice to breaking up, Deborah Hatchell covers all the basics of romantic relationships in a no-nonsense, easy-to-access way. Should be required reading for all romantically curious teenagers—which is 99% of all teenagers!"
– **Dr. Mike Riera**, Author, *Staying Connected To Your Teenager:*
How To Keep Them Talking To You
And How To Hear What They're Really Saying

"It's amazing — this book explained the *exact* problems I was going through, from what I was feeling, to even what my boyfriend was thinking."
– **Alexandra**, age 17, Florida

This comprehensive source for teenagers covers dating, relationships, and sex, and covers them well while weaving such themes as self-esteem, trust, mutual respect, thoughtful decision making, and communication throughout each chapter. It would be an excellent tool for parents, teachers, clergy, and health professionals to reach teens and prevent the problems parents dread.
– **ForeWord Magazine**

What SMART TEENAGERS Know...

About Dating, Relationships and Sex®

Deborah Hatchell

PIPER BOOKS
Santa Barbara, California

What Smart Teenagers Know...About Dating, Relationships and Sex®
Copyright © 2003 Deborah Hatchell

All rights reserved.

Printed in the United States of America

First Printing, June 2003

Cover design © 2003 Peri Peloni, Knockout Designs

PIPER BOOKS

For reprint permission, please write:
Piper Books
P.O. Box 60625
Santa Barbara, CA 93160
info@piperbooks.net

Hatchell, Deborah
    What smart teenagers know – about dating,
    relationships and sex/by Deborah Hatchell.
    p. cm.
    Includes bibliographical references and index.
    LCCN 2003101195
    ISBN 0-9722819-0-8

    1. Dating (Social customs) – Juvenile literature. 2. Interpersonal relations in adolescence – Juvenile literature. 3. Sexual ethics for teenagers – Juvenile literature. 4. Separation (Psychology) – Juvenile literature [1. Dating (Social customs) 2. Interpersonal relations. 3. Sexual ethics.]   I. Title.

HQ801.H38 2003   646.7'7'0835
                        QB133-1150

Disclaimer:

The author and publisher want you to know that this book is only one of many books and resources available on the subject of teenage relationships and sex. No part of this book is to be considered medical, psychological or legal advice. Please seek professional care from a licensed physician or a mental health professional if your situation requires it.

For Jason

Acknowledgements

Nothing worthwhile is ever done quickly or without the help of many. Many individuals supported and encouraged me while I completed this project. It was a challenge to boil down my thanks to a single line, which can't begin to express my appreciation.

My teenage son, Jason, asked me to write this book. His help in getting teenagers to complete surveys, read the manuscripts and participate in discussions was critical. Thank you, Jason, for your unending patience and encouragement. Your idea has been well received!

My mom, Linda Beckwith, whose constant enthusiasm, support and love saw me through the times I wanted to give up. My dad, Howard Beckwith, who helped me find the rhythm I needed in my second draft. My dear friends, Jim Kreider and Cindy Holland, who steadfastly inquired about the progress of the manuscript and pushed me to always think bigger than I wanted. I appreciate your editing, feedback, honesty and cheerleading. Sonja Lauren, my East Coast teen connection, I appreciate your help. Thank you all for believing in me.

Many thanks to all the teens who shared their stories with me and allowed them to be included in the book. To those who wish to remain anonymous, I respect your decision. You know who you are and I am grateful to have included your stories. To those few who were willing to have their real names used, I applaud your courage; thank you to Billy Fletcher, Daniel Cohen, Ashley Powell and, of course, Jason Gordon.

Also, many thanks to the teen and adult readers who carefully read several versions of the manuscript and provided important feedback and insight, with special thanks to Billy Fletcher, Brian Kettler, Jennifer Holland, Tiffany Werner, Tammy McKenzie, Mark Tran, Katherine Holland, Tom Tran, Miguel Elias, Chuck Stillwell, William Freeland, Ashley Powell, Michael Leon, Jan Bates, Cindy Holland, Linda Beckwith, Jim Kreider, Inga Canfield, and Dr. Clara Haignere of the Department of Public Health at Temple University.

Thank you to publicist Jodee Blanco for her evaluation and encouragement at a critical time. Thank you to Cathy Portz for her brilliant design with the 4smarteenagers.com website. Steve Klinhenn, for his help with gathering research. Rob Reilly, for saving me from an ocean of typos and commas – I owe you a box of red pencils! Rick Reeve for his unending patience with the interior design and many refinements.

Thanks also to all the others who helped, directly or indirectly, including The Leadership Group with Trygve Duryea. Finally, thank you to Jack Canfield and Patty Aubery for being such great mentors.

Contents

Contents

*Experience is a hard teacher because she gives
the test first, the lesson afterwards.*

—Vernon Sander's Law

Introduction: About Teens & Parents

Many teenagers who have gone through puberty have the physical bodies of adults. They also have many of the same needs and desires, both emotionally and sexually, as adults. A teen's biggest liability in a relationship is that they lack a frame of reference. Because these are all new experiences, they don't have a context to which they can refer back and say, "Oh, yeah. I know what will happen next because I've done this before." So, a teenager's decision-making process lacks the experience of an adult. They are more prone to make painful mistakes while in love.

Well, how *do* teenagers learn about relationships? Mostly through trial and error, which can take years (and many broken hearts) to learn from. Isn't there an easier way for teens to learn about love? Well, this book proposes a revolutionary idea: Teach teenagers relationship skills.

The goal of this book is to make you smart about dating, relationships and sex so you can avoid unnecessary heartbreak.

We'll cover every stage of a typical relationship: From the very beginning (attraction and flirting) through to the end (breaking up and grieving). The chapter on sex isn't a beginner's guide; it assumes that you understand basic anatomy and know where babies come from. You'll find a great resource section at the back of this book, which lists titles of other books that cover the basic information.

Teens Helped Write This

While doing the research for this book, I worked with groups of teenagers to find out what they wanted to know, what issues and problems they encountered in dating and relationships and, ultimately, what they thought about the book at various stages of development. Teenagers gave me **a lot** of input for this book!

The Parents Freaked Out

I also worked with groups of parents to get their feedback, as well. When I talked with parents, almost all of them freaked out when they heard the title of the book. Without even reading the book, many immediately assumed that I had written a sexually explicit how-to manual, or that sex was being "promoted" to their teens. Several angry fathers thought this book would give guys a step-by-step guide to get their daughters into bed! Some of the parents visibly squirmed with discomfort when I said the words penis and vagina. None of them understood that *relationships* were the main focus of the book—not sex.

I have to admit that this wasn't the reaction I was hoping for. So, I did some more research and found that many parents have a hard time talking to their teens about sex. Some parents are so afraid of their teens being sexually active that they even keep them out of the health (sex ed) classes at school. What shocked me was that these same parents, who don't want to talk to their teens about sex, were teenagers themselves during the '70s, when the big Sexual Revolution was in full swing!

Why It's Hard for Parents

Some parents have a hard time coping with their 'baby' growing up. For some, the idea that their 'little kid' is in love can be overwhelming because it's a big sign that their teen is creating their own identity, separate from their parents. For other parents, they want to protect their kids from experiences that could cause them pain or hurt. That's understandable, but these parents have forgotten what it was like to be a teenager. They have lost touch with the depth of emotions that they felt in their romantic relationships as teens. They forgot about the sexual feelings. They forgot about the confusion, embarrassment and feeling alone with their questions. In the effort to protect their teens' hearts, these well-meaning parents are not giving their teenagers information about how to protect themselves against potentially fatal infections.

I thought, Wow! If parents from the Sexual Revolution generation were uncomfortable talking about sex to their teens, then it's easy to guess that previous generations were even more reluctant to talk about sex. So, while this book was written originally for teenagers about relationships, its secondary purpose is for parents to use to talk to their teenagers about dating, relationships and sex.

Now I realize that your parents might freak out if they see you reading this book. You should expect it. They're just afraid for you. It's a parent thing. So, to make it easier for you, I've written a short note to your parents to help them understand the purpose of this book and why I wrote it. You'll find this note behind the last chapter. It's titled, *A Note To Parents*. Pretty original, huh?

No man is wise enough by himself.

—Titus Maccius Plautus (254 - 184 BC), Miles Gloriosus

Why Smart Teenagers?

"You! It's all your fault. If it weren't for you and that book, I wouldn't be in this mess," said Brian, with a smile on his face.

I was confused as I walked towards him. Brian is a 19 year old who had read one of the final versions of this book before it went to press. I hadn't seen him for a month since he read it. Brian was a nice guy, cute and outgoing, but had never had a real girlfriend before. Until now.

"I didn't have even one girlfriend before. Now, I have *five* girls interested in me! It's crazy!!" He sounded exasperated, but happy.

Brian went on to tell me how he liked the book, but didn't really give it a thought until he started to follow some of the suggestions. All of a sudden, girls were really interested in him. He was enjoying his newfound dating skills, but confessed that although he was dating the five girls just casually, he wanted to make a decision and start dating only one exclusively. His choice was tough because all the girls were great.

I was happy that the book was making a difference.

The Birth of a Book

Now let me tell you how this book came to be written. It's an unusual story. A story of many Post-it® notes stuck around a computer screen. It started when my 16 year old son, Jason, began his first dating relationship.

Jason is an only child and I'm a single parent, so we've always been very close. That level of closeness was about to pay off. He and his girlfriend of six months were having serious problems in their relationship. Jason and I talked a lot during that time and I gave him suggestions on how to deal with the situation. There was so much information that he asked me to write it down on Post-it® notes, which he stuck around his computer screen. Eventually, he brought all the yellow pieces of paper to me and asked if I'd type and organize them so he could have a quick reference. The typed notes ended up being about five pages long. When he read them, he said, "This is great! Why don't you write a book?" He told his friends about my 'book', and soon they too wanted to read it. You are reading what evolved from those yellow Post-it® notes.

Why I know ...

I know what it's like to be a teenager in love. In the early 1970s, when I was in the 6th grade, a miracle happened. Boys and girls suddenly saw each other in a different light. No longer were members of the opposite sex *weird*, or *gross*. By springtime, the kissing game Spin-the-Bottle was big entertainment after school, and people who held hands for more than two weeks were considered to be in a long-term relationship.

That same spring, as if everything had been perfectly planned, our teachers wheeled out the big film projector. It was time for the mandatory one-hour of *Sex Education*. Sitting in the dark classroom, we giggled uncontrollably as the female narrator over-enunciated the words "men-stru-a-tion, ov-u-la-tion and e-jac-u-la-tion." Crude comments from the boys didn't hide their intense desire to learn more than what was offered in the medically-oriented filmstrip.

My mom wanted to make sure that I didn't end up as a teen pregnancy statistic, so she had always been 100% open with me about sex. I knew all the parts of the anatomy, and wasn't ashamed of sex or my body. In fact, when I was seven years old, I got into trouble after a Brownie meeting, when I took four of the girls aside, drew explicit diagrams for them and explained all about the penis.

As a teenager, I found myself in awkward, painful and, at times, blissful relationship situations. Although I had plenty of technical knowledge about sex, I still didn't know how to behave in a *relationship*, or understand the waves of emotions I felt. Besides the emotional confusion, I had a bazillion questions about what to do on a date, how to act around a boy, or let a guy know I liked him.

As girls in junior high school, we would talk about our boyfriends. Since most of us didn't feel that we could share what was going on with our parents, we relied on each other. This peer counseling seemed like a good idea, but the problem was that we recycled misinformation. Someone could be really screwed up, and we wouldn't know it. We all dispensed wisdom to each other like Tibetan monks, and we ate up every word of dysfunctional* advice.

By the time I was a sophomore in high school, several of my friends were having sex with their boyfriends. Since I'd received plenty of sex information from my mom, I knew that the popular birth control method of withdrawal or "pulling out" at the time of ejaculation wasn't safe. I made more than one trip on the #12 bus to the local Planned Parenthood with nervous girlfriends to get birth control. While sitting in the clinic waiting room, I remember thinking that there should be an adult involved in this activity. My friends didn't think their parents would help them.

When I was a teenager, I dated quite a few guys—some were nice, some were not so nice. Today, I look back and see that the guys who I thought were boring in high school were actually great guys, and I regret overlooking them. I let myself be influenced too much by the

---

Abnormal or impaired, non-functional.

outside package—I wanted the cool or super good-looking guy. I also made choices that I regretted later. My high school dating career taught me a lot, but I hadn't learned enough to successfully navigate a marriage at age 18.

I hated being a teenager because everything seemed amplified. Problems sometimes appeared bigger than life; in fact, they could seem almost impossible to handle. Every defeat or failure felt like it was broadcast to everyone in my school. I often wondered whether I was normal. Everyone else seemed to be happy, getting good grades and had great boyfriends. People rarely talked about their disappointments and fears, and I wondered if I was the only one left behind. I suppose I would be a teenager again, but **only** if I could know what I know today. My second go-around as a teen would be much different than my first time around, because I'd know what to do—*and* what to avoid!

When I was a teenager, I used to believe that once you turned 40 years old, you would know everything about sex, love and relationships. As I got older I realized that many people never figure this stuff out, no matter what their age. I've seen 50 year olds acting no better than a 5 year old in relationships. Dating and relationships can be tough, whether you are 16 or 61.

The Inside Information

Before we go any further, let's clarify a few things so we both have the same vocabulary as you read the book. As I wrote this, the wording boyfriend/girlfriend was awkward, so instead I decided to use the term "Significant Other." In the same way, saying boy/girl sounded babyish, so instead I use Man and Woman.

Are the Stories Real?

Quite a few people heard that I was writing this book and called me to share their personal stories about their own dating experiences. I received calls from all across America. I had calls from teenagers and from adults who told me stories about when they were teens. These stories were great! I realized that there was nothing better than real-life examples to get my point across. So, with their approval, I've fictionalized them for better reading, but the situations and main facts are true. Sometimes, the names and details have been changed when people didn't want their real names used. I call these the "Teen View Stories." You'll see these in the shaded blocks in the chapters. A lot of people asked me after reading the early manuscripts, "Are the stories real?" Yes, the stories are true, and were told by real people. No, they have not been made more dramatic, but some facts are changed to "protect the innocent."

The Meaning

If you run across a word or phrase that you aren't sure of, you can look for the meaning in the *Glossary of Terms* at back of the book. Less commonly used words are marked with a footnote like this* with the definitions found at the bottom of the page. You can look at the bottom of this page right now to see what I mean. The definitions aren't meant to insult anyone's intelligence. Since the typical English word has an average of three different meanings, the definition is meant for clarity only.

The Numbers

You'll see studies and statistics mentioned in the book. These references will have a little number next to it, like this[1]. You can read where the research came from by looking in the *End Notes* section at the back of the book, which is right before the *Index*. The corresponding number in the *End Notes* will show the source for that reference. Finally, there is the *Resource Section*, where I've listed books, videos and websites that can give you more information on dating, relationships and sex.

Most of the information in this book applies to both men and women. However, there are times when a section or sentence is directed to *just* men, or *just* women. From this, you can learn about the perspective of the opposite sex! The topics in this book aren't radical, nor are they brain surgery complicated. They're just practical experience on paper, for you to read about *before* you experience them! Kind of like reading the instructions before you assemble a picnic table purchased at the hardware store.

---

*This is a footnote, to give you more information about the word or sentence you just read.

The Promise

I'm not a high and mighty relationship guru who's never made a mistake. Quite the opposite, I've hit just about every relationship speed bump and pothole you could imagine. I know first-hand how much it sucks. I don't intend to judge or preach because I hate being judged and preached to by people who have never experienced similar situations. I do plan to share my experience, and the experiences of others. Reading this book will be like a road trip. You are the driver, and I'm the navigator who will give directions to get you where you want to go, safely.

I have an open invitation to you. If at any time while you're reading this, you feel that I'm talking down to you, send me an email! Let me know the page and the sentence where you feel I am talking down to you. I'll reply. We can talk about it. If you can convince me, I'll change it in my next edition! My contact information is listed on the page, *About Deborah Hatchell.* However, my email address is *deb@4smarteenagers.com*

You're Ready for Takeoff

Okay, I think we're actually ready to start now. There is one important thing about relationships I want you to keep in mind from the beginning: The road to Love doesn't always go in a straight line. It usually takes lots of turns and curves along the way. This is what makes relationships exciting. This book will be your map. As your "navigator," I can point out a few potholes along the way so your ride isn't too bumpy. However, as the "driver" of your life, your job is to hang on tight, know when to speed up, when to slow down, and when to pull over.

To love and be loved will be the greatest event in our lives.

—Jean-Jacques Rousseau (1712-1778), French philosopher

The Learning Curve

There is a learning curve that most people go through in their first few relationships and it can make for a rough time if they're not prepared.

"What learning curve is there in dating and relationships?" you ask.

It's the learning curve that we all experience whenever we do anything new. It takes time and practice to go through the common mistakes that beginners make. After you've done something a few times, you don't even think about those basic mechanics and principles that took so much energy in the beginning. You just do it unconsciously. Like riding a bike or driving a car. When you first start, you make mistakes and have to concentrate. After awhile, it becomes second nature.

In this chapter I'll lay the groundwork for you to have a great dating experience, and I'll give you a head's-up about expectations, reality and being ready so you are ahead of that curve. Even if you're already in a relationship, reading this chapter can put you light years ahead of the average teenager.

Love Connection

Love is powerful. In fact, being loved is one of the strongest desires a person will feel in their lifetime. It's a great experience. We feel accepted and special because someone else has declared that we are worthy of their affection and time. We feel content and even safe because we have a connection to another person and we aren't alone. Other people, like our teachers and friends, even seem to like us better when we're in a relationship.

With all of these feelings swimming around inside our head, it's not uncommon to have an expectation about love and what it means.

Rebecca & Kevin

"I can't believe you're going!" said Rebecca.

Her boyfriend Kevin stood in her driveway with a basketball under his arm.

"Come on, Rebecca, it's just for a few hours. Don't be so upset. We'll go out tonight," said Kevin. It was already 2:00 and he was late to meet his friends at the court to play a game. "Call Libby!" he shouted over his shoulder as he got into his car.

Libby has been Rebecca's best friend since the 5th grade. Kevin was smart, because he knew that Libby had been dating her boyfriend for almost a year. Kevin also knew that Rebecca had never been in a relationship before they started dating a month ago. He figured Libby would be the perfect person to give his girlfriend some advice.

"Rebecca, it's no big deal. Really. You can't keep this poor guy on a short leash. He has his friends. He's not cheating on you. He treats you well. He's a great boyfriend. Relax. Everything is fine," said Libby into the phone, trying to reassure her friend.

(Continued)

Libby knew that, even at 16, Rebecca was kind of immature. Ever since Rebecca started going out with Kevin, she has been walking on Cloud 9. Libby knew that it was a long fall from that cloud back to earth for Rebecca once the reality of day-to-day life set in.

"I know, but I just love being with him. When we're apart I feel miserable. All I can think of is Kevin, Kevin and Kevin. I just worry that he doesn't feel the same way, especially when he wants to go off with his friends all the time," said Rebecca. She knew she sounded kind of whiney. Eww.

Rebecca thinks that when you are in love, you're always together and share everything. She feels hurt when sometimes Kevin has to study and can't call her at night to talk. They have a great time when they are together, but life seems to be business as usual for Kevin. Rebecca had a different expectation of going steady than what the reality was.

Reality

A relationship is doomed from the start if one person has pinned their entire happiness on it. Being responsible for someone else's happiness is too much pressure for anyone to bear. Rebecca's unrealistic expectation of Kevin and their relationship will eventually cause lots of problems for them. (This is an example of the rough time I mentioned earlier.) A smart teenager knows that a relationship is not the primary source of happiness in their life.

As we get past the learning curve and spend time in relationships or survive a breakup, we eventually get to the point where we realize that we don't *need* a Significant Other to be happy. This doesn't mean that we don't want a Significant Other, but that we feel worthwhile, safe and complete whether we are in a relationship or not. Being in a relationship is nice, but it's not essential to our existence. The realization that we are OK without a Significant Other is a sign of maturity. You actually increase your odds of romantic success when you know that a relationship is not a requirement for your happiness.

Libby & Simon

Rebecca's friend Libby wasn't always so wise. She has done a lot of growing up with Simon over the last year. Libby didn't realize that she would learn so much about herself just from being in a relationship. About two months after they started dating, much to her surprise, she realized that she could be very stubborn. This was not a quality she thought she possessed, but she did!

She learned this painful fact about herself when she was applying for her first job as a sales clerk at the local video store. She figured that it would be a great job because they paid a little above minimum wage and employees got 2 free video rentals a week! Simon, who is a year older than Libby, already has a part-time job. He had interviewed at several businesses before he found the job at Duncan's, where he works on an assembly line manufacturing guitar pickups. So, when Libby was going for an interview at Video-Joe's, Simon gave her some pointers and advice from his experience.

"No way! That is lame. I'm not going to say that," Libby said.

"Employers are listening for key words when they hire someone. Trust me, Libby, it will work," said Simon. He knew she wouldn't follow his suggestion.

Sure enough, she didn't get the job and Libby was crushed. Simon knew better than to say the old 'I told you so,' but he couldn't resist.

"Well, Libby, if you hadn't been so stubborn and had taken my suggestion we might be celebrating your new job right now!"

"*I'm* stubborn?" asked Libby. She was shocked that Simon thought she was stubborn.

"Ah, yeah. You are," said Simon.

"How?"

"Well, like not being open to my advice about the job interview.
(Continued)

And what about last semester's chemistry project when I told you that mixing ammonia and bleach would make a poisonous gas? That was almost a total disaster!" said Simon, as he began recounting all the recent examples of Libby's stubbornness.

That evening, while Libby was brooding over Simon's observation, her mother asked her what was wrong.

"Oh, it's Simon," said Libby. "He says I'm stubborn!"

"Well there's a news flash," said her mom as she tried not to laugh.

"You think I'm stubborn, too?" said Libby. It felt like a conspiracy.

"Honey, let's just say that your dad and I sometimes refer to you as 'Little-Miss-Know-it-All'," her mom said. Libby could not believe what she was hearing!

The next day at school, while passing from 3rd to 4th period, Libby saw Simon in the hall.

"Hey, you," Libby said rather sheepishly.

"Hi," said Simon. He didn't know what was going to happen after their heated conversation yesterday. Libby had left in a huff.

"I've been thinking," said Libby, "about what you said about me being stubborn." Libby paused for a moment and looked down at her blue binder in her arms. "I *can* be pretty stubborn sometimes."

"It's okay. I love you even though you're stubborn," said Simon, leaning in to kiss her gently on the lips.

Revelation

Experience will teach you that there is more to relationships than just having a regular date on Friday night. Relationships teach us a lot about human nature. We also learn some surprising things about ourselves that we never knew before. Things like, how stubborn we can be, or how selfish we really are. It's not all negative! We also learn about our positive strengths, too, such as how tender and compassionate we are, or the importance of our sense of humor. But just like it was for Libby, it can be hard to face the reality that we are less than perfect. Relationships have lots of surprises and deal with many issues, so you need to be ready for anything when you are in one.

Are you ready to date?

Wouldn't it be great if we received a letter in the mail one day that announced we were ready to date? There would be no arguing with parents about whether we were ready or not, because we'd essentially have a license to date. To make things even better, immediately after receiving the letter, we would automatically know everything about dating and relationships. We'd be completely without worry of messing up or fear of rejection. The first person we asked out would say yes, and we'd have a great time and then live happily ever after! Okay, well that was a nice little fantasy. But the fact is, nothing remotely like this daydream happens in real life.

A parent's biggest fear when their teen starts to date is that the teen will get hurt, or have their heart broken. Parents don't want their children to have pain. Some teens are frustrated because their parents have said, "You're not ready to date." Yet the teen feels ready. How do you *know* when you are ready?

Being ready is not about a certain age. It's about whether you can handle the emotions that relationships bring. Heck, if it were only about age, then it would be easy! Just like getting a driver's license, we'd all know that once we turn 16, we're ready to date. What makes it tricky is that people mature emotionally at different ages.

In a relationship you are vulnerable, and the possibility of being hurt is part of the territory. The vulnerability is because there are no guarantees in a relationship. If there was a crystal ball that could tell us whether a relationship would succeed or not, we'd have a zero divorce rate because people could simply avoid relationships they knew would fail! Since we can't see into the future, there are no guarantees. As a result, there is an inherent risk of hurt when we get into a relationship.

Actually, there is inherent risk in just about everything. Each time we get into our car, we run the risk of getting into an accident. We don't want to be in an accident, so we wear our seat belts and drive carefully. However, as we drive down the street, we have assumed the risk of the possibility of an accident. So, just like someone who plays football expects the possibility of being tackled, when you are in love you need to expect the *possibility* of heartbreak. This doesn't mean that we should live in a bubble. Millions of people still drive and play football and get involved in relationships everyday, in spite of the risks.

Does this mean that every relationship is automatically doomed? No, of course not. There are plenty of healthy, long-term relationships to prove that. However, the possibility of heartbreak is just a reality of romantic relationships. Are you thinking that you want to be single forever now? I don't want to scare you off from relationships or dating, but I would be falling down on my promise to make you a smart teenager if I didn't give you the straight truth from the start. Like I said, this is all part of the learning curve.

Just as drivers wear seatbelts and buy cars with airbags, and football players wear helmets and padding, you can also protect yourself from unnecessary hurt in a relationship by making sure you are ready. The more ready you are to handle the emotions and issues that might come up in a relationship, the less likely you are to be deeply hurt.

The Test

Now that I've made relationships sound incredibly scary, let's determine where you are on the readiness scale. I've devised a quick test so you can see how well you will handle a romantic relationship. Just because you get a green light on this test doesn't mean that you won't get hurt. It just means that you will more likely handle the emotions and issues well.

Read each question and then answer either yes or no. On some questions you might want to say, "Maybe" or "Sometimes" or "It depends." You need to answer with a yes or no. So think of the answer that *best* describes how you really are. Once you have finished, add up your points.

1. Do you get angry when your parents say 'no'? (no=1 yes=2)
2. Do you have at least one or two close friends who you talk to and do things with regularly (twice a month or more)? (no=2 yes=1)
3. Do you have at least one friend who is of the opposite sex (more than an acquaintance, but not a crush or romantic interest)? (no=2 yes=1)

4. Do you easily compromise with your friends when each of you wants to go someplace or do something different? (no=2 yes=1)

5. Are you mad if you don't get your way most of the time? (no=1 yes=2)

6. Are you understanding when your friends want to spend time with other friends, or they have homework or practice (such as sports, musical instrument, etc.)? (no=2 yes=1)

7. Do you know where you stand on sex (Meaning, you know whether you want to have sex before you are an adult/marriage partner and you've thought about what you'd do in the event of a pregnancy or sexually transmitted disease)? (no=2 yes=1)

8. Are you generally happy at this point in your life? (no=2 yes=1)

9. Do you talk to people about your feelings; you don't keep everything to yourself? (no=2 yes=1)

10. Do you hold grudges? (no=1 yes=2)

11. Do you tell the truth (You never exaggerate or make things up so a story sounds better, or to keep yourself out of trouble)? (no=2 yes=1)

Test Key*

11 to 14 points = Green light—You are ready!

15 to 17 points = Yellow light—Proceed with caution. You are close, but not quite ready. If you date right now, you might be in for a bumpy ride. Observe your own behavior and ask yourself whether you are being mature, or acting like a selfish brat.

18 or more points = Red light—Do yourself a huge favor and *wait*. If you date right now, chances are you and the person you date will be miserable.

The Important Skill

Okay, so you understand about unrealistic expectations and the revelations of human nature that occur in relationships. You also know

---

*If you don't get a 'Green Light', keep reading this book! You'll learn more just from reading, which can get you closer to the green light.

about the inherent risk of getting hurt. Now you need to know about the most important skill you can learn: How to make good decisions.

Making *good* decisions is a huge part of being successful. Every decision you make will create a specific result. Making a big decision is a process. Sometimes you'll intuitively know the answer, without much thinking. Other times you might want to use a process to find the best decision. Some people like to weigh the pros and cons of each situation before they make a decision. I've created a simple four-step process to help you arrive at the best option. This process actually takes the pro/con method two steps further, as you'll see later on. Obviously, you'll minimize mistakes (and the subsequent pain) by making the best decision possible. So, how do we make good decisions?

We make good decisions by getting the most information available. You need all of the facts before you make a decision. I call this process the fact-finding phase. Your primary resources for gathering facts and information include reading and asking people questions. As you ask questions, remember that each person's views and opinions are based on two things: Their own personal experience *and* information they gathered while reading and asking questions.

It will be up to you to sort through the various views, opinions and information and then pick out the pieces you want to apply to your particular situation. Eventually, you'll gain your own first-hand personal experience.

Five-step Decision Process

Once you've finished your fact-finding mission, you need to analyze those facts. This 5-step process will help you to analyze your facts. When you analyze something, you want to be objective. Sometimes emotions can cloud judgment, and make it hard to be objective. As a result, it's important to acknowledge that some issues have more of an emotional charge than others. For example, whether a woman should breakup with her significant other has a higher emotional charge than whether she should have macaroni for dinner. Both are decisions—one has a big emotional charge.

Writing the facts and your feelings about those facts down on paper can be very helpful in seeing the situation clearly. It's easy to do. You can use a sheet of notebook paper to make a list. In fact, here is a sample of how it might look:

5-Step Decision-Making Process:

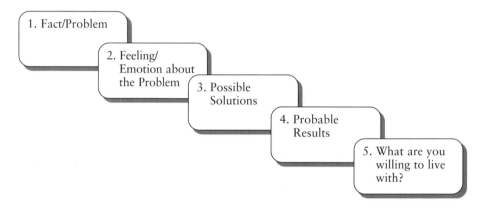

1. Write down the *facts* of the situation, **not** your feelings. It is easy to get them confused. Be as objective* as you can.
2. Write down your feelings *about* each of the facts. Many facts may have more than one emotion attached. Write them all down. Most people either ignore their feelings, or confuse their feelings with facts. By writing them down, you'll be clear about the difference between the facts and your feelings.
3. Outline the possible options or actions you can take.
4. Write down the probable results that option or action will create. It's important to be realistic and not fantasize about what we want to happen.

At this point, you have your facts laid out and the possible options with the result/consequence of those options. The next step is the *really important* part! This is where most people fail, so pay careful attention.

Ask yourself, *"**What am I willing to live with?**"* Think about how the result will affect you next week, next month and next year. Sometimes next year seems so far away that it's easy to overlook how a decision will affect us in the long run. Many people don't think about the future when they make decisions. What we're willing to live with today isn't

---

*Free of any bias or prejudice caused by personal feelings. Based on facts rather than opinions.

always what we can live with in the long term. If the result of a solution is more than you're willing to deal with in the long run, then it's *not* the right decision.

Action

Now you get to choose which course of *action* you'll take. Sometimes when we have to make a tough decision we might say, "I can't make a decision, so I'll do nothing." Don't be fooled! Doing nothing *is* doing something. Sometimes there's a big consequence for doing nothing. There are times when the best decision is to do nothing, but that is still a decision.

Do you want people to take you seriously? Then do what separates the genuine adults from the kids: *Accept responsibility* for the results or consequences of your decisions. It's an immature person who runs away from the consequence of their decisions. The mature person stands behind the result. Why did I say 'genuine adults' instead of just 'adults?' Because there are plenty of adults who make bad decisions and then blame others for their situations, instead of taking full responsibility. It's a big step to be responsible for your decision. However, this step is a significant part of completing the learning curve. If you are willing to take responsibility for your decisions, you are more likely to take care when making them.

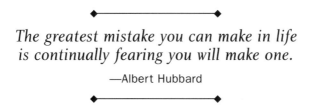

The greatest mistake you can make in life is continually fearing you will make one.

—Albert Hubbard

The Failure Factor

Will absolutely every decision you make be 100% right? That is highly unlikely. In fact, it's more likely that you'll win the lottery than never make a mistake or a bad decision in your life. Making mistakes is part of the human experience. Everyone makes mistakes. The secret is to learn from our mistakes, and not make the same one again and again. One definition of insanity is to keep doing the *same thing* over and over expecting *different results*. So, when you are faced with making a decision, take your time to gather as much information as you can and carefully think through your decisions before you make them.

◆————————————◆

You might think that this is the point in my remarks
that I issue a standard exhortation not to be afraid to fail.
I'm not going to do that. Be afraid. Speaking from experience,
failing stinks. Just don't stop there. Don't be undone by it.
Move on. Failure is no more a permanent condition than success.

—Arizona Senator John McCain, who lost the 2000 Republican Presidential
nomination, in his commencement speech to Wake Forest University's graduating
class of 2002.

◆————————————◆

 Check Point

Let's check to see where we stand at this point: We know that love is one of the strongest desires we'll feel in our lives. We also saw that we have to manage our expectations about any relationship. We know that being in a relationship won't automatically make every problem in our lives go away. We saw that we can learn a lot about ourselves when we're in a relationship. We learned that not everyone is ready to date. Hopefully you took the test to see how ready you are. We also talked about making decisions and the steps to take when faced with a decision. Okay, this was important groundwork that needed to be covered. I think you're ready for the first step: Attraction.

*Love looks not with the eyes, but with the mind; and
therefore is winged Cupid painted blind.*

—William Shakespeare (1564-1616), English playwright and poet

Attraction

Have you ever wondered what it is that makes us feel attracted to one person, but not another? How is it that our heart races a bit when just one person in particular is near us? The answer has little to do with cupid or fate. Amazingly, it all boils down to chemicals and blueprints. Who would have guessed?

Let me back up just a bit, because this involves some psychology. Many years ago, the famous psychologist Carl Jung coined the term, *Imago* (pronounced "A-Maa-Go"), to mean the "inner representation of the opposite sex."[1] Imago is also the Latin word for "image." So, our imago is actually a subconscious image that we find attractive. Kind of like a blueprint or a love map. We begin to piece this blueprint together when we are very young. The final images are fully in place by the time we are about 5 to 8 years old. The blueprint is then stored in the cerebral cortex of our brains for the rest of our lives.[2] This means that you have a good mental picture of your perfect mate by the time you are the ripe old age of 5!

The imago explains a lot. It explains why each person generally likes a certain *type* of person. It also explains why some people fall in love at first sight. Actually, some researchers believe we are built for love at first sight because of this.[3] One study showed that 30 to 40% of the people surveyed fell in love during their first meeting.[4] Because of this blueprint, everyone has their own ideal image of attractive. Once we see someone who fits our basic imago, it's like a computer search that has found a "match." Our brain sends a signal that we have found someone who fits the map! This is when the chemicals come in.

It's a pretty complicated set of neurological processes that take place, but essentially once our brain gets the signal that a match has been found, it sends a flood of hormones, including dopamine, seratonin and epinephrine into the brain's cortex, which changes our mood. We can feel elation and euphoria. Sometimes our body feels kind of tingly and our chest can feel warm and full. Our mind then interprets these emotions as attraction or love. The really amazing thing is that this is a universal human experience; the physiological process of attraction and falling in love is experienced this exact same way in all cultures, all over the world.[5]

Some people say that smell or scent plays a large part in attraction. The body produces an odorless signature, called pheromones, which are excreted in glands under the arms and in the groin and infuse the air around us. Scientists are working to determine whether pheromones are truly effective in attraction. In any event, they are a big business and lots of people buy bottled pheromones in hope of attracting the person of their dreams. Perfume manufacturers want you to buy their scents because it will drive the opposite sex wild! Ironically, using perfumes runs against the pheromone idea, because heavy fragrances would mask the natural pheromones that we are supposedly attracted to. I believe that smell *does* play a big part in attraction. However, I also believe that you have to be incredibly close to someone before you can smell the smells that will seal the deal. So, buy pheromones at your own risk. However, keep your body clean and don't drown yourself in cologne if you think that pheromones are real.

There is another aspect to the chemistry of attraction. That is when two people who match each other's imagos meet! When two people are attracted to each other, it creates an intangible spark* between them. A spark is subtle and you might *not* be knocked off your feet by it, but it's undeniable if you are paying attention. Is the person who matches your love blueprint *the* one? Have you found the love of your life? Sorry. It's not that easy. Even if you're both attracted to each other, there are still plenty of hurdles to clear on the road to love. Hurdles such as whether or not the two of you can make the relationship work, how you handle conflict and the other day-to-day realities of life, just to name a few. We will eventually get to all of these hurdles so you have the best possible set of relationship skills to make it all succeed.

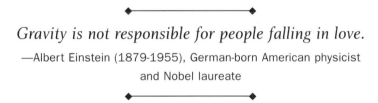

Gravity is not responsible for people falling in love.

—Albert Einstein (1879-1955), German-born American physicist
and Nobel laureate

Beauty or Type

Let's talk about the difference between beauty and type. We already know that our imago determines which 'type' we will be attracted to. But what does type mean? Most people know what beauty is, but it's easy to confuse beauty with type. **Beauty** is what radiates out from inside. **Type** on the other hand, is a style of being; it's what's on the outside. It includes hair color, height and other features that we'll talk about more soon. Remember that the type we *prefer* is rooted in our imago. A Smart Teenager is aware of the difference between type and beauty.

A spontaneous reaction of individuals to each other, especially a mutual sense of attraction or understanding.

Tammy & John

Tammy loves strong, athletic guys. Being on the track team herself, she really appreciates a physically fit man. When John first asked her out, she was excited and thought, "At last, a man from the football team!" She was glad to be dating someone in sports because she knew they'd have a lot in common. He had blondish hair and she has always been especially attracted to strong, blond guys.

However, after three dates with John, it was pretty obvious that his rugged good looks and football-star status weren't enough to keep her interested in him. He wasn't particularly nice. In fact, John was kind of mean to people. His personality detracted from his cuteness. Suddenly his chiseled features looked creepy to Tammy.

Type = The Outside Job

The initial physical attraction we experience is based on **type,** or the outside package. Physical attraction is both visual and auditory. It can be something as minor as the shape of someone's face, the way their mouth moves when they talk or the sound of their voice. John matched Tammy's imago. He was her type on the surface. He was athletic, strong and blond, and those were important exterior qualities to her.

Because physical preferences (imagos) are unique, it's important that we are authentic and not try to be what we *think* someone else finds attractive. The Smart Teenager will be themselves and let someone be attracted to them for who they *really* are.

The type we prefer is rooted in our imago:
- Some men like women who wear makeup and dress in a feminine style, while others prefer women who go natural or are athletic.
- Some women like guys with mustaches, while other women hate any facial hair on their Significant Other.
- Some prefer dark-haired people, or blondes or redheads.
- Some prefer thin people, while others prefer large people.

- Some are attracted to either tall or short people.
- Some only like those who share common interests, whether it's hobbies, extracurricular activities or religious beliefs.

Kathy & Vince

When Kathy first met Vince she thought he was kind of dorky because he played a lot of video games. She wasn't attracted to him at all. He was nice, but definitely not boyfriend material in a million years.

Her best friend liked someone in Vince's lunch group and sometimes they hung out at noontime. After a few weeks of eating lunch with the group, Kathy noticed that Vince was actually pretty smart and had a wickedly dry sense of humor, both of which she liked. She was surprised when she realized that, not only did she look forward to having lunch with the Video Geek Gang, but also that Vince wasn't as dorky as she originally thought. In fact, he was actually kind of cute.

Lust is when you love what you see.
Love is when you lust for what's inside.

—Renee Conkle

Beauty = The Inside Job

We've talked about the outside package, now let's focus on the inside package. Emotional attraction is based on **beauty**, or what a person has inside. True beauty is not something you can touch, but something you can sense. Sometimes when you first meet someone you might not find them physically attractive, but once you get to know them they become better looking. Did they suddenly get better looking? No. It's just that their personality is so attractive that it actually changes the way you see them because you see their true **beauty**.

In the same way, Kathy found that Vince was more attractive as she got to know him. His personality and character qualities played a large part in creating a spark between them. You may be emotionally attracted to someone because they are outgoing or shy; funny or serious; loud or quiet; kind, smart or athletic, or because they love animals or appreciate nature. The Smart Teenager knows that true beauty is intangible and is what people have on the inside.

◆————————◆

The most beautiful women are made for lovers
who lack imagination.

—Guy de Maupassant (1850-1893), French novelist

◆————————◆

The Universal Fear

I'm going to share a secret with you. I call it the universal fear because it's a fear that every human being experiences at least one time in their lives. Teens especially share this one fear. It's the fear of whether or not they will be accepted by others. Some teenagers have a high confidence factor due to natural good looks, athletic ability or resources such as money or family connections that can give them an edge. In spite of their appearance of confidence, even these seemingly self-assured teens worry about being accepted.

The ironic reality is that while *we* are worried about what other people think of us, *other people* are worried about what we think of them! All humans want and need acceptance. This need is just heightened during the teen years. Rest assured that this need to be accepted diminishes over the years. However, Smart Teenagers know that all teens are concerned about being accepted.

To illustrate perfectly how insecure people can be, there is a classic Woody Allen movie, *Annie Hall*, which shows that even adults worry about being accepted. In this movie, the two main characters are attracted to each other and are very nervous as they talk for the first time. While they carry on this awkward conversation, what they are really thinking and worried about (but not saying aloud) shows up in subtitles for us to read. It's incredibly funny to see this part of human nature that we can all relate to.

Stereotypes

I figure I'll get into trouble for this section because it will not be considered politically correct. This particular section might hit a few hot buttons on some folks. I'm going for it anyway because these common stereotypes* *do* exist. Obviously, not everyone will fall into these two categories. However, you might recognize these two stereotypes—because people like this may go to your school.

Bad Boys

It's often said that women find "dangerous" guys more attractive. *Some* women do like the bad boy more than the gentleman. They look for men with brooding expressions because they consider nice guys to be wimpy. Is this bad boy the slick gang member from the movie *Grease*? No. I'm talking about a guy who looks tough and is mean to women, or maybe engages in risky behaviors, such as smoking, drinking, or driving recklessly. The women who find this type of guy attractive may come from abusive families and enjoy the familiar feeling of being with someone who might hurt them, either physically or emotionally. These women tend to have low self-esteem and don't know that they deserve a better man.

The most popular explanation for why women are attracted to bad boys is 'The Beauty and the Beast' story where the love of a good woman tames the monster. For this woman, she thinks that her love will reform the sexy bad boy into a nice guy, and she will have the best of both worlds. Of course, this almost never happens. A bad boy will change only because he is ready and wants to.

Ultimately, a nice guy can't compete for the affections of a woman who holds a bad boy imago. If the person you like is attracted to the dangerous type and you aren't "dangerous," cash in your chips on that person. Unless you become someone you aren't, she will always be looking to catch the eye of the elusive bad boy.

---

*A strictly defined, preformed and unsubstantiated judgment or opinion about an individual or a group.

Hot Chicks

The men who like Hot Chicks often care more about how a woman *looks* than her heart or mind. He wouldn't consider dating anyone who wasn't considered "hot" by 99% of the men he knows.

The Hot Chicks take great pride in their physical appearance. For better or worse, they appreciate being admired. They often dress provocatively* and have the moves to match in order to draw attention. These women will argue that they don't want the attention; but like a moth attracted to a flame, it's hard to not look at them.

Men who only find the Hot Chick type attractive usually have self-esteem issues. He feels better about himself because he has a hot chick on his arm. He may need lots of visual stimulation to experience what he considers intimacy. He may also have an overbearing father figure that he needs to impress.

Rob

I've known Rob since he was a teenager. He is reasonably good looking, drives a nice car and dresses in the latest styles. Since he was 18, Rob has passed over several attractive women because he has set his standards for a girlfriend very high. Actually, he is looking for a super model look-alike, and there are not too many of those around. Ironically, whenever he does meet this type of woman they basically ignore him because *they* are looking for a certain type. While Rob isn't a loser, he doesn't fit *their* standards. He's now 30 and, of course, Rob laments that he's alone and can't find the "right" woman. If Rob weren't so shallow he could have had several great relationships by now.

The Bottom Line: Both of these stereotypes, Bad Boys and Hot Chicks, often appear confident which is an incredibly attractive quality. Additionally, these types are desirable because they are a challenge to win and keep; and some people enjoy the chase and conquest.

---

*Intending to arouse other people sexually.

*True love comes quietly, without banners or flashing lights.
If you hear bells, get your ears checked.*

—Erich Segal, novelist

Are you a Shallow Hal?

Speaking of shallow …

Actors Jack Black and Gwenyth Paltrow made a romantic comedy movie, *Shallow Hal*, where the title character is a shallow and judgmental fool who is only attracted to beautiful women. Hal doesn't care about personalities or any other aspect of women other than their looks. The irony is that *he* is no prize himself. He's not particularly good looking or well built, isn't remarkably smart, nor does he have any other redeemable feature that would make the incredibly hot chicks that he pursues respond to his advances. The movie is no Academy Award winner, but very funny and worthwhile as a way to see how you can be attracted to someone's personality.

So, are you a Shallow Hal? Do you find yourself only attracted to people that are "out of your league?" Do you, like Rob, have unrealistic criteria for a Significant Other? Are you willing to be in a relationship with someone who doesn't hang out with the popular crowd? Who is a few pounds overweight, but has a great sense of humor and is really smart? What about someone who wears glasses or is a little bit shorter/taller than you, but is a terrific person?

Increasing the Odds

If attraction is all about chemistry and blueprints, is it even necessary to make an effort? Oh, yes. You can increase your odds of attracting someone, but you can't *make* someone in particular like you (Hey, if I had figured that out this book would be completely different). What you *can* do is make yourself as attractive as possible.

Remember that there are as many different imagos as there are people, and you can't be all things to everyone. However, you can increase interest by doing a little curb appeal. Creating curb appeal is the same thing as making sure your car is in top condition when you want to sell it. Because you want to attract as many buyers as possible, you do the little things that will make it look good. It's the basics; you make sure the car is clean and has a fresh coat of wax. Before we start poking around under the hood, we need to take an inventory!

Take an Honest Inventory

When I was in high school I was a tomboy. I preferred the comfort of Levi jeans, t-shirts and sneakers to the trendy yet uncomfortable 'girl' clothes. I rarely wore makeup other than simple mascara. People used to tell me that I looked like Jodie Foster, who in the 1970s, was also a tomboy. If you get a chance to see Jodie in either Disney's movie *Freaky Friday*, or the movie *Candleshoe*, that is what I looked like.

I guess it was because of my tomboy appearance that once every school year some glamorous 'hot chick' would take pity on me and make me her pet project for a weekend. She would tell me, "I can fix you up in no time. With a little hair and makeup, you'd be sooo cute."

Well, after a few hours, I'd look like a cross between Bozo the Clown and a hooker. I'd thank the hot chick for her help and then go home and scrub my face. I just wasn't comfortable trying to be someone, and something, I wasn't.

After the second time this happened, I decided to stand in front of a full-length mirror and take an honest inventory of myself. I started at the top of my head and worked my way down, being as objective as possible. The old 'Serenity Prayer' really came in handy at that time. In case you haven't heard it before, here it is:

God Grant me the Serenity to accept the things I cannot Change
The Courage to change the things I can
And the Wisdom to know the difference

I decided to peacefully accept things I could not change (like my height and skin color) and to courageously change the things I could (such as losing a few pounds and changing my voice tone). Finally, I used wisdom to know the difference between those things I could and could *not* change.

I'm 5'3" and wanted to be taller, but I couldn't really change that and I didn't like high-heels so I accepted that part of myself. I knew I needed to stop eating so much junk food and to exercise. I wasn't obese, but I wasn't a healthy weight. I did need to get in better shape and lose about 15 pounds. So I changed my weight by making some lifestyle changes. Also, my mother had been telling me for years that I occasionally whined a bit when I spoke. I bought a book on voice control and read it word for word. I even had two sessions with a voice coach from the local university's speech department. It worked miracles.

However, I decided that I wasn't going to give up my tomboy style. I liked it because it was who I was. The only change I made was getting some shirts that were more feminine—you know, pink, light blue and yellow. Overall, I figured my appearance was okay. My clothes were clean; my stick-straight blond hair was washed every day, my teeth were straight after years of wearing braces and I brushed at least twice a day. So what if I wasn't a glamour-girl? I changed the things I could; I accepted the rest. Even though I was a tomboy, I had plenty of dating and relationship experiences as a teen, which goes to show that not everyone is attracted to the same type of person!

If you want to increase your odds of attracting someone, take a personal inventory of yourself. Look in a full-length mirror and be honest. Start at your head and work your way down. At each point, ask yourself: If you were of the opposite sex, would you be attracted to yourself as you are now? As you go over each of these items, write down what you would like to change and how.

Hair
- Clean
- Combed/brushed
- Cut (Is your hair trimmed or is it ragged, or have a bunch of split ends? This goes for guys, too!)

Face
- Clean (You don't have grape jelly on the side of your face, do you?)

- Acne controlled with Benzol peroxide or other medication
- Expression (Do you smile or have an angry frown?)

Mouth

- Teeth clean (brushed twice a day?)
- Breath fresh (You need to floss daily to control bad breath)
- Lips (soft, or dry and chapped? Use ChapStick® or other lip balm every day)

Body

- Posture (Are you humped over like a mad scientist or do you stand straight?)
- Weight (Healthy? Have you been eating too much, or not enough?)
- Body Odor (Do you shower daily and use an unscented deodorant?)

Walk

- Gait (Do you walk with your head down like you are avoiding people, or do you look up? Do you walk with confidence or scurry around like a guilty rat?)

Voice

- Tone (Are you a screecher or a whiner?)
- Volume (Do you talk so loud that you unintentionally shout or yell?)
- Laugh (Is your laugh pleasant or a grating geese honk?)

Clothes

- Clean
- Fit (Are you wearing clothes that are too small or too big?)
- Style (Your clothes say a lot about you. What are you telling the world about who you are? My son, Jason, decided in his junior year to wear only button down shirts and ties to school with his khaki pants and tennis shoes. Everyone asked him where he was going because he was dressed up. He loves it because girls talk to him a lot more—he gets an average of one random hug every day from a girl, and adults treat him with more respect! This doesn't mean that everyone should dress up everyday, but you might want to be aware of what your style is *doing* for you.)

After you've taken your inventory, look at your list and figure out what you can reasonably change and what you are willing to change. Don't lose who you really are in the process of improving yourself, or become a photocopy of someone else. You just want to highlight your best stuff. You don't want to change the essence of who you are in hopes of landing someone. This always backfires because you can't make someone like you—that is beyond your control. Make sensible changes, but don't change the heart and soul of who you are. Smart Teenagers aren't afraid to honestly evaluate themselves.

This above all: to thine own self be true, And it must follow, as the night the day, Thou canst not then be false to any man.

—William Shakespeare (1564–1616), playwright, from *Hamlet*

Sex Appeal 101

Sex appeal is the quality of being sexually attractive. Someone with sex appeal can make heads turn. Many celebrities (think Brittany Spears) ooze sex appeal for a good reason—it sells.

I wish that hunky men were always attracted to average looking women who have tons of confidence. I wish that beautiful women were always attracted to average looking guys who are really nice. Sadly and honestly, neither case is true. So, both men and women use the sex appeal methods that our society finds attractive. And they use sex appeal differently. Men use their attitude, while women use their appearance.

For Men

Okay, so you've taken an honest inventory and you've made sure that you're clean and smell good. In addition to that, you do one of **the** most important things a guy can do: Trim his fingernails every week. It's true that women talk about men when they aren't around. One of the topics that comes up with girlfriends at least once is the guy with the long and dirty fingernails. You don't have to have a professional manicure, but get the nail clippers out regularly.

While some women really like guys with fast or slick cars, most women are happy with a man who has a *clean* car that doesn't smell like a gym or get her clothes dirty when she gets in it. However, more than clothes or any other sex appeal item, the single most effective tool that men have for sex appeal is confidence. I can't emphasize this enough. Women love a confident man. They don't like a cocky jerk.

Confidence is the best accessory—it can make or break your look.

—Jamie-Lynn Sigler, Soprano's daughter, "Meadow" and author of *Wise Girl*.

Confidence, Cocky and the Nice Guy

You probably want me to define confidence. I was afraid of that. Confidence is hard to describe because it's intangible. Like beauty, it emanates from the inside out. There are subtle differences between confidence and cockiness. In the movies, the hero is confident and the bad guy is cocky. Here are some examples of the contrast.

Cockiness is arrogant and is rooted in insecurity; confidence is the belief in your own abilities—a belief that your thoughts and ideas are valuable. A cocky guy tries to prove something and ends up defensive; A confident man knows he is okay and he doesn't have anything to prove. Cocky is loud; confidence is quiet. Cockiness presses itself on others and intimidates; confidence is patient and inviting. A cocky guy treats others with contempt and disregard; a confident man treats others with respect. A cocky guy takes himself very seriously because he can't afford to let anyone see him with his guard down; a confident man can laugh at himself because he is completely sure of who and what he is. A cocky guy wants to let you know how great he is; a confident guy lets you learn how great he is.

Another way to describe confidence is assertiveness. If cockiness is aggressive, then confidence is assertive. A woman wants to know that her man is assertive enough to handle just about any situation. Some nice guys are seen as wimpy because they allow themselves to be taken advantage of. Confident men have self-respect. They're nice, but won't allow themselves to be walked on. This is where being assertive separates the wimpy guys from the confident guys. There is a great story about being assertive in Chapter 12, *Making A Relationship Work*.

A confident guy is nice, but knows when to be assertive and ask for what he wants, needs and should expect. That might be expecting good service in a restaurant or store. A confident man will be comfortable saying, "Waitress, excuse me. We're ready for the check now." The wimpy guy will sit there hoping that the waitress will read his mind or notice him.

For Women

Sex appeal, like perfume, needs be used sparingly or it can have the reverse effect you had hoped for. Too much perfume usually drives people away to get fresh air. *Too much* sex appeal usually attracts weird men. Sure, lots of sex appeal gets lots of attention, but it might be the wrong kind of attention, from the wrong men. A high level of sex appeal is like a homing device for every cocky (yet terribly insecure) man who is trying to prove to his friends (and himself) that he is okay. This macho player is the same guy who will tell another guy, "Yeah, she wants me. Just wait. I'll have her on the horizontal in two weeks."

You probably already know this, but let me explain in detail. First, you need to understand that teenage men's bodies are flooded with hormones. A teenage man may often find that his penis has a mind of its own. He can't control when an erection will happen. Men are also visual. Their bodies respond physically to looking at certain things. For example, when they see a beautiful girl, dressed in super low-slung jeans and a revealing midriff-barring top, they involuntarily react to the visual stimuli and often times get an erection (This is why your school might have rules on the type of clothing you wear—they know that certain clothes will be distracting for guys).

Now this doesn't mean that men can't control their impulses. Humans do have control over their impulses! So, men won't act like whacked out sex animals and attack a woman just because she is dressed provocatively. Hey, I'm not suggesting you dress like a nun. Heck, play up your best features. Just be aware that those super low-slung jeans and revealing, midriff-barring top *may* be sending off the wrong signal to the wrong guys.

The bigger problem for women is that these macho players just grow into *older* macho players. Women who have maximized their sex appeal know exactly what I'm talking about because they are approached by *older* men, as well as men their own age. These men are called creeps. Thankfully, not all men are this way—in fact, only a very small percentage of men are creeps.

Worse yet, a woman with too much sex appeal might intimidate the nice guys, while the players just see it as an open invitation! So, if you seem to be attracting the wrong kind of attention, adjust your sex appeal volume until you find the right balance that works for you. It's better to have nice guys, not players or creeps, flirting with you.

A woman's best sex appeal tool is, just like for men, confidence. And, just like with men, you can be too nice or you can go to the other extreme of being a cocky jerk. Like the men, you can find a middle ground of confident and friendly.

But I can't find someone like me ...

Sometimes we're attracted to someone because they're like us. It's called the Just-Like-Me effect. We are attracted to them based on our similarities. If you discount someone because they are different you'll miss out.

In the dating world, you'll rarely find a perfect match. In fact, you really don't *want* someone who holds the exact same thought on every subject or is involved in all the same activities that you are. Instead of looking for someone you think is just like you, look for someone who is a good fit. An example of a couple that might be a good fit: One of them finds it easy to make conversation, while the other one tends to be quiet. They balance each other out! Different styles or interests can bring fun, diversity and dimension to relationships. However, having similar values *is* important.

Interests or Values

Interests and values are two different things! Interests are specific activities and hobbies, such as band, football, tennis, chess club, video games, music, hunting or reading. Values are deeply held beliefs that people have about broad issues, such as the environment, health, religion, education, volunteering, children, etc.

If you both feel that doing well in school and going to college is important, that is a value you share. If she feels that volunteering is important and spends several hours a week at the local children's shelter, but he thinks that volunteering is for suckers, they don't have the same values. He is a dyed-in-the-wool evangelical Christian, and she is a dyed-in-the-wool atheist: they have a values conflict. He loves hunting, and she is an animal rights activist and member of the local People for the Ethical Treatment of Animals group: they have a values conflict.

There are couples with strongly different values that have very successful relationships. However, these relationships can have more than the usual problems if the values begin to compete for which is better, or right. A Smart Teenager understands the difference between interests and values.

Top 10 Turn-ons[6]

A leading dating service conducted an informal survey of singles to find out what was considered the biggest turn-ons. Some are predictable and some are surprising. Here are their results:

1. A nice, healthy body. So much for being enlightened. Apparently the consensus was "someone who is conscious of their body, is physically active, and dresses for their body type" is a big turn-on. The good news is that it didn't say 'Size 8'; just healthy!

2. Confidence. This is no surprise. We already know that a person who projects confidence is sexy. The cocky jerks are just rude and conceited.

3. A good job. Holding down a job shows responsibility. It's also nice to have spending money.

4. A cool car. America's love affair with the car is still in full gear. Apparently, what is considered 'cool' is in the eye of the beholder. The poll respondents had a wide range of what was considered cool—all the way from low emission hybrids to trucks. It's nice to know that a sports car isn't necessary for you to rate as cool.

5. Fashion sense. This didn't mean that only the latest and greatest designers are "it." This is undoubtedly more about wearing clothes that fit and flatter your body.

6. Nice hair. Hair? Are we a vain society or what? I guess shampoo and mousse are the way to love. This is why taking that personal inventory is important to see if you need a good haircut.

7. Good manners. Who would've guessed that manners are a turn on? People appreciate being treated respectfully. More than that, watching your date handle themselves with tact and finesse is the fastest road to Turn Me On City. Chapter 9, *Smooth Moves*, is all about manners.

8. Scent. We know about those pheromones. This is another reason why soap and deodorant are your friends.

9. Lack of neediness. This is the twin sister of confidence. Hold on to someone too tight, and they'll run for the hills.

10. Creativity. You don't have to be an artist to be creative. A creative date or a romantic poem is always appreciated.

What is everybody looking for?

Some women want a bad boy while others want a nice guy. Some men want a hot chick while others want the girl next door. There is no single, universal type that absolutely everyone wants. But it is safe to say that most people want to find someone who is confident, attractive, interesting and, most of all, likes them in return.

I love a hand that meets my own with a grasp that causes some sensation.

—Samuel Osgood

A Smart Teenager ...

- Will be authentic and let someone be attracted to them based on who they *really* are.
- Is aware of the difference between type and beauty.
- Knows that true beauty is intangible and is what people have on the inside.
- Remembers that all teens are concerned about being accepted.
- Isn't afraid to honestly evaluate themselves.
- Understands the difference between interests and values.

*The first symptom of love in a young man is shyness;
the first symptom in a young woman, is boldness.*

—Victor Hugo (1802-1885), French poet, novelist and playwright

Flirting

Once you've found someone you're attracted to, you're ready for the next step: Letting them know you like them.

"Yikes!" you say. "What if they don't like me back?"

There is always that risk. Rejection is painful, and most of us fear and avoid rejection like the plague. Because rejection is a big deal, Chapter 7, *The Big Chill*, will tell you how to handle it! But let's not get ahead of ourselves. Before we worry about whether they'll like you back, let's first concentrate on getting their attention.

Sometimes we're attracted to someone, but they don't know that we find them attractive; or maybe they don't even know who we are! To top it off, a case of sudden shyness can set in once you're attracted to someone. This makes taking the risk of rejection harder than ever. So, instead of risking everything up front and barging in like a bull in a china shop, test the water first to see if it's safe to proceed. So, how *do* you let someone know you like them? Flirt. Flirting is a safe way to let someone know you're attracted to them. It's also a way to see if they're attracted to you as well. Flirting is the age-old way of saying, "Hi, there! Do you notice me? I notice you!"

Flirting is where people stand closer than usual when they talk. They smile and look into each other's eyes. They might joke around a little bit. Flirt and then wait for them to flirt back. If someone **flirts back**, then the possibility of rejection is less and you'll feel more confident to go to the next step, which we'll talk about in the next chapters.

Kim & William

William was really nervous about talking to Kim. He thought she was very cute and especially liked to hear her laugh. William sits two seats behind her in U.S. History everyday. They always say "Hi" to each other as they pass in the halls between classes. William has noticed that Kim smiles a big smile when she sees him and holds his eye for a few seconds. He really likes that.

He felt like a coward for being afraid to talk to her, but he was determined to do something before the semester was over. One day, without a lot of planning, he summoned up his courage and finally did it. William stopped Kim when he saw her in the hallway.

"Hey, Kim," called William, "hold up for a minute!" He hoped his voice sounded natural.

"Sure. What's up?" Kim tucked her long black hair behind her right ear.

"Have you started your paper on the Civil War yet?"

"No, not yet," Kim said.

"Me neither," said William. "I'm stumped for an angle."

(Continued)

"That's why *I* haven't started," laughed Kim as she touched William's arm.

"Okay, I don't feel so bad then," said William. "I was hoping to get an idea for a topic from you, but it looks like we're in the same boat." It was working! William was really glad he took the plunge and started this conversation.

"If I think of a good idea," said Kim, "I'll let you know."

William and Kim had begun flirting. Kim was sending flirting signals to him, and William finally had the courage to take the first step.

Who's on First?

Is there a rule about who flirts first? Should the man always flirt first, or is it okay for the woman to start flirting? Some women don't want to initiate flirting as they think it makes them seem desperate or cheap. Many men are very fearful of rejection. In an independent study, over 60%[7] of the men interviewed said that they liked it when women flirted with them first. Ironically, women are just as afraid of rejection as men are and often will not initiate contact for that reason. But somebody has to start. Technically, it doesn't matter whether the man or the woman starts flirting. If you are attracted to someone, flirt with them. Flirting is a safe way to see if someone responds positively to you, which is why you should flirt *before* you ask someone out!

Flirting Basics

Flirting comes naturally for some people. They just do it. They can't tell you how, but they just do. Being able to read flirt signals is important. Once you receive flirt signals you need to respond. Let them know you are interested in them by flirting back. Let them know you are *not* interested (or not available) by *not* responding with flirt signals, or just come right out and tell them. So, for those of us who don't know how to flirt or wouldn't recognize a flirt signal sent our way, here are a few basic guidelines:

Smile. Even if you don't like your smile or think you look cool if you don't show emotion, smile. Smiling is the one universal sign that lets people know you are safe and approachable.

Eye Contact. Look the person in the eyes and hold it for 3 to 4 seconds. This is long enough to let them know that you are looking (and smiling) at them. It's not so long that you look like a drooling idiot.

Body Language. Body language lets the other person know whether you are open or closed to flirting with them. It's best if you don't cross your arms—crossed arms are a classic symbol of being closed off or protective. Be natural—don't fidget, but don't be as stiff as a board either. If you fidget too much, the person may think you are anxious and want to get away.

Touch. When women flirt, they often touch. As a general rule, men should never touch a woman when he's flirting. Let the woman initiate the touch. A brief touch on the arm is all it takes for a woman to send a signal to a man. When I say brief, I mean as in, "My hand brushed his as I reached for the salt."

Speak. Yes, starting a conversation can be a challenge, especially for those who are paralyzed by shyness. You don't have to be witty. Just say, "Hi." This is your chance to make contact, so be sincere. Be upbeat too. You don't want to say "Hi" in a depressed tone, like Eeyore from *Winnie the Pooh*. Once they say "Hi" back, then you can ask, "How are you?" If they only reply with a "Fine," then that's great for the first time. Once you've said "Hi," you've broken the ice. Now it's perfectly acceptable for you to say "Hi" whenever and wherever you run into them!

Are they flirting with you?

So, how do you know if someone is just being friendly, or is actually flirting with you? Well, there are a few telltale behaviors that men and women do when they flirt. A good guideline is that if you *think* they like you, or if you are getting the 'vibe' that they like you, they probably do. Once in awhile you will misread a sign or behavior, but it's most likely that they do like you back!

Flirt Signs

Here are a few signs someone might be flirting with you:

When women flirt, they sometimes...	*When men flirt, they sometimes...*
Touch their hair, or the man	Put their hands or thumbs in their pockets
Giggle a lot	Sway side to side, or lean back and forth
Their voices get higher than usual	Make their voices deeper than usual

Do the Obvious

There is a saying that common sense isn't so common. Here is one of the times where common sense can pay off big time. Introducing yourself is the obvious thing to do when you want to meet someone. You don't have to be cool or slick. A simple, "Hi, my name is ..." will work. When they tell you their name, you say, "It's nice to know your name," or "It's nice to meet you." If the person is not interested, they'll let you know by being distant or vague. If they act like a jerk then refer to Chapter 7, *The Big Chill*.

The next time you see them you can start a conversation. Formulate a small talk plan based on some of the *Ten Small Talk Ideas* presented later in this chapter. The important part of small talk is to RELAX (as much as you can) and be yourself. Don't worry if you're nervous. Feeling nervous is the best part of flirting.

If you ever run out of things to say in the beginning, then ask the other person something about himself or herself. Most people are experts on the subject of themselves and are happy to talk! Communicating involves more than just talking. In fact, listening accounts for more than 50% of communication. Listening involves giving feedback, and you give feedback when you nod your head, smile and laugh when appropriate.

A great conversationalist is someone who asks questions and then listens attentively. So, you just need to ask the other person questions to get them talking. If you actually listen, you will be considered a great conversationalist! For ideas, check out the section, *Ten Small Talk Ideas*.

A coward is incapable of exhibiting love;
it is the prerogative of the brave.

—Mohandas Gandhi (1869-1948), nationalist leader of India

Breaking The Ice

What is the best way to get a conversation going? The art of jump-starting a conversation requires a lot of practice and a little sense of humor. Don't hang up your jersey if you strike out the first time you attempt small talk. Even if you get flustered and forget everything else, you can easily remember these two quick guidelines:

1. Be Observant: Your powers of observation can provide great icebreakers. If she's got a noticeable accent, you might inquire where she's from or what accent that is. Caution: Some observations won't work. For instance, "I love your hair" sounds like a line*, and it's probably not going to work.

2. Be Sincere: Forget the canned and rude phrases like, "Didn't I see you in a dream?" or "I like what you're wearing. It would look good on my floor." Don't even think about asking the old cliché, "What's your sign?"

---

*Something said to deceive, impress or attract somebody.

Ten Small Talk Ideas

The best small talk ideas are open-ended questions. The answer is usually a full sentence, not just a quick "yes" or "no." When you ask a lot of yes-or-no questions it can end up sounding like an interrogation. Open-ended questions are a good way to get more conversation topics started. You can build on their answers by asking more questions to find out what you have in common.

Use the "W" approach when creating small talk. This is where you ask Who-What-When-and-Where questions to get the other person talking. "How" is another good open-ended conversation starter. Here are some examples:

1. Who do you have for your math teacher?

2. Who is your favorite actor or actress (or musician)?

3. What's your favorite thing to do?

4. What kind of music do you like?

5. Where did you go to elementary school (or junior high school/middle school)?

6. Where did you get that cool (comment on something they are wearing, have or are holding) backpack, sweat shirt, etc.?

7. How do you like your English (math, science, etc.) class?

8. How long have you lived in town?

9. Have you seen the movie _____ (insert latest popular movie)?

10. Where do you plan to go to college?

Remember: The real success factor is *delivery*—especially for the man. Two men could deliver the same line, but the one who appears sincere and genuinely interested will likely get the positive response, while the one who seems to be a player will end up "talking to the hand."

1-Minute Come-on

Now that I've said that sincerity is an important key to flirting, why would I tell you about a 1-Minute Come-on? This is not an insincere player style come-on. There will be a time or two in your life when you'll meet someone who you immediately have great chemistry with, but you know you'll probably never see them again. Don't let those chance situations become a regret. This is the time to seize the moment and go for broke. Besides, it will be one of the few times you won't have to worry about rejection! You'll never see them again, so besides a little wounded pride, what does it matter if they reject you?

The 1-Minute Come-on technique will be similar to a regular flirt, but you'll be bolder. Smile and look them in the eye for about 3 or 4 seconds. Then just come right out and say what you need to say! Say something like, "My name is (your name). I'm not normally this forward but I realize I might not see you again and I feel like we clicked. I'd like to either give you my email address or phone number, or get a number I can reach you at if you'd like to see me again."

The worst thing that would happen is they take your number and never contact you. However, at the very least, you got to practice flirting. The best thing that would happen is that they do contact you and you've cut through a lot of flirting and game playing.

If you get her number, call her! A phone number is not like a bottle of wine that will get better with time. If she's given you her number, she wants you to use it. You should call 12 to 24 hours after she gives you her number. You won't look cool by waiting, but you'll leave her wondering if you're a player.

The Sound of Silence

There is nothing worse than making your best effort to connect with someone only to have them stare silently at you. What if they don't say anything back? If this happens you may be talking to someone who is incredibly shy or scared to death of making a mistake. These people will **not** be very talkative, and you will have to carry the conversation. You can share certain things about yourself to keep the conversation going. Tell them what your hobbies are, the types of music you listen to, and why you like it.

If the person just sits there and stares at you without responding, then you can ask them if they want you to leave. If their silence is because they are deer-in-the-headlights-scared or very shy, this is their chance to reassure you that you are on track. They can say, "Oh, no, don't go. I'm kind of shy, but I like talking with you." Don't give up on someone just because they are initially shy. Shy people often have great personalities, but only show them once they get to know someone.

If their response to your question about whether you should leave is a flat "yes," then their silence was a rude way of saying, "I'm not interested." Be grateful that you know this now and move on. Don't waste a moment feeling rejected by a rude person! Be sure to refer to Chapter 7, *The Big Chill*.

Responses

You know your flirting has paid off and you're on the right track if you get a specific response such as, "Call me tomorrow," or "I'd love to spend more time with you." But what about the situation where you've been flirting with someone for a while and you get a non-specific, generic response that you aren't sure about. Do they like you? Do you have a chance? Are they playing hard to get? Should you keep pursuing them?

It's easy to misinterpret some responses. When our hearts are involved, we can read a lot into nothing as we hope to hear what we *want* to hear. If you get these standard responses, you should know what they most likely mean. Knowing this ahead of time can save you days of waiting and wondering.

---

1. **"Call me some time!"**

➢ Translation from a man: I'm not interested enough to call *you*.

➢ Translation from a woman (if she's given you her number): She's interested.

---

2. "Let's get together sometime."

➤ Translation from a man: I'm really not interested enough to actually make a plan, but I don't want to hurt you.

➤ Translation from a woman: I'd like to see you, but I want you to make the first move.

3. "You're sweet."

➤ Translation: You are nice, but just not my type and I'm trying to be polite.

4. "I'm totally busy for the next couple of weeks, but after that I'd love to see you."

➤ Translation: I am too busy to be involved with anyone. OR I've already got a Significant Other, but I'm keeping my options open and, if I become available, I'll see if I can fit you in.

Practice Flirting

I know it sounds like a scene from a bad TV show, but no joke: practice flirting. Stand in front of the mirror and practice your smile, eye contact and opening line. The more you practice, the less self-conscious you will be when your opportunity to flirt happens. If you aren't too embarrassed and if you have a cool older sister, brother or friend, you might be able practice with them. You can get important feedback when you practice with someone else. They can tell you that the line you plan to use is cheesy, or they can remind you to smile, or give you other helpful tips.

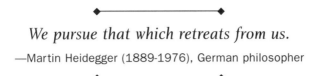

We pursue that which retreats from us.

—Martin Heidegger (1889-1976), German philosopher

Suppress the Urge to Impress

If you've taken an honest inventory and you're playing up your best features, and you're confident, then you can relax. Nothing will turn someone off faster than trying too hard to impress them. It never works. Ironically, the best thing you can do to impress them is nothing. At this point you just need to flirt.

A movie that perfectly illustrates how powerful it is to *not* impress someone is *The Tao of Steve*. I struggled over whether I should mention this movie because the main character has some habits that are less than inspiring, but the theme is worthwhile. The main character, Dex, is a loser. However, he is able to 'get' any woman he wants by using the Tao of Steve.

The Tao of Steve is about attitude and not trying too hard to win someone over. It involves a three-step process of Eliminate Desire, Be Excellent and Be Gone. First, Dex tells us that women can sense an agenda a mile away (which is true), so it's important to not be too eager. So eliminate desire. Second, he says to develop a talent or skill that you are excellent at so that you exude confidence. Third, he says to wait until the woman shows interest in you. He says the best way to do this is to 'Be Gone.' This idea is based on Heidegger's theory of "*We pursue that which retreats from us.*" In other words, we want what we can't have. So, don't try to impress someone. Remember, you want to attract someone to you, not repel them.

Chronic Flirting

Flirting is not just function, it can also be a lot of fun. In fact some people are known as flirts. They find flirting so much fun that they flirt with everyone. Indeed, it's hard to know if someone who is a chronic flirt really likes you or is just doing their thing.

If you are one of the lucky few who are a natural flirt and do it often, it's important **not** to lead someone on. If you flirt a lot with someone who you aren't interested in romantically, it can lead them to believe that you like them more than you really do. If they begin to like you and make the next move, it can be devastating for them to find out you were just playing around. Remember to be respectful of other's emotions when you flirt.

Don't Obsess

After you've flirted, it's easy to replay the scene over and over again in your mind, critiquing your performance. Don't do it. You'll drive yourself crazy thinking of all the things you woulda, coulda, shoulda said. Give yourself the chance to hash it over once, maybe twice, then put it away.

Five Flirting No-No's

1. Don't use canned lines, or lines from movies. (The person you are flirting with may have seen the same movie!)

2. Don't be so cool that you come off looking like an arrogant jerk or a player.

3. Don't boast, "Yeah, I've got 2 women who want to go out with me, but you're the lucky babe today."

4. Don't wimp out in the middle. Once you start, keep going.

5. Don't overwhelm or intimidate. Saying, "I know who you are. You are hot! I've had my eye on you." is likely to put someone on their guard, or freak them out. I had the misfortune of witnessing this very conversation as an 18 year old guy said this to a fellow classmate. She was in a panic and he didn't understand why.

Check Point

At this point, you know quite a bit about flirting. You have a good idea of what works and what doesn't. You know the role confidence plays in attraction. You also know how to spot flirting signals. If your flirting has been well received, you might be thinking about dating. You need to prepare before you ask! The next chapter shows you how to prepare before you ask someone out!

If I am not worth the wooing, I surely am not worth the winning.

—Henry Wadsworth Longfellow (1807-1882), American poet

Action Plan: Date Ideas

Okay, you've found someone who matches your blueprint. You've been flirting and they've flirted back. You're getting closer to asking them out. Before you ask, you need to do a little planning. Nothing says "I don't care" like asking someone out, but not having thought about what and when! The whole purpose of the date is to spend time together and have fun. As you relax and have a good time, you get to know each other better. As you get to know each other better, you can decide if you want the relationship to develop further.

Alex & Lily

Alex and Lily had been going steady for four months. Since neither of them had a driver's license, going places required transportation from a parent which embarrassed Alex. So, their dates were basically sitting in the park mid-way between their homes and talking. Sometimes one of them would bring along snacks. Once in awhile Alex would swallow his pride and ask his mom for a ride so that he and Lily could go to a movie. But mostly, it was talking in the park. While they had revealed their souls to each other and shared every secret imaginable, they were both getting bored. He knew they were in a rut*. Alex got nervous because he didn't want to lose Lily.

He asked his friend, Tom, who had a license if he and Lily could double date with him and his girlfriend some night. While on a double date with them two weeks later, Alex and Lily had a great time going for pizza and arcade games before seeing a movie. After that, Alex decided to arrange for more things to do even if it meant asking for a ride from a parent or friend.

Mixing It Up

Alex saw that it's easy to get bored with the relationship if you do the same thing over and over each time you go out. Activities are bonding experiences. Big corporations sponsor company sports events because they know that people bond on a deeper level when they do something physical together. Activities create special memories that you'll look back on. I know this sounds corny, but it's true: The most memorable dates will be the times you *did* something.

Does this mean that every date has to be an elaborate or expensive production? Will only high-energy, life-threatening activities build your relationships? No. Quiet times where you talk and share are important too. Keep in mind that intimacy develops on several levels: Intellectually, emotionally *and* during physical activities or events.

---

*A routine procedure, situation or way of life that has become uninteresting and tiresome.

However, just like with Alex and Lily, it's easy to let every date become a conversation date where you sit and talk for hours, especially with someone you are comfortable with. Going out and **doing** something is important for another reason: You can't really know someone well if you only see one side of them. You want to see your Significant Other in many different situations, under various conditions.

Host or Hostess

When you ask someone out it's assumed that you will be the host (or hostess) and you will pay the bill. The only exception is if you make it clear at the time of the invitation that the date is Dutch treat. Dutch treat is where people pay for their own expenses, or the bill is split 50-50. It's not uncommon in long-term relationships for couples to frequently go Dutch treat, or alternate paying the tab by saying; "It's *my* treat this time."

Jay & Kira

Kira really liked Jay. He was shy, but cute. Jay asked her out every weekend. He was nice and treated Kira very well. Jay never took her to the football field parking lot where the other teenagers in town went to park and make-out after their dates.

Kira wondered if he was rich because each date was so extravagant. He would take her out to dinner and then bowling *and* a movie all in *one night*! Every date was always dinner and two activities. It was almost exhausting, but it was always fun.

One time Jay took her home to meet his parents. His parents were old. They looked older than Kira's *grandparents*. Everything in their house seemed old. Even the furniture, but they didn't look particularly rich.

After about two months of dating, Jay surprised her by coming to her house after school one day. He asked her if she wanted to go to 7-Eleven for a Coke®. They sat in his car sipping their drinks when Jay said that they couldn't go out anymore.

(Continued)

Kira was stunned. "Why?" she asked.

"Well, I've run out of money and I can't take you out anymore," Jay said.

Kira didn't understand, so she asked what he meant.

"I've used up all the money in my savings account and I don't have any money to take you out," Jay said sheepishly.

"You spent all of your money? We didn't have to go on such big dates every time. Any one of those things we do on a date is enough! Besides, it can be my treat once in awhile."

"The man always pays. Besides, I wanted to do nice things for you," Jay explained.

It took Kira a minute before she figured out that his parents must have told him that men always pay. That explained why he was such a gentleman with her. His parents had raised him with values from the 1950s. She couldn't believe Jay had spent his last penny on her!

"Jay, we can do other things that don't cost so much or anything at all. You can come over to my house and we can watch a movie. I can pack us a lunch and go to the lake."

"Are you sure? That would be great!" Jay was amazed at this idea.

After that, Jay and Kira went on dates that were less expensive and, occasionally, Jay let Kira treat!

Expenses

Jay saw that dating can quickly become very expensive. This is why simple dates, such as getting coffee or ice cream, are a good idea. If a woman expects a man to take her out for an expensive dinner and a movie every Friday night, he might not be able to afford it after a few weeks. Men need to know that most women don't have this expectation. However, a man who picks a woman up and runs her through

McDonald's drive-thru for a small Diet Coke on the way to Lover's Lane or Make-out Point* is a user.

Who pays for the date? Usually and traditionally, men pay for dates. This tradition began many years ago when young women didn't normally work or have their own money because they lived at home until they were married. At that time dating was called courting, which was the prelude to a marriage proposal and the chance for the man to show that he was capable of providing for her.

Today, it's very acceptable for the woman to share in dating expenses. Some women will pack picnics or do other activities that create a date, but don't require them to spend cash. Smart Teenagers know it's proper to reciprocate and have give-and-take in a dating relationship.

It's All in the Details

Another reason to plan your date **before** you invite someone out is that you want to know the details. You don't want to assume anything because the first few dates are *not* the time for you to be surprised. Planning the date gives you a chance to handle important details that might affect the success of your date. You would kick yourself for being unprepared, especially when a phone call or two would have saved you an embarrassing headache. There is nothing worse on a date than to be unprepared and not have enough money, or show up on a day when the place is closed.

If you have decided on a movie, you want to see where and what times it's showing. If you are going to a zoo or amusement park, you want to know what hours it's open, and ask about parking (where and how much) and the admission fee. Don't forget to ask if certain attractions are open. If you're counting on the 'tunnel of love' being the highlight of your evening, you could be disappointed when you find out it's closed for maintenance on the night you go out to the local park. Some activities really require planning, such as concerts or plays for which tickets are sold in advance.

*Scenic spot where people sit in parked cars enjoying the 'scenery', while they kiss or fool around.

The Best First Date

The best first dates are simple and low key. Simple dates are good because the pressure is low. You will both be nervous enough without the added anxiety of eating at an expensive restaurant. It could be extremely nerve-racking to add more details to your mental list if you are worried about the right outfit to wear, where you are going and whether you'll make a mistake. More elaborate plans are good after you've been out once or twice.

The first date should be a chance to get to know the other person better than you already do. Going to a movie is just sitting in a dark room, facing forward, with no opportunity for conversation. The only good things it provides are the chance to sit next to each other and then something to talk about afterwards. Sitting in a Starbuck's sipping a Frappacino and talking is a low-key way to get to know each other. Another good first date is getting a smoothie and taking a leisurely walk.

Men: If you plan to meet your date somewhere, then be sure to make it close to her home so she doesn't have a long-distance drive or need to make special arrangements for a ride.

20 Great Date Ideas

So, you're ready to plan the date. You already know about the popular things to do in your own town. Living near a beach, lake or river opens up lots of possibilities. You can play tourist in your own town by calling your local Chamber of Commerce or Visitor's Center, or by searching the Internet to get more ideas about local attractions. Here are 20 ideas to get you started. The key at the bottom shows approximately how much each activity will cost.

1. Ice cream sundaes or cones ($)
2. Coffee house date (Starbuck's or other local coffee house) ($)
3. Movie ($$$)
4. Lunch or dinner ($$ to $$$—or more depending where you go)
5. Picnic or BBQ at a park, beach or lake ($$)
6. Long walk or hiking (F)
7. Watch a video or play video games at home (F to $)
8. Take your dog for a walk (F)

9. Attend a school athletic event: football, soccer, basketball game, etc. ($$)
10. Participate in church activity (F)
11. Bike ride (F)
12. Hit golf balls at golf course driving range or miniature golf ($$ to $$$)
13. Bowling ($$)
14. Skating (ice or inline) (F-$$)
15. Museum (F to $)
16. Window-shopping (F)
17. Bookstore browsing (F)
18. Local parades or seasonal fairs, local zoo, or other attraction (F to $$)
19. Volunteer someplace locally—homeless shelter, food bank, children's center, read stories at a senior citizen home, etc. (F)
20. Do a chore around each other's house (F)

F = Usually free $ = 5.00 to 10.00 $$ = 10.00 to 15.00 $$$ 15.00 to 25.00

Do *What?*

I know! Ideas 19 and 20 sound crazy. When I was a teenager I'd have split my side laughing at those ideas. Now that I've been around the block a few times I can tell you that these are not bad ideas at all. However, these are **not** first date ideas. These are ideas for people who have had at least 6 or 7 dates. It's a great way to get to know each other on a deeper level. You can learn a lot about someone while volunteering. Do they even want to volunteer or work? Are they lazy or selfish? Are they open-minded or stuck in their own personal rut?

Helping with a chore around your Significant Other's house is a way for their parents to get to know you. It may also give your Significant Other a way to do a dreaded chore that their parents have been nagging them about, such as sweeping out the garage, cleaning the rain-gutters, stacking firewood, or washing the car. Obviously, these are not day-to-day chores, such as doing the dishes. I don't mean you should become their housekeeper. My son, Jason, helped his girlfriend wash her mom's car! (He has never washed my car before.) However, his girlfriend had it on her chore list, and they had a good time doing it together. It also gave him a chance to interact with her mom too.

Warning: If you plan on doing less than your best work on the chore, it's best to pass on this idea. Poorly done work could reflect poorly on you!

House Dates

Who would ever think of having a date at home? Obviously you don't want every time you see each other to be a house date, but Smart Teenagers know that there are some good reasons to have a date at home once in awhile.

Getting to know the woman's parents is really important for men. The parents' confidence in you increases as they get to know you. Because they know you're a good man with honorable intentions, they'll be more comfortable when you're out with their daughter. Since it's not appropriate to invite yourself over, you each need to take the lead on this. Inviting each other over to your houses will be the chance to spend some time with your families. Either a meal, or dessert, or popcorn and a video at home is a great date idea if you aren't totally embarrassed by your family. If your Significant Other doesn't want to spend time at your house, you need to find out why. Are they afraid that your parents won't like them? Are they hiding something?

Group Dates

Some people who aren't allowed to have one-on-one dates can go on Group Dates. Group Dates can be fun because it's just a group of friends hanging out, in which several of the people are couples. It's like having a party without the effort. Even if you've been dating someone for awhile, it's nice to hang out with a group just for fun and variety.

On a Group Date you can use the same ideas as for a one-on-one date. They're usually Dutch treat and sometimes the transportation issues are easier. The best thing about a Group Date is that it takes pressure off in several ways:

- You have lots of conversation opportunities with the group.
- You typically don't have lots of privacy, so there's no pressure to kiss or be sexual before you are ready.

- You can see how the person you're dating acts with others—are they respectful and kind, or obnoxious and mean, do they have fun or are they a party-pooper?
- You can see if you really like this person before the relationship gets serious. If you aren't the match you thought you'd be, the other person is less likely to be crushed if you decline another invitation, since you didn't have an intimate, one-on-one date.

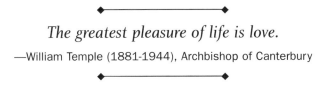

The greatest pleasure of life is love.

—William Temple (1881-1944), Archbishop of Canterbury

 Check Point

Let's see where we are: You know that the best first dates are low-key, and that elaborate plans are best saved for date #2. Plus, you've got some ideas for planning your date. You know about expenses and who pays (unless you say that it is Dutch treat at the time you invite the person out). Hopefully, you can see the wisdom in occasionally having house dates. Now that you have all of that knowledge, you're ready to actually invite someone out on a date! Our next chapter is all about asking.

If you don't ask, you don't get

—Mohandas Gandhi (1869-1948), nationalist leader of India

Asking Someone Out

Flirting was the small step. It was safe. If they didn't flirt back, it wasn't a big deal. Now we're at the big step: Asking someone out. The stakes are higher here, because this is where you'll feel the sting of rejection.

Gandhi's philosophy states that, unless you have the courage to ask, you'll never have a chance to get what you want. Look at it this way: You've got a 50/50 chance of success when you invite someone on a date. Super model Tyra Banks said during an interview that she doesn't date often because she doesn't get asked often. Men don't ask her out because they are too afraid that she'll say no. How ironic that she'd like to be asked and would probably say yes!

Rejection is so painful that, in order to avoid it, we often don't take risks. The problem with the fear of rejection is that it is unfounded until it becomes a reality, so it is a gamble. We won't know what the other person will say until we take the leap and risk being rejected. Before you actually ask someone out, be sure to read the next chapter (*The Big Chill*) on rejection, just in case.

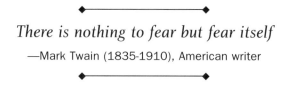

There is nothing to fear but fear itself

—Mark Twain (1835-1910), American writer

Your Insurance Policy

Before you ask, be sure you have your insurance policy in place. What insurance policy? Flirting, of course! It's best if you've had a couple of conversations with the object of your attraction *before* you ask. It provides insurance several ways: You both know each other a little bit, and the several flirting sessions will give you confidence that there's a higher possibility of getting a 'Yes' to your invitation, if they've flirted back.

Ashley's Story

Ashley is an 18-year old college freshman. Halfway through the semester, while waiting to go inside her Spanish class, the really cute guy who sat behind her in class approached her. He asked her to turn in his mid-term paper to the instructor, as he couldn't attend class that day. He had never missed a class before. She thought it was odd that he didn't just go inside the classroom himself. She said okay, and turned in the paper for him.

At the next class meeting, he approached her and thanked her for her help. She said it was no problem. Then, he said he'd like to take her to coffee that afternoon to show his appreciation.

(Continued)

"Oh, thanks," she said, "but that's not necessary. It was no big deal."

The guy got flustered and said, "No, I *want* to take you for coffee after school." Ashley again begged off.

At this point the guy finally said, "You don't understand. You have to say yes, I have it all planned out."

"Well," Ashley responded, "I can't because I'm meeting my boyfriend after school."

The guy's face turned completely white and he quietly said, "Oh."

It was a very awkward moment for both of them. She realized that the guy had probably created the scenario where he would be absent from class, need her help, and then would casually ask her out for coffee to say thank you. Very clever, she thought. However, he violated the important flirt rule. He had never before flirted with Ashley to see how she would respond, *before* asking her out. If he had engaged her in conversation, she would have either mentioned her boyfriend or not flirted back to let him know she wasn't interested. While he was very clever and courageous, he had an embarrassing 'rejection.'

The irony was that the guy was cute and Ashley knew he was smart from hearing his questions during class. If she didn't already have a boyfriend of three years, she would have said yes. Her saying no wasn't about the guy; it was about her circumstances. If he had just tested the waters first, he could have saved himself a moment of awkwardness.

On the Phone, or Face-to-Face?

Is it cowardly to ask for the first date on the phone? No, not entirely. It's always best to handle matters of the heart face-to-face, but there are times when a phone call is just fine. Calling someone that you know fairly well is acceptable. Calling someone who has given you their phone number is acceptable. It's *not* acceptable to call someone you don't know very well and whose phone number you found in the school directory. This is kind of stalker-creepy.

Women Asking Men

A long time ago, if a woman asked a man out, she might be considered "forward." Today, a woman asking a man out isn't taboo, nor does it put her in any insulting category. Many men would like women to ask them out—remember the 60% of the men who liked it when a woman initiated flirting? Those same men would appreciate it if a woman asked them out.

It may seem stereotypical and conventional, nevertheless men generally feel better about themselves when they have made the conquest. It's a strange fact of human behavior that we tend to value that for which we work. If something comes too easily, then the perceived value may not be the same. This is why some women will play hard to get. I believe that men value the relationship more if they have to take a risk by asking for the first date. So men, don't sit there waiting for a woman to ask you out. Be brave, be willing, be strong. Remember the story about Tyra!?

3 Steps to Asking

If you've ...
1. Found someone you're attracted to, AND
2. You've done some flirting, AND
3. The flirting has been received well (you haven't been rejected) ...

Then you are ready to take the next step: Asking someone out. Here are the three steps to asking. When you invite someone out, you are the asker. If you've been asked out, you are the invitee. It's probably not necessary to discuss in detail the obvious hygiene points, but before you ask someone out, make sure your breath is fresh, your teeth are clean, hair is combed and your shirt doesn't have a big stain on it.

Step One

Plan the Activity *before* **You Ask.** See Chapter 4, *Date Ideas*.

Step Two

Don't Ask in Front of a Bunch of People. If the object of your attraction always seems to be with a group, you can approach the group and ask that person to talk alone for a minute. This way, it gives both of you a little room and takes the pressure off. Remember, you're going to be nervous enough so you don't need an audience. You don't have to be alone and sealed off in another room to ask, just a few yards away, so the group isn't in immediate earshot. If the person doesn't want to leave their group for a minute, then this may be a sign that they aren't mature enough to date yet. Time to move on.

Step Three

Get to the Point. Don't beat around the bush, because you'll lose your nerve. You've made a mental plan, you haven't been rejected yet and maybe you've even rehearsed. Keep it simple: Asking should be done in just one or two lines. Make eye contact and smile. Be confident when you say something like, "Hey, I was wondering if you'd like to go to Starbuck's with me and get a mocha, or something." Be sure you have some enthusiasm in your voice. If you are trying too hard to be cool, you may sound depressed, or like you're being forced on a dare to ask them out.

◆————————◆

Do you want me to tell you something really subversive?
Love is everything it's cracked up to be. That's why
people are so cynical about it.
It really is worth fighting for, being brave for,
risking everything for. And the trouble is,
if you don't risk anything, you risk even more.

—Erica Jong, American writer

◆————————◆

71

William's Big Ask

Remember William, who was nervous about flirting with Kim from his History class? After a few friendly, flirty conversations with Kim over the course of a couple weeks, he decided to go for it and ask her out. He was 10 times more nervous about asking her out than when he first talked to her. Now he worried that she'd say no and think that he was a complete idiot, and then he'd still have to see her in class everyday!

In the planning stage, he decided that he'd ask if she wanted to see a movie on Saturday afternoon. The latest Jackie Chan movie was just released. He called the theater and they said they usually run a late matinee at 4:00 p.m. on the weekends. He knew that he was taking a big risk. What if she didn't like Jackie Chan? He also knew that a movie isn't a great 'get to know you' date, but there is a Baskin Robbins next door and they could get ice cream and talk afterwards.

On Thursday, William seized his moment. He caught up with Kim and her friend in the hall.

"Hey, Kim!"

"Hi, William! What are you up to?"

"Oh, all sorts of trouble. Can I talk to you alone for just a minute?" William asked, looking at Kim, then at her friend. Kim's friend nodded with big eyes, dying to know what he would say in her absence.

"Hey, listen," William started, as he looked down at his feet, "I was wondering if you wanted to go see the new Jackie Chan movie over at the multiplex with me on Saturday afternoon." He finally had the courage to look her in the face by the time he said "with me on Saturday afternoon."

Oh, jeez, he couldn't believe it. The sentence seemed too long, and he quietly drew in a deep breath so it wouldn't sound like he was gasping for air.

(Continued)

Kim repressed a smile, but the corners of her mouth turned up. "Oh, William, that is so sweet," she said.

Here it comes, he thought: The big blow-off. She said he was sweet. He wished he could erase the whole thing.

"I want to see it, but I can't do it on Saturday. My aunt and uncle are coming to visit. How about Sunday?"

"Oh, okay. Sure," William said trying to sound relaxed, but he was actually relieved. Somehow his left foot had gone to sleep in just those few seconds. He realized his knees were locked. "*Unlock the knees, unlock the knees*," he reminded himself.

He offered, "Is the 4:00 show okay? I can pick you up, or we can meet there."

"I'll meet you there," she said, with a full smile.

"Great," said William. "Be there about 3:30. I'll have tickets. Maybe we can go to Baskin-Robbins afterward?"

"Okay. Sounds good. I'll meet you there."

They were both smiling, and bobbing their heads to indicate 'it's cool.'

"Bye," said Kim as she turned around.

"Bye," William said as he watched Kim catch up to her friend who was waiting a few yards away. William walked to his next class with the biggest smile he could remember having. He couldn't believe that she said yes.

Change of Day or Activity

Some invitees who have schedule conflicts don't always know that they should suggest an alternative time*. Or, perhaps they just don't like Starbucks (or whatever you've suggested), but don't think to tell you that. When we're being rejected, our normal response is to get

---

*In the next chapter, the section on **Overcoming an Objection** goes into detail about this.*

out of the situation as quickly as possible. Remember to stay cool and ask for more information. Your invitee may not know to give you another option, and you may have to suggest it. They may be as nervous as you are, and can't think of the appropriate response to keep the invitation open.

If you are being asked, and the day or time of the suggested date won't work for your schedule, but you want to go out with the asker, *immediately* tell the asker when you are available to go. Otherwise, the asker may think you are blowing them off and you won't get asked out again.

The Answer

Here are the three most likely answers to your invitation to go out, and the responses you might give them.

Answer #1

Your Ask: "Hey, I was wondering if you'd like to go to Starbuck's with me tomorrow and get a mocha, or something."

Their Answer: "Sure."

Your Response: "Great! How about after school? We can walk there together."

Once the person you've asked has said "yes," then set a time and make arrangements. If it's not possible to make the arrangements right then, get their phone number and call them later that day to set the time.

Answer #2

Your Ask: "Hey, I was wondering if you'd like to go to Starbuck's with me tomorrow and get a mocha, or something."

Their Answer: "Uh, no. Thanks anyway."

Your Response: "Oh, okay. Well, would you rather do something else instead?"

Answer: "Yeah, sure."

Initially, it appears that you've been "rejected." However, this person may just not like either coffee or the activity you've suggested. If they don't suggest an alternative, then you need to decide if you want to offer another date idea. Offering another idea is seriously putting your neck on the rejection chopping block, but if you don't ask, you may always wonder "what if."

I was once asked out to go on a fishing boat as a first date. Since I get seasick, I said, "I get seasick so that isn't very appealing to me." He had the presence of mind to suggest an alternative and said, "Okay. How about a walk on the beach and a bowl of clam chowder at the restaurant on the pier?"

I said "yes" to that!

If the answer to your alternative suggestion is "no," then you can be confident that the person isn't interested in going out with you. (Refer to the next chapter, *The Big Chill*.)

<u>Answer #3</u>

Your Ask: "Hey, I was wondering if you'd like to go to Starbuck's with me tomorrow and get a mocha, or something."

Their Answer: "I can't, I'm busy tomorrow."

Your Response: "Okay. Do you want to go another time?"

Answer: "Yeah, that sounds good."

Be Gracious

There may be times when you're asked out, and you'll say "no." While it seems pretty obvious how to turn someone down, here are a few points to keep in mind before you say no. It's likely that you will cross paths with this person over the next few years. Graciousness* will go a long way towards making it easier to face them next week or next semester.

You should be honored that someone would have the courage to ask you out, and flattered that they find you attractive. You can be mean and rude, or you can be kind and thoughtful in your response. So, unless the person you are rejecting is a psychopathic stalker, it's important to be gracious when you reject someone.

---

*Kindness and politeness

The best way to say 'no' is:

1. Smile (sincerely, not sympathetically)
2. Make eye contact
3. Say firmly, "Thank you, I'm flattered, but no."
4. Give a brief and sincere explanation. If you aren't interested in dating them, let them know so they don't ask again.

Asking & Accepting Don'ts

- Don't wait until the last minute to ask someone out. Generally, women don't like to be asked at the 11th hour. It doesn't give them time to get ready, and it appears that she isn't your first choice! If you can't avoid a last-minute invitation, explain why. Be sure to say, "I know it's short notice but ..."
- Be confident. Don't ask in such a way that you expect to be rejected. Don't say this ... "You wouldn't want to go out with me, would you?"
- Don't fish. Be direct. You'll put a woman on the spot if you ask, "What are you doing Friday night?" Just go for it and ask.
- Don't be nervous asking! To be asked out is a compliment. The person you ask out might be happy to hear your invitation.
- Don't stall for time before accepting or declining an invitation. It's unfair to give an answer that leaves them wondering whether you said "yes" or "no." If you're not sure if you can accept, tell the person why ... "I have to check with my parents first," or "I have to check my schedule first because I think I have a game that night."

 Check Point

You can see that while asking someone out carries a risk, it's actually pretty simple. The hard part is the preparation—flirting and planning the date. You know not to get freaked out if they don't say "yes" right away by first asking if a change of activity or date would make a difference. You also know not to beat around the bush, but to just come out and ask. You know it's better to ask in-person and have a plan in mind before you ask. I'd say you are ready to ask for that date. But before you do, be sure to read the next chapter first!

---

*In three words I can sum up everything I've learned about life:
it goes on.*

—Robert Frost (1874-1963), American poet

The Big Chill

All this talk about dating and now we're going to talk about getting the cold shoulder. There's nothing like the big chill to cool your love jets. Don't get me wrong; I don't want to scare you out of asking someone on a date! But, I do want to live up to my promise to make you a Smart Teenager, so I'll include rejection. Rejection is one of the risks involved in dating and it's better to deal with it before it happens to you.

Outside of masochists*, I can't think of anyone who enjoys being rejected. Rejection, or the word "no," can rip into you and make you want to melt into the ground and disappear. Rejection is so painful that the fear of it keeps many people from taking risks. Whether you're a man or a woman, the bottom line is the same: Rejection sucks. All the knowledge in the

---

One who invites and enjoys misery of any kind, especially in order to be pitied by others, or perhaps admired for their tolerance and patience.

world won't entirely remove the sting of rejection. However, if you understand the dynamics of rejection and build some resistance to rejection, it can help to ease that sting.

Steve & Melinda

Melinda met Steve and she was immediately attracted to him. He definitely fit her imago. She flirted to let him know that she was interested and he flirted back! Over the next four months, they bumped into each other five times. Each time, Melinda flirted and hoped he would ask her out, but Steve never even got close to asking her out. Melinda didn't know why, and to ease the rejection she felt, she figured that he had a girlfriend and that he was a chronic flirt.

On the sixth time they saw each other, Steve worked up his courage and casually asked her if she'd like to get coffee sometime.

"Yes," Melinda answered, trying to act like it was no big deal.

They both laughed later about how he had wanted to ask her out for those four months. Steve was so afraid that she wouldn't go out with him that he wouldn't risk the rejection. He teased Melinda that she should have asked him out. But just like Steve, she was afraid of rejection.

Steve and Melinda have both experienced their fair share of rejection in the dating world, and let the fear of a single word keep them from experiencing four extra months of fun and happiness together. In looking back, they both agreed that it would have been an easy 'bullet' to take if they had heard a quick 'No.'

The Big Little Word

"No" is just a word. It's a small word, but it can knock you for a loop if you aren't prepared. "No" isn't a bullet that will kill us, but it feels terrible to hear it. Steve and Melinda realized it wouldn't have killed them if they were rejected. Yes, they'd feel terrible, but life would go on. So, how do you handle a small word that packs such a powerful punch? You develop ways of coping when you do hear it. One trick is not to take "no" personally.

The Nine No's

Salespeople don't take the word "no" personally. They anticipate it and expect it as part of their job. They realize that getting a "yes" is a matter of odds. It's a numbers game. They will hear "no" a certain number of times before they finally hear a "yes." It's just a matter of time until someone eventually says "yes."

Because salespeople receive so much rejection, they take training classes to help them deal with it. A training exercise that many salespeople learn is called *The Nine No's*. This exercise is based on the theory that 9 out of 10 times they'll hear "no." For every nine "no's" they get, they will get one "yes." In this exercise, the trainees stand together in a group and randomly walk up to each other and ask for something. "Will you give me a glass of water?" "Will you marry me?" "Will you take me shopping?" "Will you lend me your car?" "Will you hug me?" and so on. You get the picture.

What they ask for is not important since the asking is just for the purpose of getting a response. The trainees may only say "yes" on the 10th time they are asked for something. They must say "no" to nine different people, no matter how much they would like to say "yes" to the request. During this exercise, it becomes clear to the trainees that no matter how much they sincerely *wanted* to say "yes," there was an unseen and uncontrollable force that made it impossible. This understanding helps them to not take it personally when they hear "no."

You can apply this principle to your dating life. When you get a "no," just remember that it's a numbers game. You will receive a certain number of no's in your life before you get a "yes." It can help you manage your emotions (hurt, frustration, fear, anger) by understanding this phenomenon. When you are rejected just think, "One down, eight to go!" Sounds encouraging, huh? Okay, rejection still sucks, but at least you know not to take it personally.

Overcoming an Objection

Typically we can be so stunned when we're rejected that our mind immediately thinks, "How can I get out of here?" and we stop listening to the other person. If you get rejected *stay aware*! **Don't blank out!** Instead, see if there is an objection they have that can be resolved or overcome easily. In the last chapter, *Asking Someone Out*, we learned that sometimes there is a logical reason why your invitation isn't accepted, but you might have to ask why. The person you're inviting out could be very nervous too.

So, you aren't going to blank out; you're going to ask for more information. What is the reason they don't want to go out with you? Is it a schedule conflict with the date or time? Do they not like the movie you are suggesting? Are they not allowed to date anyone their parents don't know? It's better to dig a little bit and be *sure* that they're not attracted to you before giving up. Remember, they may just be shy or not know to give you more information. It's okay to ask for more information when you're rejected.

10 Reasons You Might Get a 'No'

1. They're already dating someone else, which you don't know.
2. They're not ready to date at this point in their life.
3. Their parents have forbid them to date until they reach a certain age.
4. Their religion prevents them from dating.
5. They're gay, and you are not of their gender preference.
6. They're afraid of rejection, themselves, and aren't willing to risk being hurt (or failing) by being in a relationship.
7. They aren't interested in dating because they need to stay focused on their education or activities (sports, music, etc.) and know that a relationship will distract them.
8. They aren't attracted to you in a romantic sense—you are not their imago.
9. Their association with a group or clique is so strong, that they face problems if they date outside of that group.
10. They're shallow and say something stupid like, "You are too ... tall, short, etc."

Older Men and Younger Women

Some women are attracted to men who are several years older than they are. This can be especially frustrating for guys. Emotionally, women tend to be about two years ahead of their male peers and may find men of their own age to be immature. Some women just like an older man who can drive. For men, the answer to this age-old problem is either to ask out younger women, or to evaluate whether you truly are behaving immaturely.

Shallow People and Dodged Bullets

We already know that people will say No for many different reasons and it might not have anything to do with us. Unfortunately, some people are jerks and will be mean or rude when they decline an invitation. If someone is a jerk in saying No, let me assure you that you've just dodged a bullet and have been spared a lot of misery. This person would be a nightmare to date and you are actually lucky to get off the hook so easy! If the reason they say No is "You are too … short, tall, fat, skinny, etc.," then it's important to understand that, while they may be attractive physically, they are incredibly shallow and you, my friend, would have exhausted yourself in vain trying to please them. Move on!

Kristen & Jeff

I sat in the dentist's chair as Kristen the hygienist cleaned my teeth. We were discussing the challenges we had as teenagers to keep our braces clean when Kristen told me about a guy she knew in high school named Jeff.

As a freshman, Jeff talked to her every chance he had. She was polite to him, but was completely grossed out to see the white bread and lettuce from his lunch jammed between his braces as he smiled. The guy was skinny, very smart and kind of geeky. He was nice and she knew he liked her, but he was definitely not her type.

(Continued)

The summer between their freshman and sophomore years, Jeff joined the waterpolo team, got tan, completed his orthodontia and puberty set in. Jeff looked completely different. His body had filled out and he had a great smile without braces. They had science together as juniors and were in the same chemistry lab group. That's when Kristen really began to notice him. Jeff and Kristen had a mutual friend, to whom Kristen confided that she liked Jeff. The friend went wild because she knew that Jeff had liked Kristen since they were freshmen. A few months later, Jeff and Kristen were a couple.

They broke up and got back together several times over the next four years. In their senior year of college, when they were 21 years old, they got married. They have been married for 3 years now and Kristen is really glad she hadn't been rude to the geeky, gross freshman when he talked to her.

How 'No' Can Become 'Yes'

There are times that a No can become a Yes. Someone who rejected you might have their circumstances change, or later rethink their decision and wish they had said Yes. Here are three situations where that might happen:

1. **Change:** People can change a lot in a short period of time, especially in high school. Just as with Jeff, one school year or a summer can produce lots of changes in a person, both physically and emotionally.
2. **Time:** Sometimes people become more attractive once we get to know them. Emotional attraction can increase with time. The person who rejected you initially may have a change of heart once they get to know you better.
3. **Circumstances:** The person who rejected you might have been dating someone else at the time you asked. If their relationship doesn't work out, they are available for you to ask out again.

The Two-Way Street Called Grace

I know we talked about declining an invitation graciously in the last chapter, but it bears repeating! *How* you reject someone is important. Just like with Jeff, people change. There might be some point in the future when you'd like to get another invitation from someone you've turned down in the past. So, if you've been gracious and kind when declining an invitation, there *is* a remote chance that, at some point in the future, you could be asked again.

Now, don't think rejection is a one-way street! The rejection needs to be *accepted* graciously as well. Acting like a sore sport can ruin your chances in the future. If you have an ax to grind because you were rejected, you won't be open to asking later. Worse yet: You'll look angry or bitter, or otherwise unattractive to many others around you, not just the person who rejected you.

What's the best way to react if you are rejected? If your invitation is turned down, keep it simple. Don't get mad or defensive. Remember, the 'no' might not have anything to do with you. You can say, "I understand. If you ever change your mind, let me know." This makes you appear confident and in control.

Can I Woo You?

Persistence can pay in the game of love. There are a small percentage of couples that came together because one of them wasn't going to give up easily or take 'no' for an answer. In these cases the man will "woo" or persuade the woman by courting her with little notes or flowers, flattery or a heroic act.

Some people think they can wear someone down to the point where they'll finally say 'yes' just to get their pursuer off their backs. Sure, you can wear someone down. But is that really what you want? There is a fine line between hoping to win someone's heart and being a stalker. Winning someone's heart with your kindness and humor is worth a try, but don't lose your dignity or self-respect in the process. It doesn't work if you threaten, beg or harass someone in hopes that they will go out with you. In fact, it can backfire on you big time when you are seen as a psychotic loser.

◆————————————◆

We cannot be more sensitive to pleasure without being more sensitive to pain.

—Alan Watts (1915-1973), Zen theologist

◆————————————◆

Regaining Courage

If rejection sucks, why would you want to dust yourself off and try again? Heck, you already know how much it hurts to get knocked in the chops. Why should you take that risk again? Because you are not a coward. Because you know it is a numbers game. Because love is worth the risk of being hurt.

Besides, just because *one* person says 'no' doesn't mean that *everyone* will. It is human nature to magnify rejection and assume it will happen to you every time you take a risk. This assumption seems logical to someone who has had several rejections in a row. It's easy to take your last rejection to your next at-bat and let it affect your confidence. Athletes work hard to control their emotions and not get psyched out by failure. A teen's "losing streak" can be rooted in their being psyched out by a few rejections.

While it sucks, there can actually be an upside to rejection. I wish character-building was easier, but personal growth usually follows emotional pain. This personal growth can be that you are more aware and sensitive when you are in the position to reject someone. It can make you conscious of the nature of human behavior, and you can learn a lot about yourself, such as just how emotionally strong you really are, and how level-headed you can be under pressure.

When you are rejected, you can go to one of two places:

1. Lick your wounds briefly and try again somewhere else.
2. Feel sorry for yourself and be a victim. Never risk rejection again and don't ask anyone else out again.

If you decide to take option one, you will develop strength and courage. If you decide to take option two, then you will likely become isolated and bitter. It's human nature to think that everyone in the universe knows that you were rejected. The brain has a way of making a person think that everything revolves around them. Don't let your brain trick you on this. The fact is, very few people will know that you were rejected. Rejection isn't a statement about you as a person; it's a statement about where the declining person (the person who said 'no') is at in their lives. Your last rejection has nothing to do with the next person you ask out.

Smart Teenagers Know ...

- The best way to deal with rejection is to develop coping strategies before it happens.
- Not to take 'no' personally.
- It's okay to ask for more information when you're rejected.
- How you reject someone is important.
- That rejection needs to be accepted graciously.
- That to threaten, beg or harass someone in hopes that they will go out with you never works and will only cause big problems.
- Your last rejection has nothing to do with the next person you ask out.

What's next? Well, if you've flirted and planned for a date, and asked and haven't been rejected, then you, my friend, are going on a date! One of the first things you'll do on your date is meet the parents. That's what our next chapter is all about!

> *When in love one often speaks of love too much,*
> *but does not prove it enough.*
>
> —Mathurin Régnier (1573–1613), French poet

Meet The Parents

As eager as you are to get out on the date, you will most likely meet the parents at the door first. So before we get to the chapter about the actual date, let's do some important preparation first. We want to slant the odds in your favor, right?

Let's face it, the idea of meeting the parents conjures up all sorts of negative images. Think Ben Stiller facing Robert DeNiro in the movie *Meet the Parents*. It also brings up a big question: If you meet the parents, does that mean your casual dating relationship is suddenly serious? Naaah. Mostly, it's a way to show respect to the person you are dating. Besides, family is one of the realities of being in a relationship.

When you date someone, you date his or her parents too. Well, not literally, of course. But since parents usually set rules and limitations for their teens, you will, for better or worse, deal with the parents. Trust me, you'll enjoy the benefits of having established a relationship with the parents, which I'll tell you about soon.

What is the nightmare of every parent of a daughter? That the man she's dating will take advantage of her sexually; will treat her badly or will break her heart. (Ironically, men get their hearts broken too, but it's usually the parents of women who worry most.) So, it helps the parents to relax when they have met, and know, the man their daughter is dating. They will feel comfortable when their teenager goes out with you because they know you. The benefit to you and your Significant Other is a greater chance that curfews will be extended or other privileges given if the parents trust you both.

The best way to get to know your Significant Other's parents is to spend time at their house. You don't want to become a permanent fixture, sitting on their couch all day, eating them out of house and home. On the flip side, if you only honk from the curb they will never get to know you. Attending an occasional family function, having dinner at the house once or twice, or doing an odd-job periodically will give the family a chance to know if you are a good person with honorable intentions. Now, if the person you're dating doesn't want you to meet their parents, you should ask why. Are they embarrassed of you or their family? Either way, it doesn't sound good and you might want to understand why they don't want you to meet their parents.

Getting to Know You

Kathleen's high school sweetheart, Tom, used to come by her house every Saturday afternoon to help her dad with chores. One summer, he even helped put a new roof on their house! All of his friends thought he was a fool. Actually, Tom was a genius. Kathleen's father felt that Tom was from 'the wrong family' and didn't approve of their relationship. Spending time with Tom was all her dad needed to see how wrong his judgment was. Kathleen and Tom have been married (with her father's blessing) since college graduation—and that was 15 years ago!

Eddie Haskell

In the 1960s, there was a TV show called *Father Knows Best* which is seen in reruns on stations like *Nick at Nite* or *TV Land*. One of the teenage characters was Eddie Haskell who was normally a complete jerk. However, whenever a parent came in the room, he acted excessively polite, just to get on their good side. He came off as an insincere brown-noser*. The parents, as well as his friends, saw right through his act.

When you meet the parents or spend time at your Significant Other's house, you *don't* want to be an Eddie Haskell. It's normal to worry if the parents will be scrutinizing you. Chances are, they will be. They want to see if you are good enough for their teen. Just like in the flirting stage, it's best to be yourself. If you are putting on an act, they will smell you out like a rat. While you are being yourself, you also want to put your best foot forward. Unless your parents were sticklers for proper manners, you might want to practice some of the suggestions in this chapter so you are more comfortable when you meet the parents.

The Winter Formal

Jason was excited about the Winter Formal because he really liked Tiffany. Before this, they had a few coffee dates at Starbuck's and a casual lunch date at Gina's Pizzeria, but this was a formal date. He had bought new pants, a shirt and a tie for tonight's event. He arrived with the corsage he had ordered at the florist two days ago. To add to his nervousness, he was meeting her parents for the first time.

Jason's palms were a little sweaty when he knocked on the door. He wiped them on his trouser leg before Tiffany's step-dad answered. Jason was glad he had asked Tiffany what her stepdad's last name was.

"Hi, I'm Jason. I'm here for Tiffany," said Jason as he extended his right hand. He remembered to not squeeze too hard, but Tiffany's dad had quite a grip. So Jason squeezed just hard

(Continued)

---

*A nickname for someone who 'sucks up' or 'kisses butt' to earn points.

enough to match Mr. Johnson's firm grip, but not so much to overpower him. He didn't want to get into a wrestling match with her dad on the porch.

"Hi, Jason," said Tiffany's stepdad, "It's nice to meet you. Come on in." Mr. Johnson motioned for Jason to come inside.

"Thank you, sir. It's nice to meet you too," said Jason as he wiped his feet on the mat before going inside the house.

"Tiffany has an entourage helping her get ready. It sounds like they're having a lot of fun up there," said Mr. Johnson as he looked at the ceiling, indicating that Tiffany was still upstairs. "Hopefully, she'll be down soon. Have a seat."

Apparently, Tiffany's entourage consisted of her sister, her best friend and her mom who were helping with her hair. Jason smiled and took a deep breath as he sat down on the couch. Mr. Johnson sat in what looked to be his personal recliner.

Jason thought to himself, "*Okay, this will be fun. What do I say?*"

Thankfully, Mr. Johnson came to his rescue.

"So, what are your plans for tonight?"

"Well, we have reservations at Chuck's Steak House at 7:00. After that, we'll head over to the dance. A group of us are planning to go to the Coffee Roaster after the dance," Jason said.

"Sounds good. So, are you nervous?" Mr. Johnson asked.

"Uhh, a little. I've never been to a formal dance before," Jason replied.

"Don't worry. You'll be fine. I'll check on the status of their progress. Can I get you anything to drink?" asked Mr. Johnson as he got up from his chair.

"Oh, no thank you," said Jason.

(*Continued*)

Two minutes later, Tiffany's mom came down the stairs. Jason stood up as soon as she walked in the room.

"Hi, Jason. I'm Tiffany's mom," Jason was surprised how much Tiffany looked like her mom.

"Hi, Mrs. Johnson. It's nice to meet you," said Jason as he extended his right hand to shake hers. He remembered to adjust the force of his grip for Mrs. Johnson's smaller hand.

"Oh, please, you can call me Susan," Mrs. Johnson smiled. "Tiffany is running late. She should be down very soon. I think her stepdad is up there with the video camera right now."

"Okay," said Jason. *Oh my gosh*, thought Jason.

The sound of girl's laughter came down the stairs followed shortly by Tiffany and her hair and makeup team. Her stepdad was right behind them, sure enough, with a video camera. Jason couldn't believe how incredible Tiffany looked. Her dark blue dress looked great with her blond hair. Being athletic, she didn't usually wear makeup, but tonight she did. It looked good.

"Wow, I don't know what to say," said Jason as he looked at Tiffany. "You are gorgeous." Tiffany's little sister and best friend were both giggling uncontrollably on the staircase as her dad kept the video rolling.

"Why, thank you," said Tiffany as she turned around to show off her long dress. "You look pretty good yourself." She was smiling her mega-watt smile that Jason loved.

"Is that for me?" asked Tiffany pointing to the corsage still in Jason's hand.

"Oh, yeah," said Jason, embarrassed that he had forgotten all about it. "Here, let me put it on." He had asked Tiffany whether she wanted a pin-on or a wrist corsage before he ordered it. She said wrist corsage. Jason held it up as she slipped her hand through the elastic.

(*Continued*)

"So, what's your plan for tonight?" asked Mrs. Johnson.

Jason outlined the evening again for Mrs. Johnson's benefit, even though he had already told her husband five minutes earlier.

"I have my cellphone with me. Let me leave the number for you in case you need to contact us," said Jason. He noticed that Mrs. Johnson looked at her husband with one eyebrow raised as she said she would appreciate that. Jason hoped that look was a good sign as he wrote his number on the scratch paper Mrs. Johnson handed him.

"What time do you think you'll be back?" asked Mr. Johnson from behind the video camera.

"Well, sir," said Jason, "What time would you like Tiffany home?"

"Let's say midnight," said Mr. Johnson

"Midnight?" said Tiffany. "How about 12:30. Please? It's not a school night."

"No, no. Midnight is fine. We'll be here," said Jason as he looked at Tiffany. He didn't want to push his luck on their first official date.

"We should get going if we want to make our dinner reservation. I know they'll be packed tonight," Jason said looking at his watch.

"Have fun and be safe," called her mother from the porch. The video camera was still rolling and the two girls and the parents watched as Jason and Tiffany drove down the street. "Amazing," Jason thought to himself. Just a few minutes ago he was shaking the Johnsons' hands. Now he was driving off with one of their most prized possessions.

True to his word, Jason had Tiffany home at 11:55.

Initial Introductions

Meeting the parents for the first time can be nerve-racking. When you make the initial introductions, it's best if the teen of the parent does the introduction and says, "Mom and Dad, I'd like you to meet Sarah. Sarah, this is my mom, Betty, and my dad, Frank." If the teen of the parents isn't aware of the protocol, then you should take it upon yourself to introduce yourself. You simply say, "Hi, my name is (your name)." The parents will introduce themselves. Here are the steps you should take when meeting someone:

1. **Stand.** If you are sitting when they come into a room, stand up. This is a sign of respect.
2. **Look them in the eye and smile**. Not looking them in the eye sends the message that you have something to hide. Not smiling says you are unhappy or, worse, a mean person.
3. **Extend your right hand to shake their right hand.** If you don't have a lot of practice shaking hands, practice with a friend. You want your grip to be firm. Not hard. Not limp. A bone-crushing handshake is equally as bad as a limp-wristed, wimpy handshake.
4. **Say, "It's nice to meet you."** This greeting is known as a social pleasantry. It may *not* be entirely nice to meet them since you may be very nervous. However, it's a good idea to say it sincerely anyway.

Mrs. Smith or Betty?

Up until about 20 years ago, it was considered disrespectful if you called an adult by their first name. Today it's common for a teen to call an adult by their first name. However, addressing parents as "Mr." or "Mrs." is a sign of respect and will make a good impression. Wait for them to invite you to call them by their first name. They might say something like, "Oh, please, call me Betty. Mrs. Smith is my mother-in-law."

Smith or Henderson?

Before you meet the parents, it's a good idea to confirm their last name with your date. As most of us know, parents don't always have the same last name as their kids. You could touch a sensitive "nerve" if you address a parent by the wrong last name! Jason avoided a problem by asking Tiffany before he met her parents.

Touchie-Touchie

When your relationship becomes physical, it's easy to forget where you are and give your Significant Other a passionate kiss. Here is an important tip: When you're with parents it's best to keep physical contact and touching to an absolute minimum. Parents will imagine that you do a lot more in private if you are comfortable groping each other in front of them.

A peck on the cheek or handholding is perfectly acceptable for most parents. Some parents may not even like this much, so it's best to move slowly with PDA's (Public Displays of Affection) around the parents. If you are watching television together on the couch, you don't want them to find you lying on top of each other. So, keep it cool when you are around parents.

Bad Blood

Will parents automatically like you, just because you've spent time at their house and are respectful? No. It's not a guarantee. A parent might not like the person their teen is dating for several reasons. These reasons fall into two different categories: Controllable and Uncontrollable. Some reasons you can control. Others you can't.

Category One—Controllable Reasons

These are reasons that you **can** control. If your Significant Other is important to you, you might consider what could be changed. By making reasonable changes, the parent's perception of you might change, which can make your relationship smoother. Just like taking a personal inventory, ask yourself honestly if any of these apply to you:

- You treat their child poorly, are rude, disrespectful or take advantage of him/her.

- You are rude or disrespectful to the parents.
- You create problems or get into trouble with authorities, etc.
- Their teen's school performance has suffered since meeting you.
- Their teen gets into trouble at home or at school since meeting you.
- You are a couch potato and eat them out of house and home.
- You are involved with drugs, alcohol or gangs.
- You have a school record that involves suspensions, expulsions or other behavior problems.
- You have poor hygiene or are sloppy.

Category Two—Uncontrollable Reasons

These are reasons that you **can't** control. They are the fears of the parents. Nothing you do will change the parents' perception in these cases. Since you are powerless in these situations, you and your Significant Other need to discuss how you want to handle your relationship. Will you avoid the parents? Break up? This is a tough situation and you'll have to face it.

Over-Protective Parents. These parents are fearful of their teen growing up or are overly afraid that something bad will happen to their teen.

Daddy's Girl or Mama's Boy. Some parents, especially single parents, are very close to their teens. They might feel threatened that dating will take their child away from them. It's easy for these people to misplace their fear of separation by projecting negative thoughts onto the person their child is dating.

Not MY Imago. Some parents have their own ideal, or imago, of the type of person that their teen should date. You might not fit their ideal. Perhaps you or your family doesn't have the background, education or social connections that they feel is befitting* their child. You might be a different color, religion or culture and the parents might be bigoted or prejudiced. As a result, they aren't interested in getting to know you as the good person you are. They can make your relationship difficult

---

Befitting: Suitable or appropriate.

by setting early curfews or even forbidding their teen from seeing you. Worse yet: They can make verbal put-downs or other cutting remarks to your face.

What if *you* don't like the Parents?

If *you* don't like your Significant Other's parents, then do the minimum necessary to be respectful to them. You don't have to hang out at their house or put yourself in uncomfortable positions. However, resist all urges to bad-mouth them. It's best not to say negative things about your Significant Other's parents. They may be mad at their parents and need to blow off steam about them every now and then. You should just listen. Don't judge or take sides, even if you agree with your Significant Other. Isn't it ironic that it's okay for us to criticize our own families, but usually not okay for others to criticize them? Remember, your sweetheart lives with them, so don't make disparaging remarks about the family, which can make the situation even harder for them.

Curfew and Rules

When you're out having a good time nothing is worse than to stop and say, "I have to go home." It can be embarrassing and frustrating, especially when you don't want to go home and when you know that others are allowed to stay out later. One of the challenges of being a teenager is that your parents are legally and morally responsible for protecting and guiding you, even though you might have your own ideas about how you want to live your life.

Responsible parents make decisions to protect and guide their teen. The fact is that privileges are an extension of responsibility. If you are responsible and respectful, parents are more likely to give you a longer leash. Most parents want their teens to enjoy themselves and have a good time. They really don't want to be unreasonable. Be respectful. Don't give the parents a reason to deny you permission to go out with their teen. In a healthy relationship, both partners will support each other in dealing with their parents.

Smart Teenagers Know ...

- That honoring parent's curfews and rules will most likely get your Significant Other a longer leash.
- To do the simple things that show respect towards adults, such as calling them Mr. and Mrs., and shaking their hands when meeting them.
- When you are with parents it's best to keep physical contact and touching to an absolute minimum.
- The difference between the controllable and uncontrollable reasons that their Significant Other's parents might not like them.
- It's best to resist all urges to bad-mouth their Significant Other's parents, no matter how much they don't like them.

So, you've scored points with the parents. Now, what about your date? The next chapter will give you all the right moves.

The way to love anything is to realize that it might be lost.

—G.K. Chesterton (1874-1936), British writer

Smooth Moves

I know, who cares about manners? That was for the old days, right? Well, with good manners sitting at number 7 on the *Top 10 Turn-on's* list, it's a worthy topic to discuss. Some men will probably think as they read this chapter, *"This is too much. I'll never do those things."* What they don't know is that there is nothing smoother than a guy who opens the door or helps a woman on with her coat. The guy who does this is a man, not a boy. Women know it.

You might think you're too cool to use manners. But to women, a man who knows how to handle himself *is* cool! Besides, having the right moves will make you look good and feel confident. It's easy to think in this time of gender equality that the old rules of etiquette don't apply, but good manners and respect *never* go out of style. If you really care about the person you're dating, you'll want to show it.

For Men and Women

- Say, "thank you" and "please" sincerely. These don't cost extra and go a long way.
- Smile if you're having a good time. If you're a complete downer, then your date won't have a good time and may not be interested in going out with you again.
- Make eye contact when you speak.
- Don't let your eyes wander. If you're constantly looking at other people, it will tell your date that you're a player or not really interested in them.
- Don't talk about your ex's or other dates you've had. It can make your date uncomfortable and makes you look like you are still hung up on your ex, or are bragging about past conquests.
- If you are paying for the tab, move it near you on the table as soon as it arrives. Don't let it sit there untouched for a long time. You can stay and enjoy the atmosphere for a little longer, even if the bill has arrived.
- Be sure you know how to tip. Check out the Tipping Guide in this chapter, or go to *www.tipping.org* for more detailed information.
- Don't use too many swear words. If every other word that comes out of your mouth is foul, it can be a turn-off. It also makes you look like you have to use tough words to look cool. Save the tough words for when it's appropriate, not regular conversation.
- When you run into people you know, keep the meeting brief. Introduce your date immediately and don't let your time get monopolized by people you run into. There's nothing worse than being abandoned by your date, who is busy socializing with people who bumped into you. A gracious way to end the accidental meeting is to say, "Hey, it was great seeing you. We're going to get back to our dinner. I'll call you and we'll get together soon." Likewise, when *you* run into someone who is on a date, keep it brief. Especially if they are in the middle of a meal.

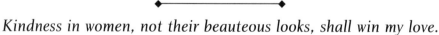

Kindness in women, not their beauteous looks, shall win my love.

—William Shakespeare, *The Taming of the Shrew* (written about 1594)

Just for Men

- Open doors and let her go first. Being a gentleman doesn't mean the woman is weak. If she makes a scene about being able to open her own door, she may be insecure and trying to prove herself, or immature and not know about manners.
- Help her get her coat on and off (if she has one). This is a very cool move.
- Let her sit down before you do, and help her with her chair.
- When walking on a sidewalk, you should walk on the street side. This originated in the horse-and-buggy days, when streets weren't paved, to protect a lady's clothing if mud or water splashed up from passing wagons. However, this is still considered good manners today.

Just for Women

- Let the man open doors for you. Say 'thank you' when he does.
- Don't always ask to go, or expect to be taken, to the most expensive places. Remember that your man is not likely a millionaire.
- Eat what you order. It is rude to order a large expensive meal and then just push it around on your plate. If you aren't very hungry, order a dinner salad and soup, or an appetizer.
- Order what you want, but don't order the most expensive item on the menu just because it is the most expensive.

The Coat

Men know that this is the coolest and smoothest thing they can do with a woman, but only if they can do it well. Think James Bond cool. Without any effort, you take her coat from her, open it up and she smiles. "*Wow,*" she thinks, "*The other guys I dated would never do this.*" She slips her arms in one at a time. Because you are skilled at this, the coat goes on easily. As you bring her coat up to her shoulders, you lean in just a bit to catch the smell of her hair. Yes, I can assure you that women really like this move.

Because it's important to do it right, I'll walk you through the steps. Be sure to practice once or twice before you do this.

1. Take the coat and hold it by the collar with both hands. You want to open the coat as far as you can without ripping it.
2. This is key: Stand behind the woman and hold it at her waist level. This will allow her to easily put her hand in the armhole. If you hold the coat up too high, she will struggle to put her hands in and the whole thing ends up like a comedy.
3. Once she has one hand in the sleeve, bring that side of the coat up a few inches, and then bring the coat around so she can easily put her other hand in.
4. Once both arms are in the sleeves, you will make a single move to pull the entire coat up to her shoulders. From here you have several options, depending on your relationship: You can lean in slightly and give a little squeeze/hug or you can nuzzle her, or you can put your hand on her upper back.

Restaurants

Restaurants have the most opportunities to display your good manners. There are also lots of hurdles to navigate. Obviously, at McDonald's or Taco Bell, you don't have to worry about a hostess, waiter, cocktail waitress, ordering dessert, leaving a tip or wondering about a doggie bag. We'll assume that you know how to handle the world of fast food and concentrate on the mid-level to upper-end restaurants.

A restaurant is a service business. It's their job to provide you with service that exceeds your expectations. Restaurant staff can make a customer's experience Heaven or Hell. However, they deal with lots of angry people every day. By being pleasant, you make their job easier and your experience more positive. Smile. Don't yell. Ask for what you want. Don't demand it.

Nine Smooth Restaurant Moves
1—Reservations

If you can, call ahead to the restaurant and ask to make a reservation. Not every restaurant accepts reservations. Many operate on a first-come-first-served basis. With restaurants like Denny's or IHOP, you won't be able to make a reservation, and if it's really busy you may have a short 5 to 10-minute wait. It's not uncommon for a popular local restaurant to have a 30-minute or longer wait on a Friday or Saturday night. A 30-minute wait can throw your evening off if one of you is starving or you plan to catch a movie at a certain time. A reservation, if it is available, will keep you from waiting.

Call the restaurant in advance and make the reservation in your name. If you have been to the restaurant several times before and know of a specific table you like, you can request that table. Most restaurants will do their best to accommodate you, but usually can't guarantee it. If it's a special occasion, like a school dance, birthday or anniversary, mentioning that will help move you up the priority list. However, be prepared when they bring a birthday sundae with a candle.

If you are planning to go out for the Homecoming or Prom, be sure to make reservations as far in advance as you can. Popular restaurants will be booked well ahead of time and you may find yourself waiting for several hours to get a table—or at Denny's at the last minute.

2—Get on the List

Once you enter the restaurant, whether you made reservations or not, you need to approach the hostess station and give your name to let them know you've arrived.

If you didn't make a reservation, the man should approach the hostess station and put his name on the list. If the hostess doesn't tell you how long the wait is, it's customary to ask. The hostess won't care if you decide to leave and go somewhere else, even if you put your name on the list.

You can check with the hostess periodically to see where you are on the list. Sometimes, on a busy night, the wrong name can get crossed off accidentally and you might end up waiting longer than necessary. Checking with the hostess will prevent that.

3—Being Seated

When the hostess calls your name to be seated, the man will let the woman go first and he follows his date as they walk behind the hostess towards the table. He will help his date take her coat off before she sits down.* The woman should sit down first. If the man wants to be

---

*The coat can then be placed on the back of her chair.

really slick, he can pull her chair out—not so far that she is two feet from the table, but just enough for her to slide comfortably into the chair. Help push her chair in closer to the table if necessary.

If the hostess has seated you at a table that isn't very desirable (perhaps it's right next to the kitchen door or a bussing station), ask for another table. It's better to wait another 5 minutes for a good table than to be miserable during your entire meal.

4—Ordering

Some men think it's cool to order for the woman. It's best for each person to choose what they want to eat. If you've asked the woman what she wants to eat and you've asked her if you can order for both of you, then it's okay to order for your date. However, it's not fair to decide what she's going to eat, unless she wants you to.

Don't be afraid to ask for what you want. If you're allergic to onions, tell the server "no onions." You can ask to have the veggies on the side if you want. Most restaurants are happy to accommodate your requests. If the menu says "No Substitutions" that means they may not be willing (or able) to substitute beef for chicken in a dish or some other request that you might have. In any event, ask.

Some dishes are messier to eat than others. When you order, think about how eating the particular dish will affect your appearance to your date. Ribs are good, but very messy. You might want to pass on those for the first date if you are self-conscious.

Hint: If your date is rude or mean to the server, it's likely they will treat you the same way once the honeymoon phase* is over.

5—Coffee and Dessert

When the meal is finished, the server will most likely offer you coffee and dessert. For some people, it can be embarrassing to admit that they want the decadent house treat. After a big meal it may be hard to

---

The early phase of the relationship when things seem perfect.

eat an entire piece of cake by yourself. Offering to share one dessert is a romantic solution.

6—Doggie Bags

You ordered what you thought you could eat and you didn't eat anything right before your dinner date. Still, some restaurants serve very large portions and there can be leftovers. Carrying around a doggie bag for hours can be awkward. If you don't plan to go home right away, the food can quickly turn bad in the time that you watch a movie. Besides, nothing smells worse than hour-old Chinese food in a car that has been closed up. Before you ask for a doggie bag, ask yourself how smart it is, considering your plans. This is not the time to be worried about the starving kids in another country.

7—Check, Please

In most good restaurants the server will keep an eye on you to see when you have finished eating. They will ask if everything is all right and if they can get you anything else. If you are ready to leave, you can ask for your check. In a busy restaurant, you might have to get the server's attention. In this case, *you* will need to keep an eye on the server. Once the server is moving in your general direction, raise your hand that is towards the outside of the table. You don't want to raise it like in school, but just slightly above your head. Hold your first two fingers together, kind of like a closed 'peace sign.' This should be enough to get the server's attention, as they will see out of the corner of their eye that something is above the rest of the heads. You never want to shout at the server, but there may be a time when you need to say "excuse me" firmly enough to get their attention without bringing the entire restaurant to a silent stop. Once they make eye contact with you, continue looking at them and slightly nod your head to confirm that you want them at your table.

8—Tipping

Tipping is not, and should not be, considered essential. It is a gratuity, which means you are grateful for the extra service that was provided. However, keep in mind that servers are usually paid about

$2.00 per hour and depend on tips to make their living. Also, if you plan to return to the restaurant, you don't want to be remembered as a bad tipper the next time. The tipping guide below will give you a sense of what is expected. A fair tip is between 15 and 20% of the pre-tax total of the bill, with 15% for good service and 20% for great service.

Even die-hard math phobics can figure 10% of a number. Let's say the pre-tax total for your dinner is $27.67. To make it easy, first round the total off to the nearest ten. In this case, round the bill up to $30.00. 10% of 30 is 3, or $3.00. If the service was good, divide the $3.00 by 2 ($1.50) to get the 5%, so you will leave $4.50 for a tip. This works out to a 16.5% tip on your bill.

For those who don't want to do headmath, you can buy a credit card sized tipping chart to slip into your wallet, which you can discreetly refer to as you are getting cash out. Most gift or greeting card stores carry these tipping cards.

Tipping Guide

Waiter or waitress	15%-20% of pre-tax bill
Restaurant owner	None
Busboy	None
Servers at counter	15% of pre-tax bill
Coat-check attendant	$1.00 for one or two coats
Restroom attendant	50 cents to $1.00
Valet parking attendant	$1-$2.00

9—The Exit

Once the meal is over, the bill has been paid, and you are ready to leave, you will reverse your actions from when you were seated. The man stands first, walks behind the woman's chair and gently pulls it out. He may offer his hand to help her stand up. Be sure to put her coat over your arm. The woman walks out first and the man will follow until they approach the door. If it's cold, once near the door, the man can help her on with her coat. Then the woman will let the man step ahead to open the door for her.

Eating and Utensils

Eating in front of a date for the first time can be embarrassing, especially if you aren't sure of your table manners. If you find yourself in a restaurant or having dinner at your Significant Other's house with their parents, here are 10 simple tips to keep in mind. I know these will seem elementary to some people, but there are a lot of people who don't know basic table manners. I've shown several of my son's teenage friends (from good families) how to use a knife!

10 Table Tips

1. Elbows off the table.
2. Sit up, don't rock back in your chair.
3. Napkin on your lap or over your leg as soon as you sit down.
4. Use the first utensils that you come to. If there is more than one fork or spoon at the setting, work from the outside in towards the plate.
5. Cut food into small bites—don't stuff your mouth so full that food falls out, or you'll look like a chipmunk packing food away for the winter.
6. Close your mouth when you chew. Seeing ABC (Already Been Chewed) food is gross and a turn-off.
7. Don't talk with your mouth full. Chew and swallow before you talk. A minute of silence as you eat is normal.

Cutting Food

8. If you are right-handed, hold the knife in your right hand. Hold the fork in your left hand with the back (curve) of the fork showing out and your left pointer finger resting down the back of the fork to give it stability. Pierce the food you are cutting with the fork and gently 'saw' the knife back and forth as you press down the back curve of the fork. If you cut too vigorously, it can shake the whole table.
9. Practice cutting food at home, *BEFORE* you find yourself on a date.
10. European-style is to keep the fork in your left hand and knife in your right hand as you eat. This takes some practice as the fork is

continually upside-down. For American-style, after you've cut the food, put the knife down across the top edge of the plate, then place the fork in your right hand to move food to your mouth.

(For more information on how to eat specific foods, go to *www.westernsilver.com* and click on "Etiquette".)

Making an Introduction

If you run into friends while on your date, be sure to introduce your date immediately. Unless you are positive that they have already been introduced, it's best to introduce them again. They can always say, "Yes, we've met." No harm, no foul. However, if you fail to introduce someone it can be rude and awkward for them as they sit there feeling left out.

1. State the names of the individuals being introduced. "Sarah, this is Bob. Bob, this is Sarah."
2. Tell them what your relationship to the person is. "I'd like you to meet my neighbor, Bob."
3. Show respect to those who are older by introducing them to the younger person: "Grandpa, I want to introduce you to my boyfriend, Tony Batali. Tony, I'd like you to meet my Grandfather, Mr. Anderson." A way to remember this is "Age Before Beauty."
4. Present a woman to a man, then present the man to the woman: "Sarah, I'd like to introduce you to my neighbor, Bob. Bob, this is my girlfriend, Sarah." A way to remember this is "Ladies First."

Manners Quick Tips

Thank you, thank you—This is the single most important thing you can do to show you have good manners. Say thank you! It's always appreciated, and it's free!

Acknowledge Others—This is the second most important thing you can do. Whenever you see someone you know, don't just give them a casual flip of your head. Actually say "Hi." When they are leaving, say "Goodbye." I know this sounds like a no-brainer, but many people fail to acknowledge others. Being acknowledged makes people feel important and is a sign of respect. Using their name when you say "hello" doubles the effect.

Movies—Get to the theater early enough so you don't have to grope your way around in the dark in hopes of finding two seats together. Always ask the other person where they prefer to sit. Some like the front row, while others prefer the back row.

Pardon Me—When you need to leave the table or get up from your seat at a theater or leave your date for any reason, let them know. A simple, "Excuse me. I'll be right back," is sufficient. It's very nice if the man stands when the woman gets up to leave.

Eating Over – For those times when you eat a meal at your Significant Other's house: Ask if you can help with anything when you arrive. The answer will likely be no. If it's a yes, you will immediately be more comfortable because you are part of the action. Practice all of the good manners discussed here, such as saying thank you, excuse me, etc. When you are done, take your plate and silverware to the sink. If you are a real gem, you can offer to help with the dishes. Again, the answer will probably be no, but you look like a million bucks!

 ## Check Point

Do you want to see what I mean about manners never going out of style? A great movie to see about how manners score big points, especially with women, is *Kate and Leopold*. Yes, it's a chick flick. But it's worth the 90-minute investment. There are two or three funny scenes where Kate's brother is given etiquette tips that revolutionize his dating life. It's a good reinforcement to everything we've gone over in this chapter.

At this point, all the groundwork for a successful date has been laid out. You know about attraction, flirting, planning a date, asking for a date, meeting the parents and manners. Whew! The rest of the book is about the actual date, the relationship and sex ... Buckle up.

A kiss that speaks volumes is seldom a first edition.

—Clare Whiting

Showtime: The Date

Can you believe it? We made it to the date! All of the groundwork we've done will pay off here. Your chance for a second date is decided on the *first* date. Now it's Showtime!

It's natural to be nervous about making a mistake or doing the wrong thing. The good news is that, just like riding a bike, driving a car or playing a new video game, once you've done it a few times you know the routine and it becomes automatic. You just do it. After you've become a dating pro, you'll still be excited or nervous with each new person you date. However, your concern will be whether they like you, instead of whether you are doing things right.

In order to master the techniques of dating, this chapter goes over each detail of a date. You should know that every date has four parts.

1. Preparation
2. Pick up/meet
3. Activity
4. Drop off/goodbye

1. Preparation

Be Clean. This is obvious, but take a shower and wear deodorant, brush your teeth and wear clean clothes. This is not the best time to try out a new hairstyle or new shoes that may give you a blister. You want to be comfortable.

Be Financially Prepared. Be sure you have more than enough money for the activity you've planned. If you're going to have pizza and a movie, $10.00 will not get you far. Before you go, add up the expected costs of your date and then bring an extra $20.00, just in case. You don't want to be short on cash. Even if you aren't paying for the date, you should have some cash with you.

Gas up. Remember that a cool car was number four on the *Top Ten Turn-Ons* List. Whether you drive a sedan or a sports car, a dirty car filled with trash that runs out of gas isn't cool. If you're driving, get your car washed and get gasoline. You don't want to be stranded somewhere late at night because you didn't think ahead. It could also potentially put your date in danger, while you are off getting more gas for the car.

Plan the Timing. Give yourself enough time to get to your destination. If you're going to a 7:00 movie, don't pick your date up at 6:45. You want to have time to speak with the parents for a few minutes, drive without rushing, find parking and get good seats together before the lights go down. In general, if you are going to a movie, allow 30 minutes *plus* the driving time to get to the theater before the show starts. Allow more time for a new movie that has been released in the past two weeks, because there will be lines and big crowds.

Check your Wallet. On top of planning your cash needs for the date, double-check that you actually **have** your wallet as you walk out the door. All the cash planning in the world won't help you if your wallet is left on your bed.

Check Your Watch. If you don't normally wear a watch, be sure you take one with you. It's important to keep an eye on the time; you want to arrive for your reservation at the restaurant or get home when you agreed.

Show up on Time. Nothing says "I don't care" like being late. If you can't avoid being late, call your date to tell them as *soon as you know* you will be late. This gives them time to slow down as they are getting ready, move a reservation back and be more understanding about the delay.

2. The Pick Up

Sometimes you'll meet your date at the agreed upon place. However, don't make a habit of this. Remember that it's important to meet your date's family. If the man can drive, he usually picks the woman up at her house. If he doesn't drive, she might pick him up or they may meet somewhere, or a parent will do the chauffeuring. Whether the man or the woman drives, the pick up is handled the same.

Go to the Door and Knock. I've said this before, but it's worth repeating. Honking the horn at the curb sends a message to your date (and their parents) that they're not important to you. Tough guys who tend to treat women badly are the ones who think this is perfectly acceptable. If someone doesn't want you to meet their parents, then you want to ask why: What are they hiding? Are they ashamed of you?

Meet the Parents. Do everything suggested in Chapter 8, *Meet The Parents.*

Log a Flight Plan. Pilots always log their flight plan before they take off. They tell the FAA when they are leaving, where they are going and when they will return. Likewise, tell the parents what your plans are and where you'll be. While this takes some of the spontaneity out of a date, it will set the parents' minds at ease and build trust for the future. Ask when **they** would like you to be back. If they say 10:00, don't flinch. Just do it. If you live up to their expectations, they will probably extend the curfew in the future as they get to know you.

Leave Your Number. Men: If you have a cellphone, leave the number with the parents. Again, this is another way for them to see that you are responsible.

3. The Activity

This part is easy: You do the activity you planned (see Chapter 5 for date ideas). But just as in life, sometimes dates don't always go as planned. If you miss the movie or if the restaurant is packed, you can opt for something different as you go along. Don't be so committed to your plan that you aren't flexible when needed. It's a good idea to have a back-up in case the original plan doesn't work out. If your plans change significantly, be sure to make a quick call to the parents to let them know. Build that trust! A one-minute phone call can earn *lots* of good will points with mom and dad.

4. The Drop Off

The last part of the date is the Drop Off. This step is as important as any, as this will be your date's last thought of your time together. The to-do points below apply for both men and women on a date, unless it's specifically mentioned otherwise.

1. For the man who drove, walk your date to the door. For the woman who drove, say goodbye in the car.
2. If you had a good time, tell your date at the drop off.
3. If you want to see your date again, tell them at the drop off.
4. Men: It's especially cool to tell your date that you will call them, but *only* if you really plan to call.
5. Thank your date for a great time—remember that there was planning, preparation and money spent on both sides.
6. Brief kiss. Heavy make out sessions should *not* be done at the door. The parents or neighbors could be watching even if you can't see them*! Many people prefer not to kiss on the first date and will say goodbye with just a friendly hug, or a kiss on the cheek.

Note: If a woman doesn't want to be walked to the door, the guy needs to wait until she is inside safely before driving off, just in case she forgot her keys, etc.

---

*See the section on PDA's in Chapter 13, **Sex in the Big City**, for more about this.

Being Chauffeured

Not everyone starts driving once they turn 16. In these cases, you may need to ask a friend or family member to drive you. It can be a little embarrassing to need a ride, but if you are cool about it and don't apologize or act embarrassed, it won't be a big deal. The pick up is handled the exact same way when you are chauffeured. Go inside and meet the parents. When you get to the car, be sure to introduce your date to the person who is driving. Both daters should be sure to thank the person who drove.

Beyond the Basics

Okay, now you have the four basic parts of a date. You must be wondering if that's all there is. No. There's more. This next section is kind of the advanced dating information. Knowing these things will elevate your dating skills several notches. You will be one Smart Teenager after this!

The Day-After Call

Men, don't miss this sure-fire winner. If you want to have another date, call the woman the day after you went out. If you get her answering machine, just leave a brief message. If you talk to her, the conversation doesn't have to be long—just a few minutes. The call is a check-in to say "hi" and let her know that you had a good time and mention that you'd like to go out again. She can say thank you for a great time again and let you know that she would also like to see you again.

In dating, it's easy to second-guess and over-analyze events. The day-after call is reassuring for both of you. Obviously, if you *don't* want to have another date *and* you said this at the drop-off, then **don't call**, as it would send the wrong message.

Light and Easy, Fun and Breezy

The overall theme to the date should be: *Light and easy, fun and breezy*. What do I mean by that? When people have a good time with you, they feel connected and will be eager to see you again. If your dates are routinely full of heavy conversations or dramatic scenes, going out with you will be considered a chore. This doesn't mean that a serious conversation during a date is a disaster; just make sure you don't have a steady diet of gut-wrenching, heavy talks. You can't force intimacy. The relationship has its best chance to develop if the time you spend together is fun and relaxing.

Don't overwhelm your date with stories about your terrible parents or mean boss. It puts too much pressure on your date if you expect them to be your therapist. Instead, turn to your other friends for comfort and support when you need it. Maintain relationships with your friends so you don't need to constantly unburden yourself to your Significant Other. This doesn't mean that you never share your feelings or what is happening in your life. But you want to keep a balance of fun in the relationship.

Miserable City

Not every date will be a huge success. If your date acts bored or withdrawn, or you seem to argue at every turn, or you both are miserable, stop and do a quick inventory:

1. Is the activity truly, miserably boring? Such as, because you are fascinated with insects you have taken your date to a lecture on the reproductive habits of Dung Beetles. (They may not find this as riveting as you do!)
2. Do you have bad breath?
3. Are you being rude, mean or obnoxious?

If you answered "no" to these questions, then you can just come right out and ask your date if they are having a good time. If the answer is no, then ask what would make it better. It may be something that can be easily fixed, such as you are going bungee jumping and your date is afraid of heights; or the pizza came with anchovies and your date hates anchovies. Is he talking too much about the RAM on his computer? Is she talking too much about her friends? These are minor obstacles that can be negotiated. Understanding and respecting each other's wants and needs is a big part of relationships. Communication and compromise are key elements in dating!

Strike Out

Don't worry; no one is making a play-by-play commentary of your date. The fact is, most people go on at least one or two dates in their lives that don't work out. If the date has been miserable and there is nothing that seems to make it right, you have a Strike Out date! A Strike Out date is where you both are miserable and are going through the motions. You and your date may not be a good match and your personalities are clashing. Dating allows you to see the person as they really are and not just as the fantasy you may have created in your mind. On a Strike Out date, you learned that you aren't a good fit together.

If the date is a disaster because of a major personality clash (and not just a minor difference of opinion), don't try to stick it out. Cut your losses early, call it quits and take your date home **before** things get downright ugly. (There is a great story about this in Chapter 12, *Making A Relationship Work*.) If your date drove you, ask to be taken home. If you don't feel safe with your date then call your parents, a friend, or a cab and get yourself home.

◆――――――◆

Only those who dare to fail greatly can ever achieve greatly.

—Robert Kennedy, former Attorney General of the U.S.

◆――――――◆

Calling It Off

By the end of the date, if you *know* that you are *not* interested in repeating the evening, let your date know. You don't need to explain all the reasons why you aren't interested in them. Whether you're a man or a woman, just say:

"Thank you for the … dinner/movie, etc. … You are a nice person, but I don't feel that we're a good match. I hope you'll understand that I don't want to go out again."

This is a difficult line to deliver, but will ultimately spare both of you the embarrassment of a future invitation. If you can't say it to their face, then call them the next day and say it on the phone. Don't let several days go by and pray they lose your number. You don't want the other person to build false hopes. They may be expecting a second date, which makes it doubly painful for them when they figure out that you aren't interested.

Dating Do's and Don'ts

- **Do** spring for parking. In some cities parking in public lots is available for just a few dollars. For women wearing high heels, walking 8 blocks to save $3.00 isn't a good bargain.
- **Do** put your cellphone on vibrate.
- **Do** ask your date, "Do you mind if I take this?" *before* you answer your cellphone.
- **Do** keep cellphone conversations short: Tell the caller, "I'm on a date. Can I call you back tomorrow?"
- **Do** turn your cellphone off when you are in a movie.
- **Do** ask your date general questions about themselves, their family, pets and their hobbies or interests.
- **Do** talk about what you like to do on the weekends.
- **Don't** take your date somewhere that you know you will run into your Ex. This can be seen as manipulative by both your Ex and your current date.
- **Don't** talk excessively about your bodily functions (such as burping, farting, etc.).
- **Don't** tell your date all about your obsessions or phobias.
- **Don't** assume that your date will share your unending fascination with the video game, *Medieval Monster*, or whatever particular passion you have.

 Check Point

This isn't encouraging, but you probably won't do everything 100% perfect on a date. Don't psyche yourself out about what you did wrong. Be sincere and honest, and you'll be fine. If you do *half* of what is suggested in this book, you'll look like a winner. If you do 90% of this, you'll be a dream date come true. String a few dates together and, before you know it, you're in a relationship. Which takes us to the next chapter!

I love you, not only for what you are,
but for what I am when I am with you.

—Roy Croft

Relationships

Now we're getting to the big stuff. This is the meat of the book.

Relationships.

A relationship is the ongoing interaction of two people in which they both derive some reward. We have relationships with many people in our lives, including parents, friends, teachers and even neighbors. These are all examples of relationships, but they each have different levels of familiarity and closeness. Of course, this chapter is focused on romantic relationships that have a deeper level of intimacy than most other relationships. We'll talk more about intimacy soon.

Each relationship is as unique as the two people involved. However, certain aspects of relationships are universal and predictable. Those universal and predictable traits are what we will focus on in this chapter.

Brooke & Sean

Brooke and Sean had been on a date every Friday night for the last five weeks in a row. Brooke really liked Sean and it appeared that Sean really liked her. They didn't hang out at lunch, but talked briefly when they passed each other in the halls. Sean would call her at home during the week to talk for about 30 minutes. That was usually when he asked her out.

On each date, they would drive to the local make-out point to fool around in his car before he took her home. The next day, Brooke's friends would call her to get the details of her date. She felt like she was on cloud nine.

Brooke's family was eating dinner at a popular pizza place one night. As Brooke took a bite of pepperoni pizza, she almost swallowed her tongue when she saw Sean and another woman walk up to the order counter. *Maybe it's his sister,* she thought to herself. Sean placed his hand on the small of the woman's back, just like he would do with Brooke. Blood rushed to her face and Brooke felt her arms go weak. The slice of pizza suddenly weighed a ton. She wasn't sure whether to be mad or scared, to run out the door or confront Sean. She decided to wait and see what he did next.

Sure enough, as Sean and the woman were walking towards a table, he spotted Brooke with her family. His face flashed red and he paused for a moment. *Maybe he's deciding how to get out of here,* Brooke thought to herself. After Sean and the woman found a table, he walked over to say hello to Brooke and explained that he was here with a friend. *If she was just a friend why didn't he introduce her,* Brooke sarcastically wondered to herself? Brooke acted very cool during the brief greeting. She wanted to cry right there, but was not going to make a scene until she had more information.

The next day, Brooke called Sean at home and wanted to know about the woman he had been out with. It was then that Sean

(Continued)

told Brooke that he didn't think that they were dating exclusively and that he had gone out with several other women in the past month. Brooke was furious and deeply hurt. She was also confused. She had assumed that, since they had been out every week for over a month and had been making out in his car, that they were boyfriend and girlfriend.

Exclusively Yours

After you've dated one person for a little while, it will become evident that you're a couple. Before you announce this to the world, don't assume that you are dating exclusively. Brooke assumed that she and Sean were a couple. She was shocked to find out that he was dating other women. If she and Sean had a simple conversation about the nature of their relationship, it could have saved her that heartbreak. To make sure that you both feel the same way about each other, you need to talk about whether you are dating exclusively. Until you have that conversation, don't assume that you are a couple.

Dating exclusively is often called going steady, which means you are seeing someone steadily without interruption. We're not talking lifetime commitment! It doesn't mean you are engaged or will get married. It does mean that you are not going to see anyone else while you date that one particular person.

Do you have to ask the other person to 'go steady'? No, not necessarily. You *do* need to have a short conversation where you essentially say this: "I really like spending time with you. In fact, I'm not interested in seeing anyone else and I want to date you exclusively. How do you feel?" If this sounds too serious, you can simply say something like, "Will you be my girlfriend?" No matter how you say it, just be sure that you both understand that you are both dating exclusively.

Is the man always the one to inquire about going steady? In the old days, a man would give his class ring, his letterman's jacket or some other prominent piece of personal property for the woman to wear as an outward sign that she was unavailable. At the time he gave her the item to wear, he would ask her to go steady or be 'his girl.' Back then, it would've been considered inappropriate for a woman to ask a man to go steady. Now, let's fast-forward about 42 years. Just like asking for a date, it's ideal if the man is assertive enough to take the lead on this. However, I feel that it's more important for the conversation to happen (so that both parties are clear) than to have the woman stand on the principle of the man should always ask, only to have someone get their heart broken. So, while it's ideal for the man to initiate the talk about dating exclusively, it's better for the conversation to happen (even if that means the woman starts the ball rolling) than to have either of them make assumptions about the status of their relationship.

So, once the conversation is started, you will both get to share how you feel. The other person will either tell you that they feel the same way or that they aren't ready to date anyone exclusively. If they say they aren't ready to date exclusively, then you need to understand that they *may* be dating other people. This means that you are free to date others at the same time! If this is your arrangement, you are "dating casually," instead of going steady.

Casual Dating

Not every date you go on will develop into a significant relationship. Casual dating is fun and allows you to enjoy the dating experience without pressure of a commitment. When you date casually, you can even date more than one person at the same time! For instance, Ben might go out with Kelly on Friday, and then next Saturday take Sandy to the movies. Casual dating may or may not involve physical contact beyond a good night peck on the cheek.

If your intention is to date casually, be sure to be up front about it with *all* the people you are dating. Let them know that you are dating several people and are not interested in a commitment to date exclusively or go steady. This will reduce the chance of someone getting hurt because their feelings became stronger than yours, or because, like Brooke with Sean, they saw you out with another person.

While you're casually dating several people, you may find that you really look forward to seeing one person in particular. That's a good sign you're ready to date that person exclusively. When you make that decision, you should tell the others that you have decided to date someone else exclusively. You need to make a point to end those casual relationships. You don't want them to have to figure it out because you don't return their calls, or worse, when they hear it as gossip from the grapevine.

Handle with Care

Three little words: I Love You. These are very powerful words and should be handled carefully. Use them wisely and only when you *are* in love. When you say it to another person, it means more than when you'd say, "I love spaghetti."

These three words are for when you're dating exclusively, after you've gotten to know your Significant Other. It doesn't mean that you're making a lifetime commitment, but it does mean that you have a level of caring and commitment that goes beyond casual dating. It's not conversation filler and can lose its meaning if you say it just for fun.

Don't manipulate people with "I Love You." Don't use it to feel more secure about the relationship, or to move the relationship to the next level in hopes of becoming sexual. Saying "I Love You" is special, and deserves to be handled with care.

The Early Stage

For the rest of this chapter, we will assume that you're dating exclusively. So, you have gone on a few dates, found you really enjoy spending time with this person and you've had the conversation about dating exclusively. You find yourself falling in love.

Remarkably, the first time we felt love was when we were babies. As infants, we looked at our parents and thought we were one with them. In the first few months of life, infants don't understand that the parent exists separately from them. Because we are helpless as infants, we rely completely on our parents for our needs. This time in our lives is usually warm and wonderful because we feel loved and the whole world revolves around us. I call this warm and wonderful feeling Infantile Love. Unfortunately for us, Infantile Love only lasts for the first few months of our lives.

When you first become involved in a romantic relationship, it's typical that the first rush of emotion feels strangely familiar and wonderful. The feeling is similar to Infantile Love. For a brief moment in the early stages of love, we feel like we are one being with our new Significant Other and the whole world is perfect. This is often called the Honeymoon Phase. Well, just as the Infantile Love period for infants is brief, so is the rush of new love. Once reality sets in and the Infantile Love feeling subsides, you are left with a real relationship. At this point, it is up to the two of you to decide whether your relationship will be successful.

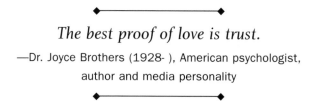

The best proof of love is trust.

—Dr. Joyce Brothers (1928-), American psychologist,
author and media personality

The Successful Relationship

You can be in a relationship, but that doesn't automatically mean it's successful. I should tell you right now that there are no perfect relationships; just *successful* relationships. So what makes a relationship successful? As you will learn from your own experience, what works in one relationship might not work in another. Remember, some aspects of relationships are universal. Two universal principles that all successful relationships have are Trust and Respect. These two elements, trust and respect, make the important foundation for you to build your relationship on. When relationships break up it can often be traced back to the trust or respect being eroded. Since these are such important elements, let's look at them closer.

Trust*

Trust is the first most important factor in a solid relationship. To have trust in someone is to have confidence that they will do the right thing.

Trust (noun): confidence in and reliance on good qualities, especially fairness, truth, honor or ability.

You believe in them and have entrusted something of value to them, because you know they will handle it with great care. In a relationship, you have entrusted your heart to another. There are two types of trust: *Implied Trust* and *Earned Trust*.

Implied Trust is where we believe someone is telling us the truth until we experience dishonesty from that person. It's hard to believe someone who has lied to you before. With implied trust, we are assumed innocent until we do something to prove that we are not trustworthy. Yes, forgiveness is important, but that is not an excuse to repeatedly betray someone's trust. We'll talk more about forgiveness in Chapter 13, *Fight Club*.

Earned Trust is where, over time and through a series of interactions, you have built a reputation for being trustworthy. Earned trust begins to replace the implied trust because you have shown, over time, that you are honorable and trustworthy.

In order to have trust in a relationship, it's crucial that both people be honest 100% of the time. It also means that you keep your word and do what you say you will do. If you are irresponsible or don't follow through with your promises and commitments, it will be hard for your Significant Other to trust you. When you trust him, you don't wonder what's happening when you see him talking to another woman. When you trust her, you won't worry whether she's being faithful to you when she's out with her friends.

Respect*

Respect is the second most important factor in a successful relationship. Respect is about feelings and behaviors. Our feelings about our Significant Other are reflected in our behavior towards them. If we don't respect someone, we will treat them badly.

Respect is what **we feel** for someone based on **their actions** (behaviors). Our respect is demonstrated in the way **we act** (behave) toward them, based on **our feelings**. It's kind of complicated, so I'll break it down a bit more.

---

*Respect (noun): a feeling or attitude of admiration and deference toward somebody or something; consideration or thoughtfulness.

1—It's what we *feel* for them based on their behaviors.

We respect someone because of what they do. They have integrity, tell the truth, do the right thing, and do things that you admire. This doesn't mean that your Significant Other is perfect, but you can't respect someone who steals when you feel that stealing is wrong. It's very difficult to respect someone who is controlling, abusive or mean, or acts without thinking about the consequences of their behaviors. You can be intimidated into pretending that you respect someone who is controlling, abusive or mean. You can even fear this kind of person, but you won't really respect them.

2—It's our *behavior* towards them based on what we feel for them.

When we respect someone, we behave in such a way that *shows* the honor and consideration we feel for them. For example: We speak to them kindly; we do things that we know they would enjoy or like; we think of them and what they would want when planning a date or a meal; and we treat them, their family and their property with great care. When we respect someone, we treat them well.

Intimacy

By intimacy do I mean sexual intimacy? Well, there are two types of intimacy; sexual and emotional. Right now, I'm talking about emotional intimacy. Emotional intimacy is closeness and familiarity. It is the beginning of love. You experience emotional intimacy when you allow yourself to be vulnerable and share your thoughts and feelings with another person. Another way to think of intimacy is "see into me."

Intimacy. See-into-me. Into-me-see. Intimacy. Get it?

You experience intimacy when you share details of your life with another person. This includes facts about your life, what you care about, your dislikes, fears and hopes. This self-disclosure creates intimacy because you allow someone to "see into you." You are exposing the deepest part of yourself. Intimacy makes you vulnerable and involves the risk of being hurt. The risk is that the person you share with could ridicule your fear or laugh at your hopes. If the person we've shared with is safe and doesn't ridicule us, we become closer to them. We begin to build a bond with them.

However, when someone hurts us while we're vulnerable, we instinctively clam up to protect ourselves. We make a mental note that the person is not safe and cannot be trusted. We don't want to share with that person again. It's important to not let one experience like this keep us from being intimate with someone else. Remember the two types of trust: Implied and Earned. The person who hurts us has lost our trust on all levels. They are untrustworthy. But be careful not to put everyone in the same boat. Judge each person on their own merits. You will cheat yourself out of the pleasure of intimacy if you are over-protective.

The Paradox

There is a paradox to intimacy. We tend to think that only the weak allow themselves to be vulnerable. The paradox is that it requires a tremendous amount of personal strength to be vulnerable with another human being. One reason why many people hate to admit that they're wrong is because it makes them vulnerable. That level of confidence is rare. However, once you've found someone you can trust, having emotional intimacy is very fulfilling.

Emotional intimacy develops between two people as they share a close, personal relationship. Over time, that intimacy will grow as deep as you've allowed yourself to be vulnerable. One of the hallmarks of true love is when someone loves us in spite of our shortcomings.

I have a warning for you! What I'm about to tell you could be good, or it could be bad. A sure-fire way to develop deep emotional intimacy with someone is to look into their eyes. Hold their eyes for at least 10 seconds, or more. This is difficult because our impulse is to look away or look at their forehead or nose or hair. While you look in their eyes, share details of your life. If they do the same (look in your eyes and share), you will both experience a wonderfully intense sense of emotional intimacy.

Now, if you **don't** want to fall in love with someone, *don't* look in their eyes and be sure to keep the conversation superficial; talk only about the weather, sports, movies or some other general or current event topic.

◆————————————◆

A friend is a person who knows all about you and still loves you.

—Albert Hubbard

◆————————————◆

Anatomy of a Healthy Relationship

We've already established that trust and respect create the foundation for a successful relationship. But, what about a *healthy* relationship? Relationships are not always good or positive. There are bad relationships too. For now, let's look at healthy relationships.

A healthy relationship is one that supports both people in a positive way. Neither one has to change their behaviors or attitudes in a way that creates problems in their lives just so they can stay in the relationship. Each is a better person because of the relationship. A healthy relationship is a dance of give and take. Both people want what is best for the other. Neither one has to have their way all the time.

As you become intimate, you'll get to know all of your Significant Other's quirks. Hopefully, you'll appreciate each other's quirks and the differences between you. Oh, you can count on there being differences. Differences are not necessarily bad. But you'll be sorely disappointed if you expect your Significant Other to be exactly like you. The relationship will be smoother if you accept and even enjoy the differences between you.

All of this doesn't mean that the relationship is perfect. Even in healthy relationships, there are disagreements and problems. A healthy relationship is where both people have the right tools to do the work a relationship requires.

In a healthy relationship, there are plenty of signs that the relationship works.

Signs of a healthy relationship:

1. They tell the truth.

2. They trust each other and don't get jealous.
3. They make sure they aren't doing anything to make their partner feel jealous.
4. They share their feelings (I'm angry, I'm hurt, I'm sad) instead of playing head games or expecting to read each other's minds.
5. They each take responsibility for themselves and don't try to make the other feel guilty.
6. They expect each other to be responsible for themselves. She doesn't do his homework for him, etc.
7. They fight fair. They can disagree and work out problems without screaming, name-calling or saying hurtful things. (See Chapter 13, *Fight Club*)
8. They don't hit or abuse each other. (See Chapter 15, *Trouble in Paradise*)
9. They are willing to influence each other without trying to control each other.
10. They spend time together, but allow each other to have the necessary space to take care of themselves and have their own lives.
11. Neither of them abuses substances.
12. They have each maintained their friendships with others from before the relationship began.
13. They are supportive of each other and their individual interests.

The Ambiguous Relationship

This sounds kind of scary, huh? Everyone is likely to have at least one ambiguous relationship during their lifetime. This is the relationship when you are more than *just friends*, but not quite a couple. Sometimes one person has romantic feelings, but the other doesn't return those feelings. Sometimes the people are afraid of ruining a great friendship by forcing it to a romantic level. These relationships are what I call the Friend Zone. It can be nightmarish because it's like being in a bad episode of *The Twilight Zone*.

The Friend Zone is awkward and sometimes painful, because the uncontrollable factor is the *chemistry*. If two people like each other, but the chemistry is missing for one of them, there is no spark to start a flame for a mutual romance. (See Chapter 3, *Attraction* for more on this.) When this happens, you can find yourself trapped in the Friend

Zone. It can be frustrating to have an unrequited* love for another person.

Bust Out of the Friend Zone

If you've flirted all you can and still can't figure out how your "friend" feels about you, then you need to take the straightforward approach. Come right out and ask them how they feel. I have to warn you: This is risky. It's risky because it can change the nature of your friendship. To minimize the risk, you want to ask them in such a way that it doesn't put pressure on them. That way, if they tell you they don't return your romantic feelings, then you both have saved faced and have a better chance to preserve the friendship. Here is a way you can approach the situation:

"You know, I really like you. I feel stuck because I don't want to ruin our friendship, but I also wonder what it would be like if we were more than just friends. Do you ever think about that?"

Your Friend Zone friend may not understand what you mean and need more clarification. If this happens, you can come right out and add to it by saying: "Would you ever go on a date with me? You know, not just as friends, but like a romantic date."

If preserving the friendship is important, you don't want to overwhelm your Friend Zone friend, so **don't** say: "I've been in love with you since I first saw you. It rips my heart out to see you with other people. I'll die if you don't love me back."

Denied

It really sucks if you get a "No, I don't think of you that way," response. It is very unlikely that your friend will suddenly change their mind next week. However, a good friend is a good friend. If you don't let your pride get the better of you, you can stay connected to the person. If they say, "I don't want to ruin what we have," then take it at face value. It's more likely that you will keep friends for a lifetime than to marry your high school sweetheart.

---

*Not felt in response, or not returned in the same way or to the same degree

In an attempt to preserve the friendship, a really good friend may say no in a way that lets you down easy. They might say, "I'm not ready yet," or, "I want to keep things the way they are right now." Don't interpret an easy letdown as the possibility of them saying yes anytime soon. It *could* happen, but be realistic about your chances for a romantic future together. Don't pine away, secretly hoping that you will do the right thing, or say the right words to change their mind. It's not about you; you are fine. It's about chemistry. The missing ingredient is chemistry, which can't be manufactured. Move on to another romantic possibility

---

 ## Check Point

Successful relationships take time and work. You can't expect the relationship to be great without any effort. As a couple, you will need to invest time and energy to make it grow. When you are in a healthy relationship, you are a better person than you were by yourself. In a good relationship, the gain is so great that the effort involved is not a chore. Now that I've fairly warned you that a relationship will take work, the next chapter looks at what will help to make a relationship work!

Love and magic have a great deal in common. They enrich the soul, delight the heart, and they both take practice.

—Nora Roberts, 21st century American writer

Making a Relationship Work

You must be saying at this point, "*Work? What? Relationships are supposed to be fun and romantic and easy and effortless, blah, blah, blah.*" Yes, you are right. In movies and romance novels relationships are easy. I want you to be smart about relationships, so I won't dress up the reality. In real life, relationships take work and practice. We fall in love because we feel that our lives will be better because of the other person. In good relationships, our lives **are** better because of the relationship. But even good relationships take work. In a good relationship, the benefits are worth every ounce of effort. The fact is, most people aren't aware of the work involved in creating and maintaining a good relationship. Once the relationship requires some effort, they get freaked out and end it because they think there is something wrong. If they knew that work was normal, they wouldn't be so surprised. So, if you aren't scared, read on.

In the last chapter we saw what a successful relationship looks like and the importance of a solid foundation. This chapter is about the work you will do on top of that foundation as you build your relationship. As I said before, each relationship is as unique as the two people involved. What works in one might not work in another. So, there really is no single, absolute thing that will make every relationship work. However, just as trust and respect are universal relationship principles, we will look at the other basic fundamentals that create a successful relationship.

Love is like quick-silver in the hand. Leave the fingers open and it stays. Clutch it, and it darts away.

—Dorothy Parker (1893-1967), American writer

Shelley & Adrian

Shelley and Adrian are high school juniors who started to date last summer. After almost seven months of dating, Shelley thought things were going pretty well.

Actually, Adrian has felt frustrated by the constant attention that Shelley expects. Most of his free time is spent with her. During the summer the intensity of their relationship was fine, and it was fun in the beginning of the school year. But now Adrian needs to be studying for the SAT's, which are coming up soon. To make more time for himself, he hasn't been calling her as often and purposely didn't meet her at their usual spot at lunch a few times.

Each time he avoids her Shelley becomes a little panicked. She's worried that he's going to breakup with her because he's been acting distant and hasn't called her as much. The worst part was when he didn't meet her at lunch. She isn't sure what's

(*Continued*)

going on and would like to talk to someone about this. But since she and Adrian started dating, she's been too busy to spend time with her two best friends, Karen and Donna. It would seem pretty selfish if she called them up out of the blue just to get advice.

After two weeks of the tension growing between them, Adrian knows he needs to talk to Shelley. He really wants to call her on the phone and talk about it, but he feels that it will be better face-to-face. While they are sitting on her front lawn on a Saturday afternoon, Adrian starts the conversation.

"Shel, I've got a confession to make."

"*This is it*," Shelly thought to herself as her mind began to race. "*He's going to breakup with me. Oh, my gosh, does he like someone else?*"

"I'm feeling lots of pressure right now with the SAT's coming up. Also, I've got tons of homework in Statistics. Between all that and the fact that I haven't had much of a chance to hang out with Mark and Shane since we've been dating, I'm wondering if we could slow it down a bit with us."

There, it was out. He had said it. Adrian waited for Shelley to say something. It seemed like forever before she finally spoke.

"So, does this mean we're breaking up?" she asked softly, looking at the ground as she pulled up blades of grass, one by one. She was afraid she'd cry if she looked at him.

"No, no," Adrian said quickly, "Heck, no. Shel, I love you. I just need a *little* more space to take care of things in my life. You're still a big part of it, but I need to do more of the stuff I used to do before we got together."

Shelley's voice cracked, "Are you seeing anyone else?"

"What? Come on. No. I'm not seeing anyone else. How can you think that? Look, I'm hoping you can understand. This

(Continued)

doesn't mean that we aren't still going together, or that I feel any different about you."

Adrian knew this conversation would be work, and it was. He was trying hard to be calm and reassuring. He could see how she had misunderstood his pulling back. He felt terrible that he had caused her to worry and wished he had started this conversation two weeks ago. There was silence as Shelley took in all of Adrian's words.

After some more questions and reassurance, Shelley agreed to give Adrian more space. They made a new plan that included a short phone call each evening, a weekend date and eating lunch together a couple times a week at school.

After Adrian left, Shelley called Donna and Karen and asked if they wanted to go to the mall and see a movie. She knew it was time to get some balance in her own life as well.

Absence is to love what wind is to a fire;
it puts out the little, it kindles the great.

—Comte DeBussy-Rabutin

Three Pillars of Relationship Doom

Relationships can fall victim to some common problems that can be avoided if you are aware of them. Here are three situations that can unnecessarily doom a relationship:

1. Balancing Act

When we are in love, it's normal to want to spend all of our free time with our Significant Other. Because our lives are comprised of several major areas, it's easy for one area to suffer as we spend all of our free time on the relationship. When this happens, it creates stress in our lives. Stress can be the doom of a relationship. Let's look at the different areas of a typical person's life:

1. Relationship
2. School
3. Family
4. Friends
5. Chores/household duties
6. Church, sports, band or other activities
7. Private time to yourself

It's important to create balance and not to neglect the areas of our lives beyond the relationship. The right balance will vary from person to person. If you're suddenly failing a class, have given up a hobby you enjoy, or are neglecting other areas of your life, you can subconsciously become resentful of the relationship and your Significant Other.

Don't cancel plans with a friend just because your Significant Other wants to see you. The relationship should not eclipse your life. It should *enhance* it. Finally, don't forget how important it is to have some quiet time alone. If you have every minute jammed with activities, you miss out on the chance to reflect on the day and its events.

Talk about your schedules together and make a plan for how you will create balance if one of you is lopsided. Be willing to compromise: If you see each other everyday at school, then maybe a short phone call in the evening after homework is done and a Saturday night date will be enough to support the relationship while allowing both of you time to attend to the other areas of your lives.

2. Neediness

The second pillar of relationship doom is neediness. Neediness is when a person is insecure and needs a lot of reassurance. The needy person may question the strength of the relationship or not believe that they are lovable. It is an overwhelming responsibility to constantly reassure the needy. The sad irony is that neediness is repulsive, not attractive. Neediness can actually drive the other person away.

I have bad news: There are no guarantees in relationships. Half of the marriages in the United States fail. You can't control how long the relationship will last or whether your Significant Other loves you as much as you love them. Love is a one-day-at-a-time proposition. Enjoy and appreciate each day you have.

If you find yourself constantly seeking reassurance or if your Significant Other seems to be pushing you away, then stop what you are doing right now! Evaluate what is happening and what you are doing: Are you calling your Significant Other several times a day for nothing in particular? Do you get anxious if you haven't heard from them in a few hours? Do you hang on them physically? Do you cry when it is time to leave? Are you the one who always initiates contact? These are telltale signs that you are acting needy.

If you *don't* have confidence in yourself or with the relationship, *act* like you do. Fake it 'til you make it. Give your Significant Other some space. Let them miss you when you are apart. It's amazing to step back and watch how they move closer when you pull back a bit. Remember the Tao of Steve? We are more attractive when we're confident. (*We pursue that which retreats from us.*—Heidegger)

3. Mind Reading

Oh, boy. This is a big one. The third pillar of relationship doom: Mind reading. It's a romantic notion that lovers should know exactly what each other wants, needs and feels. This belief brings certain hurt to those who buy into it. They are devastated when their Significant Other doesn't provide exactly the right thing at precisely the right moment. Mind reading is not real. It is not a sign of true love. While a couple might be 'in tune' with each other, the fact remains that no one will know what you want or need unless you *ask* for it. This is why clear communication is so important to the success of a relationship. We will talk about communication next.

Are you afraid to ask for what you want or need? This is a sign that the trust level in your relationship is low, or you are too immature for a relationship. Mind reading works both ways: Don't assume that *you know* what your Significant Other wants and needs. It's okay to ask them what they need in a straightforward way.

Communication

The topic of mind reading brings us to communication. If mind reading doesn't exist, how will your Significant Other know what you want, think and feel? The good old-fashioned, low-tech way: Communication. Clear, open and honest communication is crucial to a successful relationship. What most people don't know is that communication involves a lot more than just speaking. In fact, words only account for about 35%[8] of the communication process. Here are the many parts of communication:

◎ **Listening**

Listening is actually the largest part of communication. Listening is more than just *hearing* words. True listening involves *understanding*. Are you listening to understand, or just pretending to listen while your mind wanders off or thinks about what you will say next?

◎ **Words**

Although words account for only about one-third of the communication process, we still need to use words that convey what we mean. Some words have more than one meaning. Be sure you aren't being ambiguous.* It's also important to give enough information when you communicate. See the section on *Misunderstandings* in Chapter 13, *Fight Club*, for more on this.

◎ **Feedback**

Feedback is a big part of the communication process. Feedback lets the other person know if you agree or disagree with what they are saying. Nodding and smiling lets them know that you understand or are tracking with them. Shaking your head with a wrinkled brow lets them know you don't understand. As the speaker, you also need to be aware of the feedback that the other person is giving you. Do they need more clarification? Are you talking too fast, too loud, too soft, too much? Communication is a two-way street.

◎ **Voice**

Are you whispering or yelling? What tone are you using? Does your voice sound happy, angry, whiney, frightened or sarcastic? Even emphasis plays a role. How you emphasize words can change the meaning of a single sentence. For example:

This is a great relationship book. (Not just any book, but *this* book)

---

*Ambiguous—Unclear or confusing.

This is a *great* relationship book. (This book is superior)
This is a great *relationship* book. (The book is good as far as relationships go; it isn't a great literary work)

◎ **Body Language**

Are your arms and legs crossed? Is your body turned away from the person to whom you are talking? All of those are signals that you are closed off or not interested.

◎ **Facial Expressions**

Sometimes facial expressions contradict the words being spoken. If someone says, "I love you," with a sarcastic voice, eyes narrowed suspiciously and their brow furrowed, you might not believe them, or at the very least be confused.

◎ **Actions or Behaviors**

Your actions are a large part of communication. If your mouth says 'I love you,' but your action is to be disrespectful of your Significant Other, they will be confused. Integrity is when your words and actions are integrated.

Wants and Needs

Wants and Needs. This sounds like the selfish brat department of a store. "I want! I need! Gimme, Gimme." Wants and needs are not about being selfish in the way we typically think. The reality is, all humans have wants and needs. In a relationship those wants and needs are important.

Both people have to be involved in the wants and needs department. First, you have to ask for what you want and, second, you need to be sensitive to your partner's wants. We already know that people don't read minds. This is why asking is so important. If you don't ask for what you need, your chances of getting it are slim to none. Remember Gandhi's quote, "If you don't ask, you don't get."? In fact, not asking for what you want is a big mistake in a relationship. Do we automatically get absolutely everything we ask for? No. There is no relationship "law" that says your Significant Other must fulfill your every want and need. But your chances of getting it are better if you ask. Because it's easy to confuse a want with a need, let's define the difference between the two.

Need—A need is a necessity or a requirement. It's something we must have to survive, thrive or function. A need is essential to our relationship. We need to be respected. We need our partner to be faithful. We need more time alone.

Want—A want is to crave or desire. It's something that would be nice to have, but is not necessary for our existence. A want will enhance our relationship. We want to be called 'honey-bun.' We want to go to Disneyland. We want to have sex.

Common Relationship Wants and Needs:

- More time by themselves
- More time with you
- Hear "I love you" more often
- Hang out with the old group of friends more often
- More/less physical touching, kissing, hand holding, etc.
- Go out more for activities
- Don't talk about a particular or sensitive subject
- Don't give advice, just listen
- Don't complain so much
- Hear "Thank you" more often
- Want to see more action movies, and fewer romantic comedies (or vice versa)
- Be nicer to a friend of theirs, or make more of an effort with their parents
- Be told she's beautiful/he's handsome

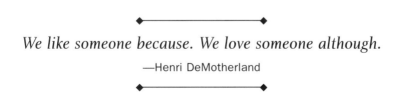

We like someone because. We love someone although.

—Henri DeMotherland

Long Distance Relationships

Long distance relationships take a lot of work. They are not for the weak of heart or character. For a LDR to work both people must have a tremendous sense of confidence, and the relationship has to have an incredibly strong foundation of trust and respect. Communication is doubly important in a LDR, as most of the communication takes place via telephone or email. Without face-to-face communication, you miss out on several dimensions of communication that include facial expressions, body language and some components of feedback. You are also missing the reassurance that comes from physically seeing and touching each other regularly.

This doesn't mean that all LDRs are doomed. Email and web cameras make communication much more immediate than back in the old days of handwritten letters sent via U.S. mail. However, both people in a LDR need to be especially aware of each other's need for reassurance. Creativity is also an important factor for those in a LDR. Creativity can make the distance seem shorter. A surprise fax or a postcard with a quick poem are little things that help couples feel connected.

Gift Giving

You're probably wondering what in the heck gifts have to do with making a relationship work. I bring this up because as a relationship develops, it's natural to want to give each other gifts or do thoughtful things for each other. Gifts can be a nice way to let your Significant Other know you are thinking of them and care.

Gift giving is easier for some. For others, it doesn't even occur to them. Don't be confused; gifts don't equal love. If your Significant Other doesn't give you gifts, don't be hurt. For those who don't naturally give gifts, you might need to stretch in this area and become aware of gift-giving occasions.

There is no absolute rule that says couples *must* give each other gifts. In fact, a problem can develop when there is an expectation to receive gifts. However, many couples give gifts to celebrate special occasions and even sometimes 'just because.' It's a good idea to acknowledge anniversaries. It's tempting to celebrate each week or month that you've been together. In the first year, some couples celebrate their "anniversary" each month. After that, they do it annually. It's also appropriate to give gifts on birthdays and Christmas/Chanukah or whatever cultural holidays you celebrate. Guys: Don't drop the ball on Valentine's Day. Missing Valentine Day is the #1 mistake in a relationship. You don't have to break the bank to let her know that she's your Valentine. A card and a flower will keep you out of the doghouse.

Okay, it's not an original observation but, truly, with gifts it **is** the thought that counts. As you get to know each other, it will be easy to think of gifts your Significant Other will appreciate. She says she loves Chinese philosophy; you buy her the book, *The Tao of Pooh*. She says she loves taking hot bubble baths; you get her an aromatherapy candle that she can use while she's bathing. He's a baseball fan; you get him a magazine with an article about Hank Aaron. He loves sci-fi movies; you buy him a copy of Terminator 2. You get the picture.

Like many other things in life, too much of a good thing isn't always good. In fact, gifts can lose their significance if they become everyday occurrences. Gifts don't need to be big or expensive. Your thoughtfulness and attention to detail will speak volumes about your love. A single rose from the flower stand presented sincerely is as appreciated as a dozen roses delivered to the door by a florist's delivery guy. Also, money is not a measure of love. A heartfelt message that you've written in a $2.00 card is actually worth more than a $20.00 gift that doesn't show any thought on your part. Use your powers of observation to come up with gift ideas. If you can't think of any ideas, then you need to start paying more attention to your Significant Other. Finally, you want gifts to be appropriate for the length of time you've been together. A gift that has deep meaning, such as a ring or something very expensive such as a $100.00 gift for your one-month anniversary, is overkill.

Hello, Jealousy

Jealousy is a green, one-eyed, people-eating monster. It's not pretty. Jealousy is rooted in a lack of trust. It is a sure sign of instability in a relationship. Acting jealous will backfire because those who are jealous look insecure. Either you trust your Significant Other or you don't. However, like everything else in a relationship, this is a two-way street. Both people have responsibilities around jealousy. You need to be aware of your part in any situation and be willing to work at making changes if needed.

The first side of the two-way street is that, if you're in a committed relationship, you need to behave that way. If you love your Significant Other, you don't want to do anything that would hurt them. Ask yourself honestly: Are you spending a lot of time with someone of the opposite sex? Do you find yourself talking a lot about one person in particular? Be honest. If you are attracted to someone else, then you need to decide whether you should continue in your current relationship. It's not fair to give your Significant Other reason to feel jealous and then act like the situation is their problem because they feel insecure.

The second side of this two-way street is to check the validity of your jealousy. Just because jealousy isn't pretty doesn't mean that it's not a red flag alerting you to a problem in the relationship. Ask yourself: Is there something going on that makes you feel jealous, or do you normally feel insecure? Once you feel insecure, it's easy for little things to magnify. Is your Significant Other simply a chronic flirt and this is what they've always done? If you feel like something is not right in your relationship, then address it directly. Don't pout or act jealous and think that the problem will disappear.

Comparisons: "Is she prettier than me?"

This is something that might come up once you're dating steadily. Both men and women do this, but more often it's the woman. It can happen anywhere: you can be hanging out or watching a movie, you can even be sitting in the cafeteria at lunch.

She might ask you about a friend of hers, a famous actress or a woman walking down the street. The comparison is just a request for reassurance that you still find her attractive and desirable. How you answer can either satisfy her need for reassurance or it can be the start of a fight. Respond in such a way that you address the need to be reassured, by saying something like, "I can't compare you. I love who you are *and* how you look."

If you are being asked to compare your Significant Other, it's a good sign that you've become complacent in the relationship. Over time, it's easy to take the relationship for granted. When this happens, we stop saying and doing the things that show each other how much we appreciate them. You might need to be more verbal or physical in expressing your pleasure with your Significant Other. The little things like saying, "You are so handsome," or "Woman, you are beautiful," are just as important one year after your first date as they are in the first month of the relationship.

No More Mr. Nice Guy

Can you really be too nice? Yes, you can actually be *too* nice. Remember that the success of the relationship is based on respect. If you act like a doormat, the other person isn't going to respect you. Here's a great story that will illustrate what I'm saying, and then we'll talk about it more.

Billy's Story

Billy was shy and had never had a date before. His friends had always given him a hard time about being 19 years old and never having had a date. His friend, Brian, suggested that they have a low-key double date by inviting two girls over to Billy's house to watch a movie with them. Billy thought this was a good idea and asked Stephanie whom he knew from high school and had been acquaintances with for several years. Stephanie was totally cute and he thought he was lucky that she said yes to the invitation.

On the fateful evening, Billy picked Stephanie up and then met Brian and his date back at the house. They made a salad in the kitchen and ate as they watched the video in the living room. Stephanie had complained several times before the movie had even started. It was minor complaining; she didn't like Billy's front yard, she was cold, she didn't think that the salad bowls were clean enough, she didn't like the video Brian had selected. Once they were seated on the couch, she asked Billy for a glass of water. He was the host, so he got up and brought her a glass of water. A few minutes later, she wanted more salad. Instead of getting up herself, she told Billy to get her more salad as she handed her bowl to him.

(*Continued*)

This was starting to wear on Billy's nerves. He felt like a slave to an unreasonable master and he wasn't sure what to do. He'd never been on a date. So he got her more salad. During the movie, she yawned loudly several times and made a big point to check her watch about every 10 minutes. She wanted to make sure that everyone knew she was bored with the video. Billy was dying. He didn't know what to do, so he sucked it up and stuck the date out until the movie was over. On the drive to take Stephanie home, she complained more. *Ugh*, he thought. *This was a total disaster.*

The Doormat

Billy's story shows why it's good not to let a bad date go too far. This story would have also been good in several other chapters, but I chose to put it here, because some people become doormats once the relationship has started. Not being a doormat is all about respect; Primarily self-respect and believing that you deserve to be treated well. Now, let's look at what happened to Billy.

Being new to the dating world, Billy didn't know how to handle the situation. He was also probably disarmed by Stephanie's good looks. There was nothing he could do that would make her happy. Billy's fatal mistake was that he was too nice! He should have put his foot down earlier in the evening. Instead, he waited until it was beyond repair. Yes, I know, it's hard to believe, but sometimes you can be *too* nice. No one, especially women, likes someone who is a doormat. The fact is, that we train people how to treat us. If you *let* someone treat you like a doormat, they will. If you draw a line, they will know next time not to cross over it. They will respect you.

Now, just to be clear, I don't mean you should be a bully in order to be respected. I am saying that you can control certain situations when you're being taken advantage of. How should Billy have handled the situation with Stephanie? He should have drawn a line when she ordered him to the kitchen with her salad bowl. That was really the last straw. He should have said with a smile, "Oh sure, feel free to help yourself. You know where the kitchen is." If Billy was already heading to the kitchen for himself, it would have been reasonable to ask him to get more salad for her while he was going there. But to order him back two minutes after he brought her a drink was manipulative. Stephanie was testing Billy's limits. Billy's mistake was not letting her know where his limit was. Notice the way that Billy could have drawn the line. It wasn't rude or disrespectful. He didn't call her names or insinuate that she was being bossy or manipulative. It was a friendly re-direct. But she would have gotten the message.

What else could Billy have done to draw a line with Stephanie? When she was yawning, he could have taken a very direct approach and pulled the covers on her act. He could have stopped the video, turned to her and said, "Hey, Stephanie, let's be honest. You're obviously bored here. Why don't I take you home now? I'll come back and watch the video with these two afterwards so we can enjoy it." Again, he doesn't need to be rude, but he's letting her know that the game she is playing won't work with him. His response was simple: If she's bored, they can call it a night. This is where you want to cut your losses before it gets ugly.

My guess is that if Billy had taken her home early, she would have completely changed her mind about him. She wouldn't have viewed him as a doormat to be abused. She might have seen him as a confident man who sets limits. This would have made him very attractive to her. If Billy played it smart, he wouldn't want to be involved with a manipulative princess like Stephanie after he saw her in action. Someone like Stephanie is rude and mean … she lacks a basic level of manners to behave politely when she is someone's guest. She is no prize and would be a nightmare of a girlfriend.

Do only women walk all over men? Oh, no. This door swings both ways. Men and women both can treat people poorly. Both men and women can act like doormats.

As a post-note to Billy's story: Does this one incident mean he's forever a doormat? Heck, no. I've known Billy for several years. He is really cute and a nice guy. More important, he is smart enough to learn from this experience and not let it keep him down. I've seen his confidence increase after this incident.

Check Point

Well, we covered a lot of the things that make a relationship work. You understand about balance, neediness and mind reading. You are practically a communications expert and you know the difference between needs and wants, and the importance of asking for what you want. You also know how important it is to not take each other for granted. You've heard about jealousy and have learned a few gift-giving techniques. Most important, we saw that to let yourself become a doormat for your Significant Other is a recipe for disaster.

You know a lot about making a relationship work, but to be really smart, you need to know how to fight! Yes, I said fight. I'll show you how to be a good fighter in the next chapter.

The course of true love never did run smooth.

—William Shakespeare (1564-1616), English playwright and poet

Fight Club

Who wants to think about fighting when they're in love? Nobody. That's why so many people fight poorly—because they haven't thought about it. The reality is that all relationships involve conflict. Yes, couples in good relationships have fights. Conflict between two people is natural and to be expected. Even in science, two or more living organisms will have conflict. It's impossible to think that two independent people with free will would never have opposing thoughts or ideas.

People who live with the illusion that they will never have a periodic disagreement in their relationship are in denial. Actually, couples that never fight are probably avoiding conflict and may be more dysfunctional than couples that fight a lot. Conflicts involve certain emotions, including hurt, frustration, anger, disappointment and resentment. Most people don't enjoy these emotions, so they try to avoid fights.

How much fighting is normal? Well, there's no right amount of fighting that's appropriate in a relationship. Some couples may have an argument once a week, while others argue once a month. Since conflict is inevitable, the challenge becomes to handle it well when it does happen. This chapter is about the common fights that happen in healthy relationships.

Deborah & Clint – Yes, this is my story

My favorite boyfriend in high school was Clint. I was almost 15 and he was my first real love. Clint was one year older than me and had a driver's license and car. He was being raised by his single dad, which was a unique situation in the 1970s. We had dated for about six months when we had our first serious fight.

Every Saturday night we went out. Clint would come to our house to get me about 6:30. My two little brothers, who were then 10 and 11 years old, would open the door and the three of them would begin goofing around. Inevitably, Clint would invite the boys to join us on our date! Since Clint didn't have any brothers or sisters, I tried to be patient. Every week, they would pile into Clint's car with us and we'd all go over to the neighborhood arcade to play video games for awhile. We'd return them home about two hours later and our date *without* the boys would actually begin.

After six months of this, I was very irritated that my brothers took up so much of the short time Clint and I had together. Because we lived across town and went to different schools, we didn't see each other a lot. Clint was kind of the silent type and he didn't call much during the week. Clint worked with his dad every weekend day, so we rarely had daytime dates. It was simple. We had our standing Saturday night date. He showed up and I was ready. He didn't share a lot about himself or his feelings, and I got the message not to pry. So we just had fun being together on our dates.

(Continued)

But these brothers of mine were taking up about 1/3 of our weekly time together, and I had had enough. My casual jokes about the situation were never met with any response from Clint, but now I had decided to draw a line in the sand. One Saturday, after we dropped the boys off, I wasted no time in telling Clint that I was sick and tired of the boys coming along. We didn't have much time together as it was and this wasn't exactly my idea of a romantic date. My throat was tight and I could hear my voice getting higher and louder with every word. I had obviously sat on this resentment for too long.

Even though we were just one short block away from my house, Clint pulled his car over to the side of the road. He turned off the engine and stared straight ahead into the dark. My heart was pounding. He'd never done this before. I knew immediately that I hadn't approached this right. I wished I could take it all back and start over.

After a thoughtful moment or two, Clint said slowly and softly, "Those kids are great. I'd love to have them as brothers. I'd give anything to have just one brother or sister and you have two. You are so lucky and so selfish." I was stunned. Clint started up the car and took me back home. With his car idling in the driveway, he said that he wanted to be alone. It was obvious that our date was over. I was afraid to get out. Afraid that I'd never see him again. I figured this was the end of our relationship. He wouldn't look at me and he didn't say anything else, so I said weakly, "Call me," and he said, "maybe."

I walked toward the house with tears streaming down my face. Two very long weeks went by and Clint didn't call or come by. I missed him. I knew he would call if and when he was ready. That's about when my mom and I saw his aunt at the grocery store. After inquiring about how Clint and I were doing and hearing the news, she explained to me that Clint had lost his mom and two older sisters in a boating accident on a

(Continued)

lake when he was about six years old. Both he and his dad watched helplessly from the dock, too far away to save them as they quickly drowned.

I felt like a total jerk. Everything suddenly made sense. No wonder my brothers were so important to him. No wonder he didn't want to talk about himself or his feelings. No wonder his dad was raising him alone. Almost a week after learning about his past, Clint and I ran into each other at the mall. With very few words and a brief apology on both our parts, we were back together. Both of us with a deeper understanding of each other's needs.

Anatomy of a Fight[*]

A conflict, argument or fight is defined as *a struggle between at least two individuals who perceive incompatible goals, scarce rewards and interference from the other party in achieving their goals.*[9] Put another way, fights happen when two people want different things and they think the other is keeping them from what they want. I perceived that Clint and I had limited time together (scarce reward). My goal was to spend as much time together as possible. However, Clint was perfectly happy to have my brothers intrude on that time. (We had different goals and he was keeping me from getting what I wanted.)

A lot of conflicts happen because of perception. We each see things differently. A conflict arises when we're afraid to let our Significant Other have a different view, or because we're afraid they won't love us if we have different ideas. Many arguments start over control, or over who is right. If you are dead set on being right all the time you can count on a very unhappy relationship. Does this mean you should give in everytime and always let your Significant Other be right? No. No one is right all the time. It is a mature and centered person who can gracefully admit when they are wrong. Be willing to recognize when your Significant Other is right.

---

*Physical fighting, hitting, or slapping is abusive and is not appropriate for couples. In this chapter, fighting means verbal arguments.

The time to repair the roof is when the sun is shining.

—John F. Kennedy (1917-1963), 35th President of the United States

A Fight to the End

On an episode of the TV show *Friends* the characters Monica and Chandler, who had begun dating, had their first fight. Chandler assumed that the relationship was over because they had fought. Monica, who had been Chandler's friend for years, immediately understood why he had never been in a long-term relationship before. He thought that a fight meant the relationship was over. She assured him that their love was stronger than a disagreement or a fight.

The first time you fight with your Significant Other can be scary. You're entering uncharted territory. You aren't sure if this means the relationship is over or not. Actually, fighting can be great! Am I crazy? No, not entirely. It's just that we learn the most about our Significant Other when we fight. We learn who they really are and what they're about. You learn the answer to such important questions as: Is your love stronger than a fight? Will they fight fair? Will they hold a grudge? Will they want to punish you with the silent treatment? If your Significant Other is fair and kind during an argument, then you have a good one. If your relationship can stand the storm of a fight, then you know you have something good.

Does this mean you should pick a fight? Oh no, please don't. It does mean that you shouldn't fear a fight. It doesn't automatically mean the relationship is over. In fact, it can make you feel even more secure if it goes well. If you still love your Significant Other after a fight, you really do love your Significant Other.

Empty the Gunnysack

A gunnysacker is someone who doesn't share their complaints about their partner as they arise. These complaints might be big problems, as well as small gripes. This is an easy trap to fall into, especially if you tend to avoid conflict.

Here's how it works: Instead of talking about the problems as they come up, the gunnysacker shoves them into a mental gunnysack and carries them around. The problem is, that one day the sack becomes so full it explodes. It's usually a little thing that sets the gunnysacker off, and they suddenly pour out all of their pent-up frustrations onto their partner. The poor partner is confused by the outburst and can't figure out why their Significant Other got so mad over such a little thing.

When I finally blew up at Clint, he didn't see it coming. I had held onto my frustration about the situation for so long that it wasn't a calm conversation. My voice got loud very quickly. If I had calmly brought up the issue as a problem, instead of hoping that he would pick up my jokes, we might have had a rational conversation about the situation. Empty your mental gunnysack regularly. Better yet, don't even carry one around!

Two to Tango

There's an old saying about fighting that goes, "It takes two to tango." If you've ever danced the tango you know that it's impossible to do it alone. You can be angry by yourself, but you can't fight by yourself. When you fight, each of you has a hand in the problem, one way or another.

Some couples find themselves arguing about the same issue over and over again. This is what I call a Persistent Argument. You argue about a particular issue, but it never gets resolved, so it comes up again and again. Persistent arguments can undermine your relationship's strong foundation. Not because your relationship lacks trust or respect, but because you are exhausted from the persistent arguing.

You don't want to just argue about the issue again; you want to get to the root of the problem so it can be resolved. To stop a persistent argument before it ruins your relationship, you need to evaluate the situation objectively. While you both have a hand in the situation, we're going to concentrate on your part. We won't worry about your Significant Other for now.

First, sit down and identify the problem. Use the 5-Step Decision-Making Process we discussed in Chapter 2, *Learning Curve*. Go through the same steps to identify the facts and your feelings. This process can help you to stay objective. At this point, resist the urge to brainstorm a solution or two. For now, just take the Persistent Argument Inventory. Ask yourself the following questions about the problem causing the argument (Answer them honestly.):

Persistent Argument Inventory

1. What do **you** do to contribute to the problem?
2. Are **you** listening to your Significant Other's needs?
3. Are **you** being respectful?
4. What are **you** willing to give or compromise on, in order not to have the situation be a problem yet again?

Notice how the inventory is focused on you? This is because you can't control others, only yourself. You want to honestly look at the situation and see your part in it. Once you have identified the issue and your feelings about it, and you've taken the Persistent Argument Inventory, *then* you are ready to sit down with your Significant Other to talk about it. If you've both read this book, it's great if you each do a Persistent Argument Inventory. Keep in mind, however, the success of working through an argument is **not** hinged on whether your Significant Other has read this book or knows about the inventory. If you are willing to be honest about your feelings and admit your part of the problem, it will go a long way towards creating a peaceful resolution.

When you're ready to talk about it, you want to sit down together at a time when you're not in the middle of a fight. Remember, your emotions are involved when you argue and it's hard to be objective when you're emotional. Be sure to use the Rules for Fair Fighting when you begin to discuss the facts of the problem.

✦————————✦

The arrow belongs not to the archer when it has once left the bow; the word no longer belongs to the speaker when it has once passed his lips.

—Heinrich Heine (1797-1856), German poet

✦————————✦

10 Rules for Fair Fighting

An argument doesn't mean that the relationship is over. Couples in a healthy relationship find that they actually have a deeper understanding of each other and feel closer after a fight than before it happened. What makes their fights turn out so positive? Fair fighting. Whether a fight ends with a productive or destructive result is determined by *how* you fight. Remember, this is the person you love. Treat them with the same respect you would in any other situation. Here are the basic ground rules to fair fighting as you work out your differences:

1. **No name-calling.** Stupid, idiot, bitch, bastard, etc., are not appropriate in a lover's argument.
2. **No violence.** No hitting, slapping, or other physical abuse.
3. **No screaming.** Your voice may get louder during an argument. Yelling and screaming will increase emotions quickly, which can keep you from resolving the issue.
4. **Use "I" statements,** instead of "You" statements. A You-Statement says: "You are a big jerk for forgetting our anniversary." An I-Statement says: "I feel hurt that you didn't remember our anniversary." With an "I" statement you take responsibility for your feelings instead of attacking the other person. It keeps defensiveness to a minimum.
5. **Be specific about your issue.** "You don't care about me" is too general. A specific issue is: "I feel like you don't care about me when you don't call for a whole week."
6. **Be brief.** Alternate talking every 3 minutes – one person talks for just a few minutes, and then lets the other person talk. This keeps the argument from becoming a monologue or lecture by one person.
7. **Don't interrupt.** If you are using the 3-minute alternating method no one will be giving a speech. Let the other person have their say.
8. **Leave the past in the past.** Stay focused on the current issue. Don't bring up past issues unless it relates specifically to the issue at hand. "You have been more than 20 minutes late for our last six dates. I feel disrespected when you show up late without calling first." This statement is current and mentions only related examples from the past.

9. **Time-Out.** If you are really hot under the collar, take a 10-minute time-out to cool off before you continue talking. Leave the room. Get a drink of water and wash your hands. Go outside for a few minutes. In this amount of time, you will have cooled off and can speak rationally. When our emotions are running high, we are more likely to say hurtful things. Taking a time-out will reduce the chance of you saying things that you'll later regret. Once you've spoken, you can't take the words back. Apologies won't erase the memory of heated comments.

10. **Feedback.** Tell the person what you'd like them to do differently. A good example is: "You have been more than 20 minutes late for our last six dates (fact and related events). I feel disrespected when you show up late without calling first (your feelings). I want you to call me as soon as you know you are running late. I won't be mad if I know ahead of time. I just hate waiting around when I can be doing something else (feedback)." Feedback can help your Significant Other to better understand your needs.

Fight Types

Arguments fall into several broad categories. The good news is, that there is a way to resolve each one. If you are aware of these classic fight types, you'll be able to identify which one you and your Significant Other are having. I've listed each of the fight types along with a framework to create a solution. The framework is just a tool for you to use. How you actually resolve the argument will be up to the two of you.

MISUNDERSTANDINGS

A misunderstanding happens when one person misinterprets what the other means. A misunderstanding, or misinterpreting actions and words, is a common fight. Feelings can be hurt in a misunderstanding. However, once the matter is explained, it can be put behind you. If you have lots of misunderstandings, that's a sign the communication in your relationship is weak. The speaker needs to give more information when they speak so that their message is clear. Clear communication is key in your relationship. (Read Chapter 12, *Making A Relationship Work*.)

◎ *Solution:* Active Listening

Active listening is a good technique to clarify communications. The listener restates the main idea of what they heard, and the speaker either confirms or clarifies for them. Here's an example of how what the speaker **means** isn't what the listener **hears,** and how to use active listening to clarify:

Example: Tom said, "When I was 5 years old, we got a motor boat to take camping one summer. A bunch of people at the lake wanted a ride, but there wasn't enough room for everyone, so my dad left my older brother and me on the dock. I was so mad, that when he came back, I bit him. I've felt bad about that ever since."

Ashley reframes Tom's statement to make sure she understands what he meant: "So, you've never forgiven your dad for leaving you on the dock?"

Tom clarifies what he meant: "Oh, no, I've always felt bad about biting my dad."

DISAGREEMENTS

This is when you each want something different and can't agree on it. When you can't agree on something, you're obviously having a disagreement. Depending on your maturity level, a disagreement can be a quiet conversation or can become a full-blown fight. If you are always determined to be right, you will have frequent disagreements. If one person always gives in just for the sake of peace, they may begin to feel resentment towards their Significant Other.

◎ *Solution:* Compromise

A compromise is where each side makes a concession to arrive at a solution. With a compromise, nobody is 100% right or gets their way completely. If you disagree about what to do on a date, one of you might choose where to eat, and the other chooses what movie to see.

Example: A man feels he never gets to see his girlfriend and wants to spend more time together, but her soccer practices seem to eat up all of her free time. Their solution is to set aside one night a week as their date night where they don't make any other plans except to be together.

DIFFERENCES OF OPINION

Human beings are opinionated. You and your Significant Other won't agree about all issues 100% of the time. This is actually a good thing! You want someone who isn't an identical copy of yourself, and has their own thoughts and ideas. Differences of opinion can range from which sport is the most difficult, to which political party is sounder, to which type of music is the best.

On minor issues that don't affect you personally, it's easy to accept these differences. On major issues that do affect you personally, you might not be able to find a solution and the situation becomes a Stalemate (see the next fight type).

◎ *Solution:* Agree to Disagree

Sometimes you may not be able to find a middle ground or compromise, so you will just "agree to disagree." You have to be willing to drop the issue and accept the fact that there is no real resolution. No one is right or wrong in this situation. This solution is difficult for most people and requires a lot of maturity, but it may be the only option for peace.

Example of a major issue: He feels that infidelity is no big deal and people need to get over their puritan attitudes about open sexuality. She feels that monogamy and trusting your Significant Other to be faithful is vitally important. This couple has a conflict on a major issue. While they have a difference of opinion, they might not be able to resolve it by agreeing to disagree, because his opinion/attitude affects her directly. It's reasonable that he might be unfaithful to her given his opinion. This couple has moved from a Difference of Opinion to a Stalemate.

THE STALEMATE

If there is an issue that you can't resolve or "agree to disagree" about, then you and your Significant Other are deadlocked in a stalemate. In the game of chess, a stalemate is a situation in which no winner is possible because neither player can move a piece without placing the king in check. The game is forced to stop in a draw. Because there is no solution, no one wins. Relationships often end because of stalemates.

Pull Over

One of the most important skills you can learn is how to stop an argument *before* it gets out of control. An argument can escalate quickly and is like a bus on a collision course. You want to be able to pull the bus over before it picks up too much speed. As mad as you are at each other, remember that you love each other and you are on the same team. Try these techniques to keep your argument from racing out of control.[10]

1. Stroke your partner with a caring remark ("I understand that this is tough").
2. Make it clear you're on common ground ("This is our problem").
3. Back down (in relationships, as in the martial art Aikido, you have to yield to win).
4. Show signs of appreciation for your partner and his or her feelings along the way ("I really appreciate and want to thank you for ...").
5. Change the topic to something completely unrelated.
6. Use humor when appropriate (obviously, making a joke about your partner will only make the situation worse).

Apologizing and Making up

Some people think that making up is the best part of an argument because they feel closer afterwards. The making up part is so popular with some couples that they subconsciously pick fights just so they can kiss and make up afterwards. While you might briefly experience that "new relationship feel" when you make up, this is a negative pattern of behavior. It can destroy your relationship over time. You could find that your relationship may not be able to weather repeated fights, just for the sake of fighting. The make up high is not an effective way to strengthen a relationship.

This doesn't mean that apologizing isn't important. Quite the opposite! In fact, it's an important step to healing. Be sincere when you apologize. Don't just look at the ground and mumble, "I'm sorry," or say it sarcastically, or begrudgingly like your mom has forced you to apologize to your bratty little brother. If your Significant Other was right, say so. If you said hurtful things during the fight, tell them, "I'm sorry for saying those things. I know they were hurtful. I didn't mean it, I was just mad." If you are apologizing for a behavior, tell them that you won't do it again, and then *don't do it again*! When you are receiving an apology, be graceful. Don't rub it in or mock the apologizer. Say, "Thank you. I appreciate that," and then drop it. Let the past be in the past.

If hurtful things were said in the heat of the moment, it's not uncommon for both people to apologize after an argument. Depending on the length and intensity of the fight, you might be ready to kiss-and-make-up right away, or it's natural to need some time to recover from hurt feelings. Once you are ready, you can kiss and be close again.

Forgiveness is giving up all hope for a better yesterday.

—Anonymous

Forgiveness

Once you've resolved a problem, one or both of you will need to forgive the other. Someone can make an apology, but unless the other party forgives the offender, the problem is still unresolved. Forgiveness is a remarkable ability that not everyone can do well.

Forgiving someone doesn't mean you condone their hurtful action. It means you give up, or let go of, any resentment and the desire to punish them. The old saying "forgive and forget" means you **forget the hurt you felt**. Forgiveness is crucial to healing a hurt. If you keep reliving the past hurt, you will have a hard time forgiving and moving towards closeness. If you keep reliving the past hurt, the issue will come up again, either directly or indirectly. However, some hurts are so deep that it takes time to heal. In these situations forgiveness may come in stages, a little bit at a time, as trust is rebuilt. Both people will need to be patient as the trust is rebuilt.

Check Point

Let's take stock of where we are. You understand that conflict is natural. You know that how the conflict is handled determines whether the result is constructive or destructive. You know about the main types of fights and the solutions. You understand the value of active listening and 'I' statements. You also learned about the 10 Rules to Fair Fighting. Finally, you saw the right way to apologize and why forgiveness is important.

This chapter was all about the day-to-day problems and routine fights that come up even in the best relationships. But it can get worse! After this next chapter, we'll take a look at **bad** relationships in the chapter, *Trouble in Paradise*. Although your current relationship isn't bad, it's worth a look because most people will have at least one bad relationship in their lives.

But first, the chapter you've been waiting for—sex!

◆————————————◆

Sex: the thing that takes up the least amount of time and causes the most amount of trouble.

—John Barrymore (1882-1942), U.S. actor. A handsome leading man
in Hollywood with a reputation for being wild; also
Drew Barrymore's grandfather

◆————————————◆

Sex in the Big City

Here we are. Two-thirds of the way through the book and we're finally at the sex chapter. It's a big chapter because it's a big topic. Be warned: This chapter gets into the nitty-gritty of sex. I haven't intended this to be a sexual technique manual or an exhaustive study of sexuality, but it's more than a basic primer. I'll give you plenty of straightforward and detailed information. This chapter tells enough to make you more intelligent than the average person is about sex, but it won't turn you into a lotherio*. If you want more information about techniques or anatomy and reproduction, you'll find titles of several books that are entirely dedicated to just those topics listed in the *Resource Section* at the back of this book.

---

*Lothario: A man who attempts to persuade women to enter sexual affairs with him.

Some people are uncomfortable talking about sex. Our family attitudes determine the comfort level we have in talking about sex. From the time you were very young, your parents (consciously or unconsciously) sent you messages about your body, your genitals and sex. Remember that my mom was very open with me and I don't have any problems talking about sex, so buckle up. I know I'll offend some people, but I have to take that chance if I'm going to live up to my lofty promise to make you a Smart Teenager about sex.

Although teen pregnancy is at an all-time low, the rates for teen STI[*] and infectious diseases are way up. This means that teens are still having sex; they're just using birth control pills instead of condoms, which puts them at significant health risk for infectious diseases. But, there is more to sex than disease, so we'll look at everything.

Sex or UnSex

It seems that sex isn't sex. In a recent study, 60% of teenage girls said they didn't consider oral sex to be sex. So what *is* oral sex? Unsex? Further, some of the girls even felt that anal sex kept their virginity intact.[11]

Well, if the technical definition of virginity is to have your hymen[**] in place, then anal sex may well allow you to be a technical virgin. The weird thing about the hymen is that it can break during a woman's period or while she's riding a bike or a horse. Hmm. Does that mean the woman who has never had intercourse, but had her hymen break during her first period isn't a virgin?

We get stuck on the idea of sex being intercourse. For the record, anything that involves sexual activity *is* sex. This includes oral sex, anal sex, mutual masturbation and petting. Smart people acknowledge this fact. Don't think I'm a prude or against sex, because I'm not. But we need to be honest with ourselves. So that we're clear, when I use the word 'sex,' I mean anything that is sexual in nature, which includes oral sex, mutual masturbation or other forms of petting.

---

[*]*Sexually Transmitted Infections.*

[**]*Hymen: A thin mucous membrane that completely or partially covers the opening of the vagina.*

Sex is great, and it has an inescapable reality: It comes with responsibilities. The three biggest responsibilities are pregnancy, sexually transmitted infections and managing the emotions that can arise during and after sex. Some people choose to wait until they are better prepared to handle the responsibilities of sex. Some people have guidelines for sex set by their religion or family, such as no sex before marriage.

During the 1970s there was something called the Sexual Revolution. During this time, it was common for young people to have casual sex with multiple partners, without condoms. The only known STI's then could be cured with a quick shot of penicillin. At that time, a virgin over the age of 16 might have been considered a social outcast or a complete nerd or loser. Since then, the STI's have gotten serious, even lethal*. Herpes was the big, serious STI when it was discovered in the early 1980s. Of course, Herpes was dwarfed by the fatalness of HIV. Herpes and HIV have made the teenage virgin no longer the social outcast. There's no such thing as safe sex, only safer sex. More on that soon.

The Emotions

Besides physical pleasure, what emotions could be involved with sex? More than you might think! Remember how during attraction we aren't aware of the chemical reactions going on inside our head? Well, during sex and even kissing, a lot more of that is happening! Neurobiologists and other scientists have found that a hormone called Oxytocin is released in the body during sex. This chemical is kind of like a 'love drug.' It makes the participants feel emotions beyond just sexual response or an orgasm. Oxytocin actually promotes bonding between the couple[12]. This bonding creates feelings of euphoria, intense love and a deep sense of connection towards their partner. So, during sex the body is dealing with this incredible chemical reaction.

Meanwhile, the logical brain can be conflicted by this emotional bonding and connection if it's unsure about what the sex means to the relationship. If there is concern about the security and future of the relationship, the conflict that the brain goes through can be overwhelming. Add to that the concern about protection against STI's and the

---

*Cause death.

uncertainty of what would happen in the event of a pregnancy. Whew! Yes, it's easy to feel confused. If someone is going against the rules set out by their parents or religion, they can feel guilty or remorseful after having sex. It's no wonder that some people have a hard time dealing with the emotions during and after sex.

One high school administrator observed that teen couples have more arguments and problems on Mondays. These tensions, she felt, were undoubtedly due to sexual encounters they had over the weekend. Just so you know, this experience isn't limited to teenagers; adults experience these very same emotions and conflicts if they haven't taken the time to discuss these issues with their partner.

The Conscious Conversation

In order to keep you and your Significant Other from being overwhelmed with all of these emotions, you will want to talk about the three Big Realities. I call it the Conscious Conversation. I'll tell you more abut the Conscious Conversation soon. First, let's take a short detour.

Sex is one of the most powerful urges you will experience. It feels good. Once you read the part on kissing, you'll understand how one thing leads to another and the urge of the moment can carry you away. It's kind of like when you're driving a car along a nicely paved road and the traffic is light. The vehicle gradually gains speed before you realize how fast you're going. Sure you know the speed limit is 65 miles per hour, but as you casually glance at the speedometer you realize that the car is hurtling along at 85 mph. It's the same with sex. It's very easy for one thing to lead to another and, before you know it, you are going faster than you want. Sex feels good and all the steps that lead up to intercourse can move along quickly. Before you get carried away on the Expressway to Sexville, you need to think a few things through first.

Take time *alone* to think about what you believe, value and want in regards to sex. You need to know where **you** stand on the three Big Realities that come with sex. How would you handle an unplanned pregnancy; are you willing to risk an STI; is sex a casual activity or does it have a special meaning? Do the thinking part on your own. The answers need to be yours. You want to decide how far you want to go *before* you get on the road to Sexville. This way, you are in control. You are making a **conscious choice** and it's not something that "just happened." You *never* want to be the victim of circumstance, especially with sex.

Once you have a clear idea, then you are ready for the Conscious Conversation. The Conscious Conversation is where the two of you sit down and share your *individual* thoughts on the three Big Realities. This is why you want to take time by yourself to think through what you want. As a Smart Teenager, you don't need to get talked into anything.

The Conscious Conversation is where you and your Significant Other talk openly and honestly about the three Big Realities of sex. I know it's no fun to talk about reality because it takes all the spontaneity out of sex. Actually, my friend, it will **enhance** it. Enhance it? Am I crazy? No. I'm smart. I don't want to be worried about whether my Significant Other loves me or is just having a good time. I don't want to have to argue about condoms and whether they are latex or lambskin, or is that old condom in the faded wrapper he's got the same one his big brother carried around all through high school. I don't want to be worried about what will happen if a pregnancy occurs.

I'm smart because I know that, by talking about these three Big Realities, I will be more likely to relax and enjoy myself. I already know the answer to those questions, because we talked about it. I won't be upset the next day or worry about whether he loves me. I'll know where we stand. I won't have to worry about my relationship being strained by a misunderstanding. That Conscious Conversation is priceless.

Obviously, the Conscious Conversation is not appropriate for the first date. Also, you want to have this talk in a non-sexual setting. Non-sexual means you aren't in the throes of passion, the heat of the moment, ripping each other's clothes off and gasping, "Baby, we need to talk," as you go for the next button. By conscious, I mean *aware,* not just awake! You have to be aware of the three Big Realities before you can start this talk. I know that some people are very embarrassed to talk about sex. But since you are going to take off your clothes and be stark naked in front of this person and expose the most intimate parts of your body, talking about an uncomfortable topic for a few minutes will be easy! Besides, this talk can make or break your relationship. Are you willing to let go of your embarrassment for the sake of the relationship? The relationship needs to be more important than your embarrassment.

If you are too embarrassed to have a Conscious Conversation with your Significant Other, then you might want to reconsider whether you are ready to be sexual. If you can't have an honest conversation about your feelings, then you need to know that someone will likely be hurt and that someone is probably you, because you aren't being smart about sex.

The Three Big Realities

When you have that Conscious Conversation, there are the three topics you need to cover.

1. Meaning
2. Protection
3. Pregnancy

Let's break each one down so you know what you're talking about when you have the conversation.

Meaning

This is the emotional side. You want to talk about what sex means to each of you. Sometimes the two partners may have completely different interpretations about the *meaning* of sex. One can think that sex is a declaration of their commitment, while the other may think they are just having a good time. It could be hurtful if both people had different ideas about the meaning of sex.

You want to talk about what having sex with you means to them: Do they love you? Are you making a commitment to date them exclusively? Are you both in agreement? What if you break up? Can you handle the possibility that you will see each other around (at school, etc.) after having been intimate?

It's easy to stereotype men and women when it comes to sex. While men generally think about sex more often than women, some women do like to have sex for fun and without a commitment. Having the Conscious Conversation applies to both men and women. Men can, and do, get hurt just as easily as women. However, be aware that if someone wants sex, they might say what they think you want to hear just to get you to in the 'sack.' This is why having a relationship where you've spent enough time together to have Earned Trust, not just Implied Trust, is important (Chapter 12, *Relationships*) before you make the decision to become sexual with someone.

Protection

The second topic that needs to be discussed during the Conscious Conversation is protection. If you wait until you are at the hot-and-heavy stage, it's easy to say "forget it" and dive into unprotected sexual acitivity, which can create a future crisis. Abstinence is the only way to 100% avoid STI transmission. So, if you are sexual, use condoms.

Protection is everyone's responsibility, not just the woman or just the man. You are protecting yourselves against pregnancy *and* STI's. With the realities of Herpes, Hepatitis, HIV and other diseases, *condoms are an absolute **must**.* Using a condom shows that you respect your Significant Other enough to protect them. Using a condom is also about self-respect and shows that you respect the value and quality of your own life enough to insist on protection. *Only condoms provide safer sex.*

Are you or your partner too embarrassed to buy condoms? If so, then you should reconsider whether you are too embarrassed to have sex. Sex is a mature act. If you are not mature enough to go to the drug-store, stand in the aisle reading the boxes and pay for condoms at the cash register, then you are likely not mature enough to be engaging in sex.

Pregnancy: Truth or Consequences

No birth control method is 100% effective in preventing pregnancy. Because there is always a chance of a pregnancy, a good measuring stick to use in your decision is this: **You should have intercourse only if you are ready to deal with a pregnancy.**

For every decision we make, there is a result or a consequence. The decision not to do homework usually results in a poor grade. If we decide to show up to work late, the consequence might be getting fired. When we decide to have sex, we might get pregnant.

But what about birth control pills? They're 99% effective, right? It still isn't 100%. Plenty of babies have been conceived in that 1% with birth control pills. You should know how birth control pills work. The pills are hormones that tell the woman's body not to release an egg during ovulation. As a result, the body needs to get the hormones from the pill on a daily basis. One missed day and an egg might be released. Also, the body needs to have the hormones for 30 days *before* a woman can rely on birth control pills for protection from pregnancy.

You and your Significant Other need to discuss what you would do if a pregnancy resulted. Would you get married and raise the child? If so, how would you support yourselves? Will you be able to finish school? How would a baby affect college? Do you consider abortion as an option? Do you both agree that adoption is a good solution? Will your parents be supportive—emotionally, physically and financially? Remember, that this baby would belong to both of you: Forever. A baby is not a toy that can be put away when you feel tired. Being sexual is a mature action and requires mature thinking.

Six Bad Reasons to Have Sex

Okay, we've reviewed the three Big Realities that need to be discussed before you engage in sex with your Significant Other. You understand about the emotional and physiological effects that sex has on a person. Now let's look at some negative reasons why people choose to have sex:

1. Because your Significant Other will break up with you if you don't
2. To be more popular with the opposite sex
3. Because your friends have all had sex
4. To feel loved
5. To hurt someone, or get revenge (such as your ex, parents, friend, etc.)
6. Just to get it over with

Make sure that the reason you decide to have sex is based on a positive, or from a place of strength, not fear. You'll regret your choice if it's for a bad reason. This is especially true for those considering having sex for the first time. There is only one chance for a first time and you can't take it back. You should never say yes because you feel pressured.

Consensual Sex

You're probably wondering when we get to the good details. We're three steps away. But first you need to understand what consensual sex is. This is especially important since a lot of high school seniors are 18 years old. Consensual sex is where both parties freely consent (agree) to have sex. It usually means that both parties are of legal age, which is 18 years old. It is very important that both parties are 100% clear that having sex is something they both want to do. If it is not consensual, then it becomes rape.

This is important to you because it is considered illegal for minors to have sex. Therefore, anyone aged 18 or *older* who has sex with anyone *under* age 18 could go to jail. This means that an 18 year-old man with a 16-year-old girlfriend could find himself in trouble if things went bad. Consensual or not, the parents of the minor may press charges against the adult teenager. Be clear that you are engaging in consensual sex.

Know the No

We know that consensual sex means that both people want to have it, and that no one is being forced to have sex against their will. Another reason why you want to make sure that it is consensual is that someone could claim that you raped them. While its usually men who rape women, there have been documented cases of women forcing men to have sex with them. The only time that sex is not rape is when both parties have clearly agreed to engage in intercourse. Because of this you need to listen for the magic word of "no." If you hear someone say "no," you need to stop immediately. Check in with them. Have they changed their mind? If so, you need to respect that.

People who are abusive or who have control issues will rationalize to themselves that the words "no" and "stop" are a person's way of being seductive or playful. "No" does not mean that they will say "yes" if you try a little harder. "No" is not a secret code for "yes." The reality is that no one is entitled to sexual favors. Just because you are in a serious relationship or bought them dinner, does not entitle you, or anyone, to sexual favors. If either person says "no" or "stop," even during a heated make out session, you need to STOP immediately. If you continue on, it can be considered attempted date rape. Even a minor can be prosecuted for date rape.

No one has a right to be sexual with another person against their will. This includes couples who are dating or married. Yes, rape can even occur with married couples. Taking someone out, spending money on them, or doing them a favor does not mean that sexual favors are part of the transaction. Sex must always be consensual.

Your Mouth Says 'No', but Your Body Says 'Yes'

If you find yourself saying "no," be clear. Firmly say, "STOP." Don't whisper it, or hope they figure out that you want them to stop. Be 100% clear about where you stand by saying 'no' loudly.

If you say 'no,' be sure that your actions and your words are integrated. If you feel that the situation is getting out of control, don't keep kissing or petting. If you are with someone who is abusive or has control issues, this will encourage them to continue.

Stand up when you say, 'no.' Excuse yourself to go to the bathroom to change the mood. If you think that the mood won't change, ask to be taken home or call someone to come and get you. This is why I believe that every teenager should have a cellphone, so they always have access to call home from anywhere at anytime.

The Silence

Date rape occurs more often than most people realize. This is because date rape victims are embarrassed or afraid to report it. They think that they deserved the rape, or that sex was expected of them. Sadly, the same person often commits date rape with multiple people because no one reports them.

If you are raped while on a date, you need to know that it is not your fault. You might feel shame or be embarrassed, but you need to get support immediately. It's not worth it to be silent. Even if you don't want to press charges against the person, you still need to talk about the event. If you don't talk about it, your feelings of shame might turn into depression and affect other areas of your life. If you've been raped, tell any adult you trust: your parents, a friend's parents, a teacher or a school counselor. They will help you get medical attention and counseling, and at least make sure you are safe from the person who raped you.

PDA's

No, this isn't a Palm Pilot or other Personal Digital Assistant. PDA is the abbreviation for Public Display of Affection. As you become closer to your Significant Other, you will find that hugging, touching and kissing might happen without thinking. It's almost automatic. When you and your Significant Other hold hands, hug, kiss or walk arm in arm in public, you are giving a PDA. You're publicly letting people know that you have a romantic relationship. PDA's are one of the many fun things about being in a relationship. However, not everyone is comfortable with PDA's.

Some things are private and personal. Being intimate, making out, petting* and sex are private activities. It's something special between the two of you. In a relationship of trust and respect, both parties value the privacy and intimacy of the relationship. They aren't interested in sharing it with others. If your PDA's become a public make-out session, people will become uncomfortable. You've probably seen couples in a clutch and thought to yourself, "get a room." If the people around you aren't uncomfortable then **you** should be, since you are giving them a free peep show**.

Remember, parents can get pretty upset when they see their teen being intimate with a Significant Other. It's actually normal for a parent to not want to think about their teen being sexual. How many times do you

---

*Petting: Touching between people that causes sexual pleasure but does not include sexual intercourse.

**Peep show: In strip clubs, customers can anonymously view sexual activities, like a peeping tom. This is called a 'peep show' because the performers know someone is watching them.

want to imagine (or see) your parents being sexual? So, do everyone a favor and limit your PDA's to handholding and a brief peck on the cheek. You don't want them to wonder what happens when they aren't around. When you are hanging out with friends, you can be more relaxed, but remember to be aware of what is appropriate. You don't want them to think, "get a room." Besides, it's not your friend's business how advanced you are sexually in your relationship.

The Santa Effect

Remember the line in the song, "Santa Claus Is Coming to Town" that says, *"He sees you when you're sleeping, he knows when you're awake"?* When you're out in public, keep in mind that even though YOU don't see anyone you know, someone who knows YOU (or your parents) may see you.

There have been many occasions when someone I know told me that they saw my son at a movie or a restaurant. He didn't even know they saw him! You don't want your parents to hear, *"Hey, Bill, I saw your daughter making out with some guy in the grocery store parking lot yesterday."* Be aware that others can be watching you in public without your knowledge.

Kissing

From a purely logical point of view, it seems odd that two people would be compelled to put their mouths together. Why not their hands? Or elbows for that matter. The fact is, kissing is a powerful event. Remember how we talked about the imago being a powerful love map in attraction? Well something similar, yet more potent, happens during a kiss. By the end of this chapter, you'll see that your brain is a big player in the love game. The kiss is pretty influential in love and it's because the lips are the most sensitive part of the body. They are paper-thin and covered with something called touch-receptors.

When lips touch, these receptors are activated and your brain becomes busy with transactions. The activated touch receptors sends out neurotransmitters from four very small areas in your brain. These neurotransmitters carry messages to another part of your brain called the limbic system. The limbic system controls your emotions. Once the limbic system has received the messages, the brain then tells the pituitary gland (also in your brain) to release the hormone called gonadotropin. This hormone creates sexual stimulation or excitement, including erections. This is why kissing can quickly lead to petting and other sexual activity. If you understand this process, it can help you to be more conscious when things get 'hot.'

It's no wonder that the lips are so sensitive; the brain has more 'cells' devoted to the sensations in the mouth than anywhere else in the body. The final stage of this complex transaction (which all started with a kiss) is where yet another part of the brain gets a message: the amygdala, which imprints a memory of the whole experience in your brain.[13]

Kissing utilizes smell, taste and touch. Three of our five senses are overwhelmed as our brain and body are inundated with all sorts of electrical signals and chemicals. Now it makes sense why kissing is so powerful. This is why a killer kiss is important to a budding romance. It can make it or break it. If the kiss isn't great, then the memory that gets imprinted won't be powerful.

Holy Halitosis

The mouth is a warm, damp and dark area. It's the perfect breeding ground for bacteria. These bacteria, along with certain foods, can create a foul smell. Since taste and smell are a huge part of kissing, it goes without saying that a clean mouth will produce a better kiss. It's common knowledge that daily flossing is the key to fresh breath because bacteria loves to grow between teeth! Brushing twice a day is a no-brainer. Once you have a clean mouth, then you want to understand the basic mechanics of a great kiss.

10 Steps to the Killer Kiss

The main thing to remember is that you want the kiss to be gentle and inviting. You want the person to want more, not less. For the most inviting kiss, follow these steps:

1. Go slow.
2. Be gentle.

3. Slowly bring your face close to the other person's face.

4. Slowly touch the side of your nose with the side of their nose. (You can breathe here—don't hold your breath or you'll pass out.)

5. Keep your lips closed very lightly (not tightly)—don't go in for a big, open mouth kiss right away. Build up to that. No one wants to kiss a fish.

6. Pucker ever so slightly. If you pucker up really hard (like when you have to kiss your Great Aunt Zelda) your kiss will not be very inviting. Ick. Pretend you are softly whispering the word 'who' in someone's ear. Practice this on the back of your hand a couple of times to get the feel.

7. With your faces close together, gently touch your lips to theirs and press in for about 1 to 2 seconds. When you press in, you don't want to mash them, but not so lightly that you tickle them and make their lips itch. This is a gentle kiss, not a grinder kiss.

8. Pull away slightly, just until your lips no longer touch, and then gently ...

9. Press in again and repeat. Your lips might begin to open slightly as you repeat this process. Both of your lips might even 'grab' their lower lip.

   From this point the passion will likely begin to build because just inside the lips are even more of those touch-receptors. Don't rush it. Resist the urge to jam your tongue into your partner's mouth. Going slow is what creates the Killer Kiss.

10. When you are ready to stop kissing: If you've been doing French kissing (open-mouth/tongue kissing) Close your mouth and give the person one or two short closed-mouth kisses before you pull away. If you don't, there can be a string of spit between you. Gross. Not very attractive.

"Houston, we have Spit Control"! You want your lips to be moist, not wet. A kiss is no time for excess spit. Nobody wants a goober baby drool kiss. Some mouths are wetter than others and controlling it can be a challenge for those. If you do have a wet mouth, be sure to slow down when you kiss and swallow frequently to keep yourself from floating away in saliva.

Kissing Questions

- **Should I keep my eyes closed?:** There is no right or wrong way. About one-third of people like to keep their eyes open during a kiss[14]. Others think it is creepy.
- **Can I get Herpes, HIV or Hepatitis from kissing?:** Only if the person you are kissing has infected lesions on their lips. Otherwise, these viruses cannot be transmitted via kissing.
- **Should I breathe while I'm kissing?:** Yes. Most definitely. You'll pass out if you don't. However, you want to breathe through your nose.
- **What if I burp while I'm kissing?:** This is embarrassing, but it does happen sometimes. It's usually not a ripper belch like after a soda. When you've been kissing for a few minutes, it's not uncommon to swallow air while kissing, which will come back up. (Breathe through your nose to reduce this problem.) Women will do this as well as men, so don't be shocked. A kissing burp doesn't happen every time you kiss, but everyone has had it happen to them at least once! The best way to handle it is to laugh and say, 'Sorry.' Your kissing partner will laugh and say, 'Don't worry.' You'll be kissing again in about half a second. If your partner gets mad or freaks out about a kissing burp, they may not be mature enough to be in a relationship. Little kids get excited over bodily functions.
- **I get really aroused sexually when I kiss. Is this normal?:** Oh, yes. Remember, your brain is releasing gonadotropin while you kiss. Passionate kissing can get you so excited that you are ready to have intercourse in no time. This is how one thing can lead to another quickly. Be aware of this neuro-physiological reality before you start kissing passionately. You want to have that Conscious Conversation *before* the hormones make a decision for you!

Foreplay and Petting

Once you've been kissing for awhile, sexual excitement can be high. Foreplay (also called petting) is all the fooling around that happens before actual intercourse. It includes touching the breasts and genitals. This can be a time of intimacy and closeness for the couple. If you rush through this phase of lovemaking, you are cheating yourselves out of a special experience. Foreplay gets your mind and body in synch.

When couples don't love each other, they usually avoid this part of sex because it is intimate and not just physical.

Foreplay is an important element for most women as it helps to gets them sexually aroused, which is crucial to lubricating the vagina. It can be very painful for a woman to have a penis or even a finger, enter her vagina when it's dry. Penetration is easier and sex much more enjoyable if there is enough lubrication. However, not all bodies produce enough lubrication, even with foreplay. It's tempting to use Vaseline, but this can clog the urethra* and cause infections. It's better to use specially formulated water-based products such as Astroglide or K-Y Liquid (available at most drug and grocery stores) to help with lubrication. Lubrication is a delicate balance. Too much lubrication reduces the friction and therefore sensation. If you've used too much lubricant, wipe some of it off. A towel or dry washcloth nearby can come in handy!

Breasts

The breasts and nipples are sensitive areas on both men and women. Most people (yes, including men) enjoy having their breasts caressed or their nipples gently pinched, rubbed and sucked. Of course, you noticed that the word "gently" is the key. Some inexperienced men will grab and twist a nipple so hard that you'd think they were tuning an old radio. You don't want to inflict pain on your partner. Slow and gentle is key.

Just as much as some people love to have their breasts touched, some people don't. It's not a universal pleasure. *Most* people enjoy it, not all. If your hand gets pushed away, don't be surprised and don't take it personally. Also, some women experience extreme breast sensitivity during their periods. The sensitivity is so severe that it's painful to have their breasts touched. Always be aware of what your partner needs.

Masturbation

It's no surprise that most people are embarrassed to talk about masturbation. The definition of masturbation is to give one's self sexual pleasure by stroking the genitals, usually to orgasm. How often do you

---

*The tube that carries urine from the bladder out of the body, and in the male also carries semen during ejaculation.

talk about that? Some people say it's embarrassing or desperate to resort to masturbation instead of having sex with another person. For all this embarrassment, it's estimated that 97% of females have masturbated by age 21.[15] I'd be comfortable saying that at least an equal percent of men have also masturbated.

Many years ago, teens were told that masturbation caused blindness or hair to grow on the palms of their hands. Some religions consider it a sin or a sign of a weak character. Other beliefs about masturbation include that it creates sex addicts, or is the source of infidelity* in relationships. Some people feel inadequate if their partner masturbates.

Just to dispel some of these myths, let's look at them. Nothing takes the power away from something like dissecting it! As we already know, most people have masturbated at least once in their lives. People may not talk about it, but they do it. Does this mean that 97% of the population are social and sexual losers? I doubt it. After thousands of years of medical experience, there has never been a documented case where someone went blind (or hairy) due to masturbation. If that were the case, we'd have a lot of hairy, blind folks in the world! We also know that people's beliefs and attitudes about sex are handed down through the generations from their families. Some people have a lot of shame about their bodies and sex because they were taught that sex is dirty. It's hard to change generations of conditioning. Ultimately, you'll have to decide for yourself what you think about masturbation and sex.

Masturbation is the best way for someone to get to know their own body. Especially for women, masturbation is often the way to learn how to have an orgasm. Once a woman knows how to bring herself to an orgasm, she can show her partner. Beloved advice columnist, Ann Landers, even supported masturbation as an alternative to intercourse for teens.

Frequency of masturbation is connected to an individual's sex drive. Each person has a different level of sex drive. There is no absolute 'normal'; some are high and some are low. People with a high sex drive may enjoy a sexual release once to several times a day, while those with a low sex drive only desire it once a month, or even less.

An act of unfaithfulness or disloyalty, especially to a sexual partner.

Those with a higher drive may find that masturbation provides them with a quick sexual release. Even people involved in a committed and loving relationship will masturbate. Masturbation doesn't reflect on the quality of the relationship. It doesn't mean they care less about their partner. It just means that they have a higher sex drive and masturbation allows them to satisfy themselves while respecting their Significant Other's individual drive and needs.

Communication

Communication is so important to a relationship that it even happens during sex! Just like with any other type of communication, you can't expect your partner to be a mind reader. Don't be afraid to ask for what you want and need. You want to be involved in your lovemaking and not lie there silently like a dead fish. When your partner does something you like, let them know! Moan, groan, say "yes" or, "I love that." Give your partner feedback. Tell him what feels good. Tell her that you like it when she moves that way. Tell them if it hurts. Most guys actually appreciate direction in the bedroom.

Some couples like to talk during sex. Sometimes the talk is gentle and loving; sometimes is can be a little raw with slang terms. However, lovemaking is not the time you should be recounting your bad day to your partner or telling them about the really funny thing your friend did. If you can't focus on what is happening in the moment, then you should not be making love at that moment. Sometimes you'll find that silence can be exciting and romantic too. You'll find the right balance.

Oral Sex

Oral sex has become an alternative to intercourse for many teens. They don't consider oral sex to be *sex* because it doesn't involve penis-vagina penetration.[16] Just because pregnancy will not result from oral sex, doesn't mean that it isn't sexual.

With oral sex, infection transmission is still a risk. Did you know that cold sores on a mouth can transfer to the genitals*? For instance, if

---

*Genitals are the penis and testicle scrotum on the man, and vagina, clitoris and labia on a woman.

someone has an active cold sore (cold sores are herpes) on or inside their mouth and gives oral sex to their partner, the chance of their partner contracting genital herpes is very high. Gonorrhea, HIV, hepatitis and other infections can be transmitted during oral sex. Yes, you can get gonorrhea of the throat! Yummy.

To prevent STI's, condoms and vaginal dams should always be used for oral sex. A dental dam is just a square of latex or thin plastic that is placed over the vagina before oral sex. You can easily make a dental dam by using a piece of Saran Wrap! The CDC* says that only non-microwavable Saran Wrap is effective.

Some women are very self-conscious about receiving oral sex, as they may be worried about the odor or taste of their vagina. Women: If a man likes giving oral sex, he likes the smell and taste. Don't worry about what's going on for him. All you need to worry about is whether *you* enjoy the feeling. Many men enjoy both giving and receiving oral sex. Men need to be aware that, just as women have genital odors, so do men. Some women enjoy the musky smell that is typical around the testicles and penis, while others don't.

Semen is a different story. Most men's semen has a highly acidic taste and smell similar to bleach, and burns in the throat. While a man may enjoy ejaculating into a woman's mouth and feel very satisfied when she swallows his semen, he should be aware that this isn't always pleasant for the woman. (Would you like a shot of a hot bleachy substance?) He should *never* pressure her to swallow it and shouldn't feel rejected if she chooses not to swallow. Some women do enjoy it, but not all.

Only you know how you feel about oral sex. If you don't like to give or receive oral sex, then let your partner know. Your partner should be sensitive to your wants and needs sexually, as well as emotionally.

Cleanliness and Taboos

Talk about the taboo of taboo topics. Anal sex is certainly at the top of the taboo list. More than 30% of teenagers consider oral and anal

---

Centers for Disease Control.

sex to be 'safer sex' than traditional vaginal intercourse[60], so it's important that we cover this topic, even if it makes some people uncomfortable. For many people, anal sex is more shameful than masturbation. Some religions consider it a sin, and in some states, it's even a misdemeanor as 'sexual misconduct.' There are plenty of jokes about anal sex, but it's no laughing matter because it presents some very complicated health issues that vaginal sex doesn't.

First, what is anal sex? It's the penetration of the rectum (anus) with a finger, penis or other object. Now for the important part: Protecting your health. The skin inside and around the anus doesn't have the elasticity the vagina has. Also, the anus doesn't produce lubrication like the vagina does. These two factors make the skin in the rectum easy to tear. Plus, the rectum has a dense blood supply that is very close to the surface, so the risk of infection is even greater than with vaginal intercourse. All STDs can be transmitted through anal sex. Unprotected sex, whether it's vaginal, oral or anal, is a high-risk activity; a condom should be **always** be used, even with anal sex.

It surprises people to learn that pregnancy can occur from anal intercourse. Yes, I said pregnancy. No, sperm can't get to the uterus from the rectum. But, sperm stays viable (alive) for some time after ejaculation. Those little guys are good at their job – swimming! Sperm can leak, or spill, out of the rectum and onto the vulva. Sounds impossible? The rectum and vagina are only about an inch apart. That's nothing compared to their swim along the fallopian tubes! This is called "splash contraception." So, don't be misled into thinking that anal sex is safe, or 'safer,' sex.

Now for the part about cleanliness: Have you ever heard of E-coli? E-coli is a bacteria that's found in the bowel and feces, and can make someone very sick if ingested. In fact, there are documented deaths from E-coli. While there may or may not be feces near the anus opening, the microscopic bacteria *are* present. Once something (finger, penis, object) is inserted into a rectum, both it and the rectal/genital area must be washed with warm, soapy water and rinsed well **before** continuing. If someone has anal sex, and then has vaginal or oral sex without washing first, they can spread E-coli. E-coli in the vagina can create infections and other complications for both partners. Hepatitis

A can also be transmitted when bacteria is transmitted to the mouth or vagina.

Some people enjoy anal sex, *but not everyone does*. So, be sure to discuss this **before** you attempt anal sex with your partner. You don't want to surprise them in the middle of your effort. If you don't like anal sex, or don't want to try it, then don't feel pressured to do it. This is a personal preference, and not something you'll learn to like.

If you decide to engage in anal sex, it's **very** important that you're careful to protect yourself from infections and E-coli, and to know the correct way to keep both you and your partner safe. Remove the condom that was used for anal sex, and then use a fresh condom before continuing with oral or vaginal sex. Oh, and be sure to wash your hands after you remove the condom so bacteria doesn't get on the fresh condom.

Because the skin in and around the anus is thin and can easily tear, using a lubricant such as Astroglide or KY Liquid with the condom will reduce tears and rips (anal rips and tears heal slowly, are very painful, and can get infected). You'll find these condom-safe lubricants at any drugstore and most grocery stores. Well, I did say that anal sex was no laughing matter. Even though some people might be grossed-out reading about this topic, it's too important to leave it out.

Be Smart: HIV and all STIs transmit during anal sex, so always use a condom!

The Big O

Orgasms are kind of like God*. You can't see them, but you can feel them and everyone talks about them with reverence and amazement. Of course, the bigger problem in describing an orgasm is that the experience of orgasm is a little different for everyone. One person might describe it as an earth-moving event, while the next person says it feels kind of tingly. Hmmm. That's a big difference. Let's look closer at

---

*I don't intend to offend anyone's beliefs, but this is such an accurate description that I couldn't pass it up.

orgasms and first identify the basic definition. An orgasm is a sexual climax whereby the body experiences a release of muscle tension after the genitals have been stimulated for a period of time, during which fluids are discharged from the penis or vagina.

There is an orgasmic inequity between men and women: It's fundamentally easier for a man to have an orgasm than a woman. The penis is an external organ, which the man can easily see and touch. Most men learn to orgasm through masturbation in their early adolescence. Unlike the penis, the organ that brings a woman to orgasm is the clitoris. This little, baby pea-sized thing is carefully hidden away in the folds of her vulva. No wonder it's easier for men. Women practically have to go on an Easter egg hunt just to locate the right button. Case in point: My friend, Sharon, confessed that she didn't have an orgasm until she was 40 years old. She intellectually knew what an orgasm was, but hadn't physically experienced one.

While this inequity seems like bad news for women, the truth is that women are actually lucky in regards to orgasm. Once we figure out how to work our equipment, we are able to have *multiple orgasms* in a single lovemaking session! Even better, unlike men, we can have more than one kind of orgasm—which I'll tell you about soon! The poor men generally only get one orgasm per turn. Once he has ejaculated, the man is at the mercy of his body, which needs to regenerate sperm and other fluids before he gets another shot (excuse the bad metaphor).

I wasn't surprised to hear my friend Sharon's story. Actually, only about 30%[17] of women can have an orgasm through intercourse. Until she was 40, Sharon had never used masturbation to figure out what she needed in order to experience an orgasm. Additionally, she didn't have a relationship with her husband that included open communication. He never asked about it and she never mentioned that she hadn't had an orgasm.

Now, if you were hoping that I'd give you a play-by-play on how a woman can achieve orgasm, I'm sorry to disappoint you. That topic is a book in itself! Dozens of books have been written entirely on the subject of orgasm. I've listed a few of them in the reference section of this book. You can do a search on *Amazon.com* using the words 'sex' or 'orgasm.' You'll be amazed.

What does it feel like?

The definition I gave before was kind of a dictionary description. Now I'll give you a more detailed picture. Like I said, an orgasm is a giant release. The release is kind of like when you finally scratch an itch that is driving you crazy; or when you have a really big sneeze. Contrary to the hype, the world doesn't stop, the sky doesn't open up, and angels don't sing. It just feels good.

As the body is building to climax, muscles in your arms, legs, back and even face may tense up. Blood vessels around your genitals are engorged with blood and, once the area is stimulated long enough, in just the right way, it's kind of like going over the edge of a roller coaster. The combination of the release of the built-up blood along with any fluids, such as semen, and all your muscles relaxing simultaneously, feels very good. For most people, it takes about 3 to 15 minutes of stimulation before they achieve climax or orgasm.

The G-Spot

Okay, by now you're probably wondering, "What in the heck is the G-Spot?" No, it's not a nightclub. It's a small spot inside the woman's vagina that produces a powerful orgasm. Women primarily have two types of orgasms. Clitoral, which occurs when the clitoris is stimulated; and a G-Spot, which occurs when the G-Spot is stimulated.

The G-Spot was named by three researchers who presented their findings on this area in the vagina at the 1980 national meeting of the Society for the Scientific Study of Sex. They chose the name G-Spot because the first physician to identify this area was a German gynecologist named Dr. Ernest Grafenberg, who first wrote about it in the 1940s.[18]

What is this spot? Well, similar to the prostate gland in men, the G-Spot is a small dime-sized area in the vagina that, when stimulated properly, can bring incredible pleasure. The G-Spot is located an inch or two inside the vagina, toward the naval. (Remember that the prostate in men is located an inch or two inside the *rectum,* toward the naval). It has a soft, spongy feel. When pressure is applied, the woman might feel like she has to pee. When stimulated to orgasm, the woman will experience a much deeper and more intense orgasm than a clitoral one. One of the best ways for a woman to have an orgasm with intercourse is in the female-on-top position. This enables her to have at least a G-Spot orgasm. It's not uncommon for a woman to have a G-Spot *and* clitoral orgasm simultaneously while on top of the man.

A G-Spot orgasm is very intense. The woman will even experience an ejaculation response. No, women obviously don't ejaculate sperm like men do and it's not thick in texture, like a man's semen. But she does "ejaculate" or discharge a fair amount (about 1 or 2 ounces) of watery fluid from her vagina. It seems like more, but this is all. It's easy to think that the woman has urinated because of the volume of this watery fluid. Relax! This fluid is *not* urine. It has a distinctive odor, which is kind of pungent sweet. You may want to put a towel or two down before you make love to help absorb the fluid that can be produced during sex. If you empty your bladder (peeing) before you have sex, it will help you to relax and not worry if you are peeing.

The three researchers who presented their findings went on to write a book called *The G Spot Orgasm*. I've listed it in the *Resources* section. Because they are research scientists, it is full of scientific and medical background, which includes references from famous sex and reproductive researchers, including Masters and Johnson, Alfred Kinsey, Shere Hite and Sigmund Freud, among others. However, it also includes very clearly how to achieve the G Spot orgasm for both men and women! It is worth the read.

Faking an Orgasm

Pretending to have an orgasm is a trick older than calling in sick to work! There is a classic scene in the movie, *When Harry Met Sally*, where the two friends are having lunch in a restaurant. Harry and Sally are arguing about women faking orgasm. Harry says he can tell when a woman is faking. To prove him wrong, while sitting in her chair, fork in hand, Sally goes on to loudly fake an orgasm, throwing her head around and screaming rather convincingly, while all the restaurant patrons stare with their mouths open. It's a great scene and worth watching the movie for!

Though both can do it, women are more likely to fake an orgasm than a man. It's generally easier for men to have orgasms; in fact men worry about premature ejaculation. The fact is, not all sexual stimulation leads to orgasm. There are times when having an orgasm seems about as possible as winning the lottery without buying a ticket. Factors such as stress, feeling tired, being sick (flu or cold) or having problems with friends or family can make it difficult to reach orgasm. Especially for women, emotions play a role. She needs to relax and let go in order to achieve orgasm. Her ability to relax is another reason why trust and respect in the relationship are crucial. Never are we more vulnerable than during an orgasm. If you don't have a strong level of trust, she will be worried about the relationship. Her mind is on other things and she can't relax.

Women also need more time than men. Many men rush through sex and don't take the time women need. You can have all the technique in the world, but if you rush and she can't relax and allow herself to let go emotionally, it will be very difficult for her to have an orgasm.

If you are unable to reach an orgasm, it's better to just tell your partner that it isn't happening. You may be tempted to make your partner feel good about themselves or reinforce that they are good lovers, but it's not smart to fake an orgasm. Not achieving an orgasm doesn't mean that the lovemaking experience wasn't pleasurable or satisfying. Orgasm does not need to be the absolute end-goal of each and every lovemaking experience between you and your partner. Sometimes, just being close and enjoying each other is terrific. Some couples have to practice before they can have orgasms with intercourse.

Premature Ejaculation

Premature ejaculation is when the man ejaculates either before entering the woman, or almost immediately upon insertion. Yes, this happens to almost every man at least once in his life. This is most likely to happen the first few times a man has a sexual experience. Premature ejaculation occurs because the man becomes so excited as he anticipates the event that his orgasm happens spontaneously. As men have more sexual experiences, they develop the ability to control their ejaculation.

Two thousand years ago, the Chinese believed the woman's orgasm to be sacred and men practiced the art of having an orgasm without ejaculation. They found that if they controlled their muscles, much like stopping urine mid-flow, they could have an orgasm without ejaculating, which allowed them to maintain their erection. The purpose was so the man could give his lover as many orgasms as she desired before ejaculating and having his penis become flaccid*.

The opposite of premature ejaculation is *Inhibited Male Orgasm*. This is when a man cannot have an orgasm despite being highly aroused and stimulated even over a long period of time. The inhibited male orgasm may have psychological origins and the man might benefit from talking with a physician about it.

Breast Size and Penis Size

Men are worried about penis size, premature ejaculation, and their ability to satisfy a woman. Women are usually worried about their breast and body size. Obviously, breast size is a matter of personal preference. Bigger is not always better. Some men prefer small breasts and are actually turned off by large breasts.

The average penis size, just for the record, is between 4" to 6" long when erect. Most men equate the size of their penises to their lovemaking abilities. A penis that isn't large enough to enter the vaginal canal and pass over the G-Spot is not likely to satisfy a woman. Keep in mind that the G-Spot is about two inches from the vaginal opening. Given this, the average sized penis is more than adequate. Ironically, if a man's penis is too large, it can actually be painful for a woman to have full penetration. This can be equally unsatisfying for both the man and woman.

More than the size of his penis, a man's ability to satisfy a woman lies in his ability to control his ejaculation and his awareness of (and responsiveness to) his partner's needs and wants. The few *Dirk Digglers*** of the world, with bizarrely large penises, have little to do with an average or real-life man.

After Play

Intercourse that happens quickly and without foreplay and after play is known as a "quickie." After you've made love, it's nice to be able to

---

*Soft or limp.
**Mark Wahlberg's character in the film "Boogie Nights" about the pornography industry.

relax and enjoy the moment of closeness. After play is cuddling, kissing, gentle touching and kind words. It brings the lovemaking to a close with some emotional bonding, instead of immediately falling asleep or getting up and moving on with the next order of business. Sometimes a quickie is practical, such as when you're in a hurry. But if quickies become your normal sexual routine, one of you is likely to be left emotionally unsatisfied and possibly feeling used.

Rough Sex

Some couples like to have rough sex once in a while. This is where the physical contact is not gentle and loving, but aggressive and forceful. A little bit like wrestling.

Rough sex is fine as long as both partners have expressed a desire for it. It's very important that during rough sex, you don't get so carried away that one of you gets hurt. With a petite woman, a large or strong man can inadvertently cause bruising or even fracture of a bone. Rough sex can also quickly become rape, so it's important that both partners listen carefully to each other in case one needs to stop at any point.

Slang Names

The parts of the body have many slang names. Some of them are offensive and degrading to people. It's best to use their clinical names when having your Conscious Conversation. If you are embarrassed to use the clinical names, then that is another sign of immaturity.

Clinical Name(s)	Common Slang Name(s)
Vagina	Pussy, bush, cunt, hole
Penis	Dick, tool, prick
Breasts	Tits, boobs, jugs
Buttocks, butt	Ass, bootie
Clitoris	Button, clit
Semen	Cum, seed
Intercourse, coitus	Fucking, screwing, bootie
Oral Sex	Giving head, eating out, blow job
Orgasm	Cum, jism, climax

Sexually Transmitted Infections/Diseases

When we're in love, we don't like to think of our Significant Other as possibly being the carrier of an infection. When you have unprotected sex with someone, you are microbiologically having sex with everyone they've ever had sex with. Your Significant Other may not know that the last person they had sex with was infected with Chlamydia, Herpes or HIV because that *other person didn't know!* It's not that your Significant Other would intentionally mislead you, but since it's hard to know if we have a dormant disease, it's best to proceed *as if both* people have a disease.

The National Center for Disease Control (CDC) currently has a campaign called "Healthy People 2010." The campaign's objective is to significantly reduce the population of young adults, aged 15 to 24 years, who have Sexually Transmitted Infections by the year 2010. They've been monitoring the teen cases of STI's every year since 1997. Sadly, as of their update in 2000, the numbers have, in all categories, increased.[19] This means that teens are not using condoms. Teen pregnancy is down, so they are probably using birth control pills instead. Only a condom, properly used, can reduce the risk of STI's.

Some STI's cannot be cured with antibiotics. An example is Herpes, is a virus that can be spread from the mouth to the genitals, and from genital to genital. It can be managed with a lifetime treatment of medications, but it **never goes away.** The carrier is left to deal with herpes for the rest of their lives. Outbreaks are generally painful and highly contagious. The carrier will need to tell every subsequent sex partner that they have genital herpes before having sex. For women, a herpes outbreak can complicate childbirth as the baby can become infected if delivered vaginally. If not treated, some STI's develop into serious health issues. For instance, Human Papilloma Virus (HPV), which is commonly known as Genital Warts, can grow into cancerous cells if left untreated. In fact, 93% of all cervical cancers are related to HPV. Herpes and HPV can also be present on the groin, where a condom can't protect you!

If left untreated, some STI's, such as chlamydia, can cause sterility[*]. STI's are not to be taken lightly. So, if you are sexually active, be sure to get regular medical exams and use condoms.

---

[*]Permanent condition of not being able to produce children.

Health Check

If you don't want your parents to know you need to get a physical exam (or you don't feel comfortable going to your family doctor), then visit your local neighborhood medical clinic or Planned Parenthood for a confidential, low-cost (and maybe free) exam and consultation. Talk with a doctor about the risks and what you can do to reduce them. The clinics also dispense condoms and other birth control measures. But, not all STI's are automatically tested. You have to ask to be tested.

What you discuss with any doctor is confidential; they won't call your parents and tell them you came in. If you are worried, just ask what their confidentiality policy is with teenagers. Most physicians won't contact your parents unless there is a medical emergency. If you get regular care, you won't have an emergency!

You are responsible for your body and health. Use the appropriate protection and get regular checkups when you are sexually active. Remember, engaging in oral and anal sex *is* sexual activity!

Brew and You

Alcohol is another factor in STI's. You must be wondering what beer or whiskey has to do with STI's. Mixing sex and alcohol can be a big mistake because alcohol can increase your chances of having unprotected sex. We all know that alcohol impairs judgment, so it's not surprising that a report revealed, "more than a third of sexually active teens and young adults in a new survey admit that alcohol and drugs have influenced their decisions about sex. Nearly a quarter say they have had unprotected sex while under the influence."[20] Don't let Jim Beam or Miller High Life make your decisions!

The best website to get accurate information about STIs, their cause and treatment is the American Social Health Association. They've given me permission to reprint a portion of the STI Frequently Asked Questions page in this book. If you have access to the Internet you might want to go to their site to read more at *www.ashastd.org/stdfaqs/index.html.*

STD Chart

STD Name	What it is ...	Treatment
AIDS and HIV	Human immunodeficiency virus or HIV, is a virus that attacks the immune system resulting in Acquired Immunodeficiency Syndrome, or AIDS.	No cure. Medications available to manage symptoms. Expected lifetime varies from case to case.
Chancroid	A treatable bacterial infection that causes painful sores.	Antibiotics
Chlamydia	A treatable bacterial infection that can scar the fallopian tubes affecting a woman's ability to have children.	Antibiotics
Crabs	Also known as pediculosis pubis, crabs are parasites or bugs that live on the pubic hair in the genital area.	Special body shampoos. All clothing and bedding must be washed in hot water, or isolated for 2 weeks.
Gonorrhea	A treatable bacterial infection of the penis, vagina or anus that causes pain, or burning feeling as well as a pus-like discharge. Also known as "the clap". Can be passed orally in the form of 'Throat gonorrhea.'	Antibiotics
Hepatitis	A disease that affects the liver. There are more than four types. A and B are the most common.	Vaccine to prevent. Depending upon the type, there may be no known cure.
Herpes	Genital herpes is a recurrent skin condition that can cause skin irritations in the genital region (anus, vagina, penis).	No cure for herpes. Medications can manage outbreaks and reduce pain over an individual's lifetime.
Human Papillomavirus/ Genital Warts	Human papillomavirus (HPV) is a virus that affects the skin in the genital area, as well as a female's cervix. Depending on the type of HPV involved, symptoms can be in the form of wart-like growths, or abnormal cell changes.	Because it is a virus, there is no cure available. Treatment options include removing the warts via cryotherapy (freezing), acid (burning them off), cutting them off. This is the most common form of STD.
Nongonococcal	Nongonococcal urethritis (or NGU) is a treatable bacterial infection of the urethra (the tube within the penis) often times associated with chlamydia.	Antibiotics
Pelvic Inflammatory Disease	An infection of the female reproductive organs by chlamydia, gonorrhea or other bacteria. Also known as PID. Can cause sterility or infertility.	Antibiotics

Scabies	Scabies is a treatable skin disease that is caused by a parasite.	Special body shampoos. All clothing and bedding must be washed in hot water, or isolated for 2 weeks
Syphilis	A treatable bacterial infection that can spread throughout the body and affect the heart, brain, nerves. Also known as "syph".	Penicillin
Trichomoniasis, or Vaginitis	Caused by different germs including yeast and trichomoniasis, vaginitis is an infection of the vagina resulting in itching, burning, vaginal discharge and an odd odor.	Depending upon infection, either oral medication, topical cream or combination of both.

STD Statistics[21]

☞ One in five people in the United States has an STD.

☞ Two-thirds of all STDs occur in people 25 years of age or younger.

☞ One in four new STD infections occur in teenagers.

☞ 93% of the cases of cervical cancer in women is linked to Human Papilloma Virus or HPV (Genital Warts).

☞ Hepatitis B is 100 times more infectious than HIV.

☞ STDs, other than HIV, cost about $8 billion each year to diagnose and treat.

☞ At least one in four Americans will contract an STD at some point in their lives.

☞ HPV (Genital Warts) is the most common STD in the United States. More than 5 million people are infected with HPV each year.

☞ Less than half of adults, ages 18 to 44, have ever been tested for an STD other than HIV / AIDS.

☞ At least 15 percent of all infertile American women are infertile because of tubal damage caused by pelvic inflammatory disease (PID), the result of an untreated STD.

☞ Two-thirds of Hepatitis B (HBV) infections are transmitted sexually. HBV is linked to chronic liver disease, including cirrhosis and liver cancer.

☞ One in five Americans have genital herpes, yet at least 80 percent of those with herpes are unaware they have it.

> **Protect Yourself!**
>
> Know what your protection provides you with:
>
> | Form of Protection | Protects From |
> | --- | --- |
> | Condoms | Pregnancy and STDs |
> | Sponge | Pregnancy only |
> | Diaphragm | Pregnancy only |
> | IUD | Pregnancy only |
> | Pill (hormones) | Pregnancy only |
> | Morning After Pill (hormones) | Pregnancy only |
> | Norplant (hormones) | Pregnancy only |
> | Injectable (hormones) | Pregnancy only |

Condoms

Condoms sure check your ego at the door. Although condoms are only 95% effective in protecting against infections, with correct use, they are the best defense available. The fact is, abstinence is the only 100% way to avoid pregnancy or infections. So, if you plan to be sexual, plan to be safe. Use a condom every time!

Many people don't like to use condoms. There are plenty of arguments for not using them. Unfortunately, the risks of infection make those arguments look weak. If you actually care about your Significant Other as much as you say you do, you will insist on using a condom. As most of us know by now, having sex without a condom is like having sex with everyone your partner has ever had sex with! It's just not worth the risk to have sex without a condom.

Here are some of the arguments: They break, they're not big enough for me, they take away all the feeling, I'm allergic to latex, it takes away from the mood. These are good arguments. But none are good enough to risk your life, or the life of the one you love. Let's look at each of these good arguments and see if there is a solution.

- **They Break:** Yes, sometime they do. That is why you want to buy quality, brand name condoms. A rip or tear is always a risk, but since it doesn't happen every time, it's not a valid excuse to not use condoms. Be sure to use lubricated condoms to reduce rips.

- **They're not big enough:** Good news, big guy! The industry recognized that men come in different shapes and sizes. Extra large or Magnum-sized condoms are available even at grocery stores. Check it out. Also, condoms are *supposed* to be snug.

- **They take away all the feeling:** Yes, they do reduce the sensitivity. But for the 15 minutes that the average sex act lasts, it's not worth a lifetime of misery. Check out the new thin polyurethane condoms. They're approved for STD/HIV prevention and the sensation is better! However, it'll cost you at the cash register because they're more expensive.

- **I'm allergic to latex:** This is a serious consideration for those with latex sensitivity. Again, check out the new polyurethane condoms. Unlike lambskin, they prevent STD's!

- **It takes away from the mood:** Yeah. Kind of like having to take out the garbage in the middle of your favorite show. Smart lovers know how to make the condom part of their foreplay. Learn to incorporate it into your lovemaking.

How to Use a Condom[22]

1. Treat condoms gently and keep them out of the sun because the sun will deteriorate them.
2. Use a pre-lubricated condom, or apply a small amount of water-based lubricant—such as K-Y jelly or Astroglide—inside and outside the condom to help prevent rips.
3. With latex condoms, never use lotions, baby oil, vegetable oil, Vaseline or cold cream—the oil in these products can cause the latex to breakdown. If you use a lubricant, use one made with water (such as Astroglide or K-Y Liquid).
4. Open the package gently by tearing it on the side (Don't use your teeth or scissors, which could tear the condom) and pull the condom out slowly.

5. Put the condom on *before* the penis touches the vagina, mouth or anus.
6. Hold the condom by the tip to squeeze out the air. Leave some space at the tip to hold the semen.
7. Unroll the condom down the entire length of the erect penis until it reaches the base. Be sure to smooth out any air bubbles along the way. The condom should fit snugly so that it won't slide off during intercourse. If you start to put on a condom inside-out, throw it away. You'll know it's inside out because it won't roll down the length of the penis easily.
8. As soon as the man has ejaculated, the man should hold the condom at the rim and pull out slowly while the penis is still hard. If you wait until the penis is flaccid, the condom can come off inside the woman!
9. Wrap the used condom in tissue and throw it away in the garbage —don't dispose of condoms in the toilet as they cause a clog!
10. Use a new condom if you want to have sex again or if you want to have a different type sex (for example, switching from anal to vaginal).

Condom Sense

Buying condoms can be almost as difficult as buying a car. There are so many options it can be confusing. Here are a few key points when buying condoms:

Latex or polyurethane only! Lambskin is organic and doesn't protect against STD's or HIV.

Brand name. While not always a guarantee of quality, it's best to stick with a brand name when buying condoms. Don't go for cheaper varieties. Look for the words "machine tested" on the box.

Have more than one condom with you. If you have only one condom and it breaks, tears or has some other mishap, you don't want to be tempted to have unprotected sex.

Fresh. Don't rely on the old condom that your big brother carried in his wallet all through high school. Get your own. Don't store them on your car dashboard or anywhere in the sun. The heat will break them down and make them weak.

Men: Practice putting on a condom when you are alone. Don't wait for your first sexual experience to fumble around, trying to figure it out. You should also get an idea of how much friction the condom can handle before coming off or tearing. Yes, I mean masturbate with it. Practice removing the condom without spilling semen. Sperm are still viable even if exposed to air. If you spill semen near the woman's vaginal area, there is a risk that the sperm can 'swim' and cause pregnancy/infection.

Sex Fast Facts

- Most young people begin having sex in their mid-to-late teens, about 8 years before they marry; more than half of 17 year olds have had intercourse.[23]
- A sexually active teenager who does not use contraceptives has a 90% chance of becoming pregnant within one year.[24]
- The method teenage women most frequently use is the pill (44%), followed by the condom (38%). About 10% rely on the injectable, 4% on withdrawal and 3% on the implant.[25]
- Each year, 10% of all women aged 15-19—19% of those who have had sexual intercourse—become pregnant.[26]
- The overall U.S. teenage pregnancy rate declined 17% between 1990 and 1996, from 117 pregnancies per 1,000 women aged 15-19 to 97 per 1,000, but the incidents of teen STD cases have gone up.[27]
- 78% of teen pregnancies are unplanned, accounting for about 1/4 of all accidental pregnancies annually.[28]
- Every year 3 million teens—about 1 in 4 sexually experienced teens—acquire an STD.[29]
- In some studies, up to 15% of sexually active teenage women have been found to be infected with the Human Papillomavirus, many with a strain of the virus linked to cervical cancer.[30]
- Teenagers are less likely than older women to practice contraception without interruption over the course of a year, and more likely to practice contraception sporadically or not at all.[31]

Check Point

Well, now you've had the advanced course on sex education. There is a lot more information about sex available, and I encourage you to read more about it. Again, I've listed some good books in the *Resources* section. You've read about sex from the emotional, physical, physiological, intellectual and psychological perspectives. However, this is just knowledge. What you do with it is ultimately up to you.

Whether you decide to have sex now or wait until later, **you** are the boss of your body. Sex is a wonderful way to be close to someone and express your love. But we know that it also comes with responsibilities. If you decide to have sex, be smart. It's your responsibility to make sure that you are emotionally ready, that you are adequately protected and that you are choosing the right person to share yourself with, for all the right reasons.

Now that you've finished the chapter on sex, you might be tempted to put the book away. Before you do, ask yourself these questions: What if sex isn't enough? What if your relationship hits some rough road? What if you begin to experience *Trouble In Paradise*? That is what the next chapter is all about.

Choose your mate wisely. This one choice will bring you 90% of all
your happiness and misery.

—Unknown

Trouble in Paradise

A good relationship can feel like paradise.

A bad relationship can feel like Hell.

Have you ever wondered why in the world anyone would ever get involved in a bad relationship? I don't think it's a conscious choice where they woke up one beautiful morning and threw open the windows and said, "Yes, I think today is the day I'll get involved in a bad relationship and be miserable." The truth is, very few relationships *start out* bad. If they did, no one in their right mind would ever willingly get involved. The typical story is that the relationship starts out okay, but slowly degenerates in a downward spiral until it's officially bad. By the time it's bad, the people are involved emotionally and physically. Just as it's difficult to appreciate how big the forest is when you're standing among the trees, it can be hard to see that your relationship is bad when you're right in the middle of it.

In Chapter 13, *Fight Club,* we looked at the disagreements and fights that most couples encounter while in good relationships. In this chapter we will examine bad relationships and the problems that accompany them. You may not be in a bad relationship, but this short chapter is worth a few minutes of your time. Armed with the information from this chapter, you might be able to help a friend or someone else who is in a bad relationship.

Amber's Story

Amber and Todd dated for a full year. They were 14 years old and in the eighth grade when they got together. Both were good looking, smart and popular. Neither Todd nor Amber had brothers or sisters, so they frequently spent time at each other's houses. The school year was almost over when things started to get crazy. First it was just simple disagreements, and then Todd's personality began to change. Normally he was easygoing, but he became controlling. Before long, the relationship was more hurtful than fun and Amber eventually ended the relationship. Todd wasn't happy about the breakup. It was hard for both of them and they wanted to remain friends, even though they weren't together as a couple.

They tried several times to work it out and get back together, but Todd's controlling behavior increased. He told her who she could be friends with and what she should do. He was acting aggressive and it made her uncomfortable. She had to admit that the good friend she had known and loved was slipping away, and was replaced by this angry person who she barely recognized. She finally realized that they couldn't work it out and weren't ready to be friends yet. It was like another breakup all over again.

Todd became even angrier than before. It scared Amber that he changed so quickly. One day he showed up at her house after school while her mom was at work and asked to come in to talk about their relationship. Amber said, no, it was over. Day

(Continued)

after day, Todd came over wanting to be let inside. Amber talked to her mom about the situation. They both were sad that they had 'lost' the old Todd. Amber's mom talked to Todd's parents about his uninvited visits and then told Amber to never open the door to him when she was alone. Just after her mother warned her about this, the dreadful day happened.

Todd was banging on the front door pleading for Amber to let him inside. He was very angry. Amber knew something was different and was so scared this time that she called her mom at work. Her mom immediately called Todd's parents and then left work to come home to Amber. Thankfully, Todd's folks showed up at Amber's a few minutes later and took him home. His parents realized the problem was out of hand.

An hour later, while Todd's parents discussed their crisis situation, he committed suicide in his room. Everyone was devastated by his death. Amber wrestled with feelings of guilt. She wondered if she shouldn't have broken up with him, or if she had opened the door would he still be alive?

The counselors assured her that Todd's choice was not her fault and that she did the smart thing. She was safe. The counselors told her that she was smart to talk to her mom and not open the door that day. No one knows what may have happened had Amber opened the door, but the fact remains that she listened to her gut and did what she needed to do to feel safe and secure.

About Teen Suicide

Males between the ages of 18 and 24 have the highest risk of killing themselves[32]. If you, or someone you know, are overwhelmed or hopeless to the point that suicide is a thought, please contact either of these resources for more information or help:

http://www.metanoia.org/suicide/

http://www.befrienders.org/suicide/warning.htm

◆————————————◆

It isn't the mountain ahead that wears you out;
it's the grain of sand in your shoe.

—Robert W. Service (1874-1958), Canadian poet

◆————————————◆

Anatomy of a Bad Relationship

No one wants to admit that their relationship has gone bad. Bad relationships can range from mild to severe. The mildly bad relationship might simply be where the communication is so poor that the couple fights constantly; or it might include dealing with a drama queen or someone who is very irresponsible or is in trouble a lot. A severely bad relationship might include chronic jealousy or abuse of any form.

As I said in the beginning of this chapter, relationships rarely start out bad. The relationship will disintegrate slowly for one reason or another; maybe because the person isn't mature enough to handle a relationship. Maybe it's the dynamic between the two people. This is when you have two people who are great by themselves, but put them together, and it's like mixing gasoline and matches: Kaboom! It's Disaster and Fight City. (These couples often have a high level of sexual tension*.) Another reason that a relationship would go bad is when one person changes. They might get involved with a gang, or they might begin taking drugs. When people change, it can be scary. Amber was smart to not try to handle Todd by herself and knew when to get other people involved in the situation.

Whatever the degree of "bad" the relationship is (whether mild or severe), there are a few telltale signs that are like red flags to alert you to a bad relationship. Since it's hard for us to see when our relationship has gone from *The Love Boat* to the *Titanic*, being aware of these red flags can help you know when it's time to dock the ship and dump the relationship overboard.

Three Red Flags (or 3 ways to know you're in a bad relationship):

———————————

They are highly attracted to each other sexually and have intense sexual experiences together.

1. **Listen to your family and friends!** Your family and friends will say things about your relationship. If you're in a bad relationship, you won't want to hear what they're telling you. Their statements are important clues about what you can't see. Smart Teenagers won't allow themselves to be blinded by their love or ignore the truth.

2. **Listen to your gut!** Your gut never lies. You know when you're in a bad relationship, because your gut will tell you. Your stomach will hurt or you might have a general sinking feeling. Listen to your body. Smart Teenagers aren't so afraid of being alone that they ignore or rationalize away a sinking feeling.

3. **Look at the evidence!** Evidence is based on facts. In a good relationship, there's usually lots of evidence that it works. Do the facts about your relationship point to how well it works, or to how bad it is? If you're not sure, read the list of signs in the section *Anatomy of a Healthy Relationship*, found in Chapter 11, *Relationships*. Can you honestly say yes to those items? Do those signs, when applied in the opposite, describe your relationship? That is your hard evidence. A Smart Teenager is willing to look objectively at *all* the evidence.

Abuse

Of course, not all bad relationships will include abuse. However, just like a bad relationship, abuse starts out slowly. Let's face it, if someone smacked you around on your first date, you wouldn't go out with them again.

Abuse is not prejudiced. It happens everywhere and to anybody. Abuse will cross over every demographic and geographic line you can imagine: Women, men, old, young, rich, poor, black, brown, white, intelligent, illiterate, ugly, beautiful, tall, short, skinny, fat, North, South, East, West, in big cities and small towns. No one is exempt.

We tend to think that abuse only happens to married people. Think again! Abuse can happen to people who are dating. It happens to dating couples so often that the FBI has actually given it a special name! The FBI calls it *intimate violence*, instead of *domestic violence*[33].

Abuse isn't just for adult relationships. It affects teenagers as well. University researchers found that 20% of dating teens had experienced psychological violence—most often name-calling, intimidation or threats. An additional 12% reported being physically hurt. The study noted that victimization rates were similar for men and women.[34] While abuse affects both men and women, a study published by the U.S. Department of Justice showed that the most common victims of intimate violence are younger women, between the ages of 16 and 24. As if abuse isn't enough, it gets worse! Murder by intimates accounts for about 9 percent of all homicides in the United States each year. More disturbing is that researchers believe that the extent of violence between intimate partners is higher than reports indicate.[35]

The fact is, abuse gets more intense and extreme over time. It doesn't just go away by itself. The abuser thinks that hitting their partner is reasonable and justified; that they were forced or pushed to hit their partner because their partner wasn't behaving, or that it is their right to hit their partner. They don't consider or acknowledge it to be abuse. Because of this thinking, there is no way to reason with an abuser.

When people think of abuse, they immediately think of the obvious physical abuse that includes hitting, slapping, punching or any other act that causes physical pain. However, there is another type of abuse, which doesn't leave scars or marks. It's what I call *invisible abuse*.

Invisible Abuse

Invisible abuse usually doesn't show bruises, but it can cut and harm just as deeply as physical abuse. Invisible abuse comes in three different packages: Verbal, Emotional and Playful Torture. Usually, two or all three of these invisible abuses occur together. Invisible abuse is also a component of physical abuse. Like physical abuse, all three of these invisible abuses start out slowly and gradually become more severe over time.

Verbal Abuse

Verbal abuse is the first type of invisible abuse. It uses words to mistreat someone. It's a recurring pattern of verbal put-downs that hurt the victim. These put-downs are usually aimed at the person's key insecurity. If we're honest, everyone has at least one insecurity tucked away in their mental closet. In an intimate relationship, it's normal and even healthy to share our fears and insecurities with our Significant Other. We trust that person and they know us pretty well. So if they say something that happens to play into our insecurity, we would logically believe them. Our mind reasons that they love us and wouldn't hurt us, so when they make a hurtful comment that hits our insecurity button, we think twice and wonder if they know something we don't.

Remember, these verbal put-downs don't happen on the first date. They start gradually. So, be smart and know how to recognize the signs of verbal abuse. The Smart Teenager isn't afraid to confront someone who says things like:

- "You're stupid."
- "You're dumb."
- Calls you names of any kind: "You're a bastard" (or whore, bitch, idiot, ass).
- Put-downs or other aggression, including passive-aggressive *teasing*.
- "You don't know anything."
- "You don't know how to take a joke."
- "You're too sensitive."
- "You don't have a sense of humor."
- "You're fat" or skinny, or other description that is hurtful to you.
- "You're ugly."
- "You better do what I want/say."
- Threatens you, your family, or friends in any way.
- Threatens to harm themselves if you don't behave a certain way.

Emotional Abuse

Emotional Abuse is the second type of invisible abuse. Emotional Abuse is where the abuser tries to manipulate and control their victim by using a combination of emotions and verbal abuse. This can include criticism and humiliation, telling you what do, who to be friends with, how to behave and what you think or feel. Just like verbal abuse, emotional abuse slowly undermines the self-esteem of the victim until they begin to doubt or second-guess themselves.

What's an Emotionally Abusive Relationship Like?[36]

What are some of the situations that are typical of an emotionally abusive relationship? Someone who is being abused would answer 'yes' to some or all of these questions:

1. Do you feel that something is wrong with your relationship, but you don't know how to describe it?
2. Do you feel that your partner controls your life?
3. Do you feel that your partner does not value your thoughts or feelings?
4. Will your partner do anything to win an argument, such as put you down, threaten or intimidate you?
5. Does your partner get angry and jealous if you talk to someone else? Are you accused of having affairs?
6. Do you feel that you cannot do anything right in your partner's eyes?
7. Do you get mixed messages, such as the reason you are abused is because they love you?
8. Are you told that no one else would want you, or that you are lucky your partner loves you?
9. Do you have to account for every moment of your time?
10. When you try to talk to your partner about problems, are you called names, such as bitch or nag?
11. Does your partner threaten to break up with you?
12. After an argument, does your partner insist that you have sex as a way to make up?
13. Does your partner blame you for everything that goes wrong?

How Emotional Abuse Affects You[37]

How does someone who is being emotionally abused feel? These are questions that someone who is being abused would answer 'yes' to:

* Are you unable or afraid to make decisions for yourself?
* Do you do everything you can to please or not upset your partner?
* Do you make excuses for your partner's behavior?
* Are you forgetful, confused or unable to concentrate?
* Have you noticed changes in your eating, sleeping, alcohol or drug use?
* Have you lost interest or energy to do the things you used to?
* Do you feel sick, anxious, tired or depressed a lot of the time?
* Have you lost contact with your friends, family or neighbors?

* Have you lost self-confidence and feel afraid that you could not make it alone?

Emotional abuse is very confusing because there are no broken bones to point to, but you are hurting. It's also confusing because your confidence and self-esteem has slowly been eroded away. You might think that the problems in your relationship are your fault. This is why listening to your gut is important. If your relationship doesn't *feel right*, it probably isn't. The Smart Teenager *never* gives up their personal power to anyone else.

Playful Torture

Playful torture is the third type of invisible abuse. Playful torture is the passive-aggressive's favorite game. A passive-aggressive person is someone who is angry but, instead of being direct about it, they express their feelings in ways that hurt the person they are angry at. These behaviors often look playful or accidental and appear isolated or unrelated to anything. Sadly, the passive-aggressive usually gets great pleasure from inflicting playful torture and would never admit what they're doing is hurtful.

Playful torture is basically torture disguised as play. It looks like everyone is having a good time. However, someone is doing something that is painful or "torturous" to someone else. Have you ever heard someone repeatedly say, "Stop, stop, please, stop!" and the other person *doesn't* stop what they are doing? That is playful torture. When the victim asks for the behavior to stop, the passive-aggressive person will ignore or laugh at their pleas. If their victim cries or is seriously hurt by the behavior, the passive-aggressive dismisses the incident by saying that they didn't mean it, or were just playing, or it was accidental. They often belittle their victims who complain about this torture by saying, "You don't have any sense of humor" or "Can't you take a joke?" Playful torture is the passive-aggressive's favorite game because, for that brief moment when they're hurting their victim, they have total power and control.

If someone is doing anything that causes you pain or distress, ask them firmly and clearly to stop the behavior and explain why you don't enjoy it. If they continue with the behavior after you've asked them to stop, then it's fair to say that they are passive-aggressive. Below are some typical forms of playful torture.

You should know that playful torture includes:

- Twisting or pulling arms, legs, hands, fingers.
- Hitting in any way.
- Tickling to the point where it is painful and they don't stop even when begged.
- Putting hand(s) or arms around the throat.
- Biting, pinching or squeezing.
- Hugging or holding so tight that it causes either pain or difficulty in breathing.
- Hiding or keeping your personal property and then taunting you about it.

Excuses

One certain sign that you're involved in a bad relationship is that you make excuses or rationalizations* for the problems. These excuses are the fuel of denial. If you're making excuses, you are in denial about the reality of your relationship. At some moment you'll hear yourself trying to explain to yourself or others why you are in the relationship. Take advantage of that moment to step back and examine the facts (evidence) more carefully. When someone wants to be in denial, there are endless excuses and rationalizations. Here are just a few common excuses to explain the relationship:

- ◎ It'll get better—soon, tomorrow, next week, when s/he gets a job, or a raise, etc.
- ◎ It's because of—his/her mother, father, brother, teacher, boss, school.
- ◎ It would be different if—we didn't live in this neighborhood, city, state.
- ◎ This wouldn't happen if I—lost weight, were smarter, was more attractive, or was more attentative.
- ◎ It wouldn't be so bad if s/he didn't—do drugs, drink so much.

A defense mechanism whereby people attempt to hide their true motivations and emotions by providing reasonable or self-justifying explanations for irrational or unacceptable behavior.

◎ This wouldn't happen if we had—sex, a car, better teachers, more money.

The White Knight

One of the extraordinary occurrences in abusive relationships is that the victim will protect and defend their abuser if someone tries to intervene on their behalf. I didn't understand this until I saw it with my own eyes. I had just moved into a new apartment complex two days before when I was awakened at about 2 a.m. to screaming and a loud banging on the wall behind my bed. It took me a minute before I realized that it was coming from my next-door neighbors who were three college girls. The sound was really close. It sounded like someone's head was being smashed into the wall on the other side on my bed. I could hear a girl screaming for her life. I immediately called 911. Apparently, eight other people had already called in the last four minutes. The police were on their way. I could hear every word between the cops and the woman at their front door (which was right next to mine). To my shock, the girl told the cops that there was no problem! I couldn't believe that just a minute ago she was pleading with this jerk to stop killing her and now she was lying for him. The cops arrested her boyfriend because the girl was visibly bleeding from her head. I later found out that this 19 year old girl's relationship with her boyfriend had degenerated over a year. She was convinced that he loved her. It's easy to get mad at abuse victims because they can't see the obvious. This blindness is all part of the craziness and confusion that slowly creeps up on otherwise level-headed people.

If someone comes to defend you against an abusive person, *don't* shoot your hero! If someone is intervening on your behalf, this should be a wake-up call. A bucket of cold water. A cup of coffee. You need to be intervened on! Hello!!! This is another red flag that the relationship is bad and you need to get out. Don't wait until you are dead before you finally get the message.

Getting Out

Of course, not everyone wants to get out of a bad relationship. Sometimes the payoff for them is greater than the effort and pain to end it. If they are enjoying spending their valuable time in a bad relationship—"power to them," I say! Let's face it, you can't talk anyone out of something they want. If they want a bad relationship, they've got a bad relationship.

Abuse is a different story. It's common for abuse victims to feel "crazy" and behave in ways that they wouldn't normally behave in a healthy relationship. The crazy feeling can confuse the victim and make them feel responsible for (or that they deserve) the abuse. This crazy feeling can also make it hard to confront the fact that the relationship *is* abusive. The crazy feeling and confusion of this makes it hard to have the courage to end it. On top of the crazy and confused feeling, the abuse victim may have 'lost' their family and friends' support. Classic abusers will work to alienate their victims from family and friends. They do this because they're smart. The abuser knows that family and friends will give their victim feedback. Feedback that the relationship is bad. The abuser can't afford for the victim to hear this. So in addition to feeling crazy and confused, the victim is alone and doesn't have outside support.

Staying in an abusive relationship can cost you more than just a few months or years of your life. It can cost you your entire life. Abusive relationships are dangerous because they never get better. Sure, there might be moments of sweet peace, but the cycle of abuse will start up again. Because it can be hard to end an abusive relationship, you need to involve adults you can trust to help you through it. You can get help from your parents or guardian, an adult family member or school counselor.

Support

Even if you've alienated your own family and friends because of an abusive relationship, go to them for support. Trust me. They'll be there. They have painfully sat by and watched you suffer. They have tried to tell you about what they saw, but you were under the spell of the abuser and wouldn't hear them. While you were in the middle of the forest (relationship denial), they have been sitting outside waiting for you to summon up the courage to ask for help. They will understand and be more than happy to help you get out of the relationship. But you have to ask. Put your pride away and get support.

The reason that support is needed when ending an abusive relationship is twofold: First, the abuser can become enraged or even more abusive when they realize they won't be able to control their victim. If you are breaking off an abusive relationship, I can't emphasize this enough: **Don't do it alone!** Get plenty of ongoing support from family and friends. They can provide you with physical protection and tremendous emotional support. The second reason you need support when ending an abusive relationship is because it's not uncommon for the abuser to suddenly become very nice after a breakup to lull the victim into believing that they are "changed." Many abusers promise, "I won't hurt you again. Really. You have to believe me. This time it will be different. Please, I love you." The support from other people is crucial so the couple doesn't get back together after they've broken up.

If someone wants to continue in an abusive relationship in any capacity, then they need counseling. If someone counsels you to *stay* in an abusive relationship of any kind, get a second opinion! The Smart Teenager does not tolerate abuse. It's important to get other people involved if a relationship becomes abusive. A Smart Teenager will get help from an adult they trust.

The Payoff

The next chapter is devoted entirely to relationships that are not necessarily abusive, but deal with heavy drama. It also speaks to the fact that sometimes a partner in a dysfunctional or unhealthy relationship will decide to stay in the relationship. When this happens, it's usually because there is some payoff for them. The other person is getting something intangible from the relationship that makes it worth putting up with all the hassle. I'm not addressing the payoff in this chapter, because, in my own experience, abusive relationships are not something that get better. So, I hope you will read the next chapter, not just for the information about dealing with high-drama relationships, but also for the part about why someone would choose to stay.

What a Smart Teenager Knows about Bad Relationships & Abuse:

- Listens to their family and friends, and won't allow themselves to be blinded by their love, or ignore the truth.

- Isn't so afraid of being alone that they ignore or rationalize away a gut feeling, and is willing to look at the evidence objectively.
- Recognizes the signs of various types of abuse (verbal, psychological, etc).
- Knows that abuse has **no** place in a love relationship and won't tolerate it.
- *Never* gives up their personal power to anyone else.
- Knows when to get others involved.

 Check Point

At this point, it's pretty clear that abuse has **no** place in a love relationship. Someone who abuses you does not love you. In fact, they lack respect for you. While it's sad, it's a fact that abusers have often been abused themselves. They usually have low self-esteem and get power from hurting or controlling others. The abuser is sick and needs counseling and you are not responsible to help them. You are only responsible for yourself. If your relationship involves abuse of any kind, it is important for you to be safe. Remove yourself from the relationship *immediately*.

Now that you've been thoroughly drilled about abuse, does this mean that every relationship that involves bad communication or has common arguments is abusive? No. Absolutely not. That is why I put the chapter about typical relationship problems first. I want you to be able to identify the difference between abuse and plain old problems that couples have. It takes a very Smart Teen to be aware of the differences.

The next chapter is about relationships that may, or may not, be abusive but have high levels of drama. In this next chapter you'll learn how to handle Drama Queens!

Age is no guarantee of maturity.

—Lawana Blackwell, author, *The Courtship of the Vicar's Daughter*, 1998

The Drama Syndrome

The last chapter focused on abuse. This chapter is about relationships that have high levels of drama. While a high-drama relationship might be bad, it's not necessarily abusive. A high-drama relationship always has a Drama Queen. These are the people who always seem to have a crisis happening. In spite of the name 'Queen', both men and women can be Drama Queens. However, women tend to be Drama Queens more often.

Am I suggesting that women are 'emotional?' Yes. It's a fact that scientists have known about for quite some time. It all goes back to the brain again. Women's brains are set up a little differently than men's. The areas of their cerebral cortex (which is linked to language, judgment and memory) are more densely packed with nerve cells than men's brains. This allows them to process information more effectively than men. It also gives them greater access to their emotions. As a result, women are more verbal and more in touch with their emotions. Thus, they tend to be more emotional[38]. This doesn't mean that they are weak or hysterical, but it explains why women are more likely to be Drama Queens than men. Does this mean that *all* women are Drama Queens? Oh, no. Absolutely not! Later we'll see how someone (man or woman) becomes a Drama Queen.

But back to the relationship! Those who've had a relationship with a Drama Queen will tell you, it's pretty exhausting being in a relationship with one. When a Smart Teenager feels overwhelmed, they put the brakes on. They know this is a good time to pull over and take stock of the situation before they continue.

Jason & Nina

Jason and Nina had been dating seriously for almost eight months. It was the first serious relationship for both of them. The problem began so gradually, that it was almost unnoticeable. Things would be fine for awhile. Then a problem would come up for Nina, and she would fall apart and Jason would help her through the situation. The problems or issues that plagued Nina varied. For one, she hated her parents, although Jason didn't think they were so bad. Sometimes the problem-of-the-moment was about her family or a friend. Sometimes it was about school or her weekend job. She complained a lot about almost everything and her problems became more frequent over several months. None of the issues was actually serious or life-threatening, but they were to Nina.

Sometimes Jason felt overwhelmed by the situation and would get frustrated with Nina. When this happened, she would suddenly chill out and the situation would quickly resolve. Things would be back to normal for awhile until another problem came up and the whole thing started all over again. Jason could see that it was becoming a vicious cycle.

Each time an issue came up Jason listened to her and tried to help whenever he could. He had even called in sick to work twice in

(Continued)

the past so he could help with her problems. Nina's emotions increased to the point where she cried a lot, or would be mad at Jason for nothing. Jason had become very confused about the situation. Worse, he felt tired and consumed by the relationship. In fact, Nina had suddenly broken up with him three weeks ago without explanation. It broke his heart. Just as mysteriously the very next day, she called him and begged for forgiveness and wanted to get back together. He said, "Of course." He loved her. Jason wondered if this was normal for relationships.

He really loved Nina and hoped he could break this cycle of high emotion. He decided he would confront her about the high drama in their relationship. So, he calmly told her that her problems were wearing him down and asked if she would talk more to her friends about her situations, and involve him less. She was mad about his request, and said he was pushing her away and was being mean to her. Jason assured her that he wasn't pushing her away, but that he just couldn't deal with the drama anymore.

The next time Nina started with one of her situations, Jason knew he had to stand strong and not play her "game." He acknowledged her problem, asked her what she was going to do about it, and then told her he had to leave, but to call him when she had a solution worked out. Nina was shocked. Jason wasn't participating as he usually did! She was speechless as he drove away. A few days later, while at her house Nina started up again and she began crying. He hated it when Nina cried like this and normally would rush to comfort her and take care of her. Jason had to hold onto his resolve to not get involved or play her drama game.

Just like the last time, Jason acknowledged her situation and asked her what *she* was going to do about it. At that point, Nina stopped crying and lovingly put her hand to his face and smiled. Then suddenly, she *slapped* him hard across the face with the hand that had just a moment ago rested lovingly on

(*Continued*)

his cheek! Jason was the one in shock this time. The slap stung, but it was nothing compared to the pain of his heart sinking. He knew she had crossed the line from crazy making to abuse. It was a defining moment. That was when he realized that the situation would never get better. He looked at Nina with disappointment and determination.

"That's it, Nina," he said. "It's over. I'm out of here." He then walked toward the front door to leave.

"Wait," Nina screamed, "Stop! Don't go!"

Jason turned around just as she was throwing herself to the floor screaming and crying. He was disgusted at this point.

"I'll die without you," Nina was sobbing. "Don't leave me."

Jason shut the door behind himself. He was numb, angry, sad and glad all at the same time. He felt sick to his stomach.

Nina called Jason many times every day over the next week, but he wouldn't talk to her. She sent him emails apologizing for slapping him, begging him to take her back. She said she knew she had made a mistake, and would he please forgive her? She even called his friends to try to get find out what he was thinking or to relay messages to him.

None of Nina's efforts worked. Jason now saw her as a manipulative and high-strung Drama Queen. He wasn't going to play the game with her anymore. Jason continued to ignore her until the calls and emails finally stopped. He was sad about the relationship ending, but, within a few weeks, he felt much better than he had in months. He knew it was for the best. Jason also knew that he would never tolerate a relationship with a Drama Queen again.

The Drama Syndrome

Jason was caught in what I call a Drama Syndrome. A Drama Syndrome is the three-stage cycle of emotionally charged events that center on a Drama Queen. The three stages are similar to the pattern of physical abuse. The peak is the second stage, or the actual event or scene. The Drama Syndrome is certainly exhausting, but it *may or may not* be abusive.

Drama Queens are essentially the lead actors in their own show. However, they can't have an episode without someone to play the part of Supporting Cast. They need at least *one* other person to play their game. This is why Nina was so mad when Jason was going to leave. She knew she wouldn't be able to play the game by herself! For clarity, we'll call the high-drama event an *Episode*. Let's look at each stage of the Drama Syndrome:

Anatomy of The Drama Syndrome

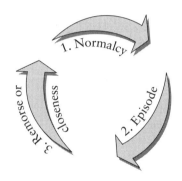

Stage One: Normalcy. This is when things are going good. There is no drama. The routine of life goes on as normal.

Stage Two: The Episode. This is the peak, or the actual episode of the drama playing out. It's when thing start to go bad. The Drama Queen will exhibit strong emotions, which are usually anger or fear. At their worst, they may cry, yell, scream, whine or whimper. They may even throw things during the Episode. Drama Queens can have rage or anger management issues. A single episode can last a few minutes or a few days, depending on the issue at hand.

Stage Three: Closeness or Remorse. This is when things are lovey-dovey. The episode has subsided. The Drama Queen may feel bad about the episode and apologize. Strong feelings of love and closeness are typical during this stage. This stage quickly gives way to normalcy and the cycle starts over. It's easy to see the pattern.

The Cycle Tightens

Over time, the Drama Syndrome cycle becomes shorter and shorter. It's not uncommon to eventually have the period of normalcy shrink to the point where it lasts for only a few days. To add to the confusion, you can't predict when the next Episode will occur. The cycle becomes exhausting for those who play the game, as they have to keep up with the erratic emotions of the Drama Queen.

Never Help *Anyone*?

Does all this mean that anyone who is going through a tough situation is a Drama Queen? Of course not! Does this mean that we shouldn't help anyone when they're in a jam? No. Part of being a good friend is to be available when someone needs a shoulder or a hand. This chapter is not about the times when someone needs a hand. We are talking about the person who is *constantly* in a crisis and demands that you be involved. Everyone has "stuff" happen that's beyond their control. Some common dramatic events that everyone will go through in their lives include:

- A car or bike accident.
- Getting laid off from work.
- A family member develops a life-threatening illness.
- A friend or family member dies.
- A natural disaster, such as a fire, earthquake, flood, tornado, etc.

During and after, the person at the center of the event receives extra attention from their family, friends, co-workers, acquaintances and sometimes even strangers. People want to hear the story of the event, or offer their condolences, support and help. It's good, and important to get extra support when going through a rough time.

Physiology of an Episode

When an Episode happens, hormones such as adrenaline are released into the body, which creates a feeling of being overwhelmed. It makes the heart beat faster and the blood race faster. You can feel perspiration under your arms and on your upper lip. Your mouth might get dry. This is known as the **fight or flight reaction.**

An Episode is very upsetting, and it can take anywhere from a few minutes to a few days to feel normal again, depending on the size of the Episode. People usually *don't enjoy* this feeling. On the other hand, Drama Queens *do enjoy* it. They enjoy the attention they get from an Episode. After awhile, they become accustomed to the physical rush of being overwhelmed by their emotions. Many Drama Queens don't feel alive if they don't feel the rush. They begin to create Episodes just to get a "fix" of the physical rush, and attention from others.

Drama Queen Undressed

Drama Queens either have emotional issues that need to be worked out with a professional counselor, **or** they are incredibly immature and need to do a lot of growing up. Emotionally, the Drama Queen acts like a five year old. They may pout, throw temper tantrums, burst into tears, blame, withhold, taunt, tease or get mean.

As people move out of childhood, they develop the ability to recognize, identify and talk about their feelings. They can tell whether they are afraid or mad. They are able to resolve issues or get support. They've become emotionally mature. An emotionally mature person isn't controlled by their emotions. An emotionally mature person knows that they are not going to be impacted by their emotions forever and that powerful feelings are fleeting. Powerful feelings are kind of like a commercial break during a television show. A 30-second commercial doesn't mean that the show won't come back. In the same way, most people are truly angry for no more than a few minutes before they cool off and return to their regular selves.

Have you heard the saying, "Count to 10 and take a deep breath before you speak when mad"? This is because rage passes quickly and you're then able to handle the situation sensibly. This doesn't mean that you're no longer mad. It does means you're no longer caught up in the high level of emotion that would cause you to say or do something irrational that you'd regret a few minutes later.

Crying is an expression of intense emotion. It's fleeting too. When people cry, it is usually in small spurts. Someone grieving the death of a family member or coping with another significant loss will cry hard for a few minutes and then regain their composure. Just because they stopped crying doesn't mean they aren't sad anymore, or that they won't cry about it again. It does mean that their emotions are moderate and appropriate.

The Drama Queen is emotionally *immature*. They are controlled by their emotions. Unfortunately, there is no "Relationship License" one needs to qualify for before starting a relationship. A Drama Queen isn't emotionally mature enough to handle a relationship. Remember the test to see if you are ready to date from Chapter 2, *Learning Curve*? That test was to see if you had the emotional maturity to navigate a relationship successfully.

Drama Queen Styles

There are three different styles of Drama Queens. Some are specifically just one type, though most will exhibit a little bit of all three styles. Drama Queens are amusing to watch from afar, but they can be emotionally draining for those in a relationship with them.

1 – Hypochondriac – This Drama Queen has imaginary illnesses. They may involve medical doctors and their entire family in their ongoing health issues. A headache is sure to be a brain tumor, an upset stomach is certainly a bleeding ulcer. The comic actor, Woody Allen, often plays characters that are hypochondriacs.

2 – Magnifiers – For this Drama Queen, the slightest day-to-day problem becomes a catastrophe. A minor headache is cause to stop their daily routine. A broken shoelace is the end of the world. Poor service at a fast food restaurant creates a scene. Spilled milk is treated as a criminal offense. They worry about and get upset at small things. These people are often unaware of their behaviors.

3 – Psycho* – This category isn't very complimentary and for good reason. These people lie and manipulate others. They use psychological tactics to keep those around them confused. They can cause a tremendous amount of pain and suffering to those who are willing to play their game. These Drama Queens can also be emotionally abusive.

A negative slang name for someone who has significant psychological problems, such as schizophrenia or mania that is marked by delusions, hallucinations and distorted perceptions of reality.

Roots

So, where does this high-intensity, dramatic behavior come from? What makes the Drama Queen tick? How did they get like this? Why do they create Episodes? Most of the Drama Queen's behavior is rooted somewhere far away from your relationship. The pattern was probably set long before you came on the scene. In fact, their pattern of behavior may have more than one cause. Here are 5 possible causes:

1. They may have grown up in chaotic households where they witnessed unhealthy marriages.
2. They may feel most alive, not to mention important, when an emergency is unfolding. They thrive on arguments, dissension* and high stimulation.
3. They may be so afraid of silence and loneliness that they will put up with anything to stay busy. They will provoke arguments just to fill up the void. An unpleasant situation is a distraction, and they need a distraction because they are terrified of their own company. If they had a quiet moment, they might have to examine their life and the direction they are moving in. That prospect is very scary to them.
4. They may just need time to grow up and mature. A Drama Queen hates to hear this. In their mind, they *are* emotionally mature. This isn't about age. Some people are emotionally mature at age 14, while others still haven't grown up emotionally at age 41!
5. Their behavior may have a chemical nature. Remember, our brains are like chemical factories. Sometimes moods can be controlled medically with hormone supplements or other drugs. Only a doctor can make this determination.

Seven Symptoms of The Drama Syndrome

Smart Teenagers know when they feel overwhelmed. They are too busy to deal with a Drama Queen and can identify the symptoms of the Drama Syndrome. If you can relate to two or more of the items below, you may be involved with a Drama Queen.

---

*Disagreement or quarreling.

1. Your **life is neglected**—you have incomplete business, such as unfinished homework, missed deadlines, piled up laundry, etc.
2. Your **health is suffering**. You find yourself not doing the things you need for your own health, such as exercising, eating right, taking vitamins or getting enough sleep.
3. Your **relationships are neglected**—Your friends and family wonder where you've been, complain that you haven't been in touch with them, or suggest that you are too involved with issues around your Significant Other.
4. Your **work is suffering**—You show up late to school or work. The quality or amount of work you produce has dropped because you can't concentrate. You skip school or work to take care of the Drama Queen or the details of their latest Episode.
5. You can't remember your life ever being this **hectic**.
6. You **feel overwhelmed and tired**, like you are juggling too many things.
7. You begin **making excuses** (to yourself and others) about why the Episodes are happening.

The Reward

If it's so terrible, why would anyone want to be involved in a Drama Syndrome? Like abuse, the Drama Syndrome starts out slowly and builds over time. Those who find themselves playing the role of supporting cast to a Drama Queen can also become addicted to the "rush" of the Drama Syndrome. They can actually begin to *enjoy* their part in the game, even if it isn't healthy.

But there are other rewards. As humans, we rarely do things without ulterior* motives. So, there is *some* reward, *some* benefit to the decision to stay involved in a Drama Syndrome. People don't stay in a relationship unless they are getting something out of it. So, what kind of reward would you get from being with a Drama Queen?

It can be an excuse for why you are doing poorly in school or other areas of your life. Maybe you feel powerful, important or loved because you get to save the Drama Queen from their latest crisis.

---

*An underlying motive, usually a selfish one.

Maybe you've become addicted to the feeling of excitement that the Drama Syndrome brings. Sometimes the biggest "reward" is that you get to be a victim yourself! You might get sympathy when you complain to your friends and family about how hard it is to deal with your Significant Other. Jason didn't complain to anyone to get sympathy. He was just miserable, so he decided to end the relationship.

If you are involved with a Drama Queen and you aren't sure what your reward is, then try this quick two-step process to narrow down the possibilities:

1. **First, Observe** yourself complaining about your situation to others. How do you feel when you complain—do you feel validated, listened to, or important? How do you feel when you are in the middle of the Drama Syndrome—do you feel powerful or needed?
2. **Second, Stop** complaining to others. If you eliminate the "oh, poor me" benefit, you will either get bored with the situation or the real reason for your payoff will be staring you in the face!

If you decide to stay in a bad relationship, don't be a victim. Be clear about what you are getting out of it. Start writing in a journal; write honestly about your relationship and what you get out of it. Then, do everyone around you a big favor and don't complain about how bad your relationship is! Trust me, they are tired of hearing about it.

Breaking the Drama Syndrome

Ending the relationship is the quickest, easiest way to untangle yourself from a Drama Syndrome. However, some people want to save the relationship and hope to change the dynamics. Keep in mind that people *rarely* change, so have realistic expectations if you attempt to change the relationship by breaking the Syndrome. Be open to whatever happens as a result of attempting to break the Syndrome. If you are expecting a particular outcome, you could be hurt if those expectations aren't met.

When breaking the Syndrome, the relationship has the possibility of moving in one of three directions. In any scenario, you will come out the winner! Here are three possible results of breaking the Syndrome:

1. The Drama Queen stops the game and the relationship becomes healthier.

2. The Drama Queen gets mad that the game isn't being played and decides to breakup.
3. You get tired of the game, and decide to breakup.

The Three-Step Solution

So, how can you break the Drama Syndrome? Well first, remember that the Drama Queen is essentially an emotional 5 year old. The best way to deal with a 5 year old is with a time-out. Parents take control of a 5 year old's emotions by creating a cooling off period for them. Of course, it's easier to call a time-out with a 5 year old who gets sent to their room, than with someone who can get into a car and drive off.

So how do you give your Drama Queen a time-out? You need to **remove yourself from the scene.** The game needs two people. Without someone to react, the game doesn't work. The time-out removes the Queen's supporting cast from the equation. When the Drama Queen begins an Episode, they get a time-out by having their Significant Other leave. Follow the same steps that Jason did with Nina.

1. **Acknowledge it:** "Sorry to hear about that."
2. **Place the responsibility on the Drama Queen's shoulders:** "What are *YOU* going to do?"
3. **Take a time-out:** Remove yourself physically and tell them to contact you when the situation is resolved. "Honey, I'm going to go. Call me when it's all worked out."

After the third step, the you **must** *leave immediately*. You need to be **away** from the Drama Queen. The Drama Queen should be ushered to the door or taken home. This will surprise the Drama Queen, just like it did Nina. Remember, if there is nobody to play the game with, the game is over! The Drama Queen will probably get mad. The best response is to act cool and don't take their bait*.

---

*The Drama Queen may protest, begin yelling, insisting that they need to talk, or need help, etc. They will try to lure the other person into an Episode.

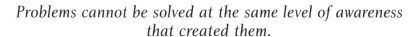

*Problems cannot be solved at the same level of awareness
that created them.*

—Albert Einstein (1879-1955), German-born American physicist
and Nobel laureate

Boundaries

Why give the Drama Queen a time-out? For two reasons: First, the
time-out takes the responsibility of the situation off of you. This creates a very important emotional boundary. Second, it puts the responsibility of the situation back on the Drama Queen. They will quickly
learn that, when they are dramatic, they are on their own. I've said it
before and I'll say it again: The Drama Syndrome only works with the
participation of another person. Without someone to react to them,
the Drama Queen will either stop the game or find a new player.

The Three-Step Solution is a way for you to set a healthy boundary
with a Drama Queen. You need to be prepared to use the Three-Step
Solution as many as **10 times** before the Drama Queen changes their
behavior. Why 10 times? It's like advertising. Commercials run regularly because companies know that repetition is important when getting someone to decide to buy. It's the same with setting boundaries.
You want the person to buy into a new way of being, and it will take
more than once for them to warm up to the idea.

I have to tell you the truth: setting this boundary with a Drama Queen
is very hard. It's easy to write about, it's easy to talk about. It takes
some kind of spine to do it. It takes another kind of spine to do it over
and over, like 10 times.

A boundary sounds like a negative thing, huh? Like something to
keep someone out. Actually, boundaries are important. They are even
essential to our survival. Skin is a good example of our most basic
boundary. Emotional boundaries are the ability to say 'no' and set
limits. They are healthy and necessary for self-preservation. It allows
you to take responsibility for what you are really responsible for. If

we didn't have emotional boundaries (the ability to say 'no') then other people would take advantage of us. If you spend all of your time and energy taking care of someone else, you will neglect yourself. In this light, boundaries are not a negative thing. In fact, they are very positive.

 Check Point

Let's check in and see where we are. You saw how a high-drama relationship is different from an abusive relationship. We also learned that Drama Queens are essentially the lead actors in their own show. We looked at the anatomy of a Drama Syndrome and saw the three phases and how it creates a cycle. We also learned about the physiology of an Episode and how some people can get hooked on the feelings it produces.

Most important, we saw that the Drama Queen is emotionally *immature*. We know about the different styles of Drama Queens and what might cause someone to become so dramatic. We also looked at why someone would stay in this kind of a relationship. We talked about breaking the Syndrome and the Three-Step Solution. Finally, we briefly looked at the important role of setting emotional boundaries. The bottom line to all of this is that we can't change others. We can only change ourselves.

So, what if all of your efforts to make your relationship work have failed? How do you handle a breakup? Fortunately, the answers are a page away because that's our next chapter.

'Tis better to have loved and lost than never to have loved at all.

—Lord Alfred Tennyson (1809-1892), English poet

Breaking Up

By the time you contemplate a breakup, you've been through the wringer. A lot of water has gone under the bridge. Breaking up is a sad and painful experience. It's not to be taken lightly. Tennyson's famous quote about lost love is a hard one to swallow when your heart is breaking. Most people don't understand or appreciate the quote until they have fully recovered from a breakup. This chapter will focus on reasons why people breakup, the way to break with someone, how to tell when your Significant Other might be getting ready to break up with you, and what to do after a breakup.

Kristi & Paul

Kristi waited on the swings for Paul to meet her at the park. This was the park where they first kissed 10 months ago. Almost a year. Breaking up with Paul was a really hard decision for her to make. He was nice and sweet, but they seemed to be drifting apart over the past few months. There was no big event to blame. No one was cheating. They fought like most couples she knew, but that was becoming more frequent. They were also getting on each other's nerves more often. Kristi used to laugh at his Elvis impersonation when he said, "Thank-yooou. Thank-you-very-much." Now it grated on her. She told him that it wasn't so cute anymore, but it was a habit for him and he wouldn't stop. All the things she used to think were so charming about him, were now annoying.

Kristi knows that things about her are grating on his nerves too, like her regular knuckle cracking, which she just can't stop. She's done it since she was eight years old and, like Paul's Elvis impression, it won't stop. Breaking up would be easier if she hated Paul. But she doesn't. She just doesn't love him anymore. Even kissing and making out doesn't have the same excitement.

She saw Paul's car pull into the parking lot and her heart began to beat faster. She really didn't want to hurt him. In some ways, it would be easier to not breakup and just stay together. She actually tried to breakup with Paul last week, but lost her nerve. *Don't be a coward*, she thought to herself, *end it now before it becomes a disaster.*

"Hi, you," Paul smiled as he walked up to her, giving his standard greeting.

"Hey," Kristi said back.

"What are we doing here?" He asked as he draped his arm around her shoulder and planted one of his giant kisses on her cheek.

"*Oh, God!*" Kristi groaned inside. "*Please help me.*"

(Continued)

Kristi blurted it all out as she turned to face him, "Look, Paul, I'm going to get right to the point, 'cause there's no easy way for me to say this."

Paul looked surprised by her sudden announcement and serious voice.

"I like you, but I don't love you anymore. You've never done anything to hurt me and I don't want to hurt you, but I don't want to go out with you anymore." Kristi had practiced this speech like a bazillion times in the past month.

Paul was frozen for a moment. He was in shock and didn't know how to respond. Kristi was dying to say something, but knew she should keep her mouth shut.

"I know things haven't been so hot between us lately," Paul said, "but I don't want to breakup." His eyes were getting teary. "Honey, I love you. We can work this out. Can't we?"

"Oh," Kristi worked to keep her resolve. She hates confrontation. "I don't think there is anything to work out."

"Well, *why* then? I don't understand." Paul's voice was getting louder.

"I just don't feel the same way anymore," said Kristi. "I don't know if I can explain it entirely. All the things I used to love about you seem to get on my nerves. We fight a lot more than we used to. And even when we make out, it's not as exciting. I feel like we're drifting apart." Kristi wasn't sure her explanation made sense to Paul.

"I know. I know," said Paul, "But Kristi, I love you. I'll change. I'll do anything you ask. Tell me what it is that I do that gets on your nerves."

"No, Paul," said Kristi, "I don't want you to change. I just want to be your friend. I mean, I like you, but I don't love you. I don't want to date you anymore."

(*Continued*)

Paul sat down on the grass. Kristi wasn't sure whether she should sit or stand. This was awful. Finally, she sat down beside him.

"God, this is terrible. I feel like I've been knifed," said Paul. A few tears ran down his cheek.

"I'm so sorry," said Kristi. "I've struggled with this decision. I'm just afraid that if we keep going we'll end up hating each other. I'd rather end it now before it's a total mess. I don't want to lose you as a friend." At this point, Kristi had tears running down her face too.

They watched a man throwing a Frisbee to his dog for quite some time.

Paul broke the silence, "Okay. We're not together. I'm really mad. No. No, I'm really hurt. I just can't believe it."

"Can we be friends?" said Kristi. She wanted closure, but mostly to feel good about the whole breakup thing.

"Not now," said Paul, "Maybe later. I'm not ready to be friends yet. I have to get out of here." Paul stood up, didn't look back and walked to his car. Kristi watched as his car pulled out of the parking lot.

Reason, Season or Life

As a teenager deeply in love you don't want to hear what I'm about to tell you, but it's true. I haven't spared you yet and I won't stop now. Ready? The chances that you'll marry your high school sweetheart are highly unlikely. In fact, you'll probably have several significant relationships in your life before you decide to settle down and commit to one person. Okay, I suppose its not earth-shattering information. The reason I tell you this is that teenage love is different from adult love.

The main difference between teenagers and adults in love is hope. It's the hope for love. For many teens, this is their first real love. They have high hopes for this love and see themselves together forever. I don't want to pop your love-bubble, but it's important to know that only a very small percentage of the human population marries their high school sweetheart. As you are suffering the heartache of a breakup, know that while this relationship was important, it isn't your only chance at love. You just had high hopes for it, which makes it extra painful.

It's a fact that not everyone we have a relationship with will remain directly connected to us for our entire life. People come into our lives for various periods of time, and then we lose touch with them. These periods are either for a Reason, a Season or for Life. The person who comes into our life for a *reason* is there long enough to accomplish a purpose, perhaps to teach us something, to help us with a situation or maybe we are to teach them something. The person who is there for a *season* will be there for a period of time—3 months, 1 year, 10 years, etc. The last and most rare one is *Life*. This is where the person is with us for the duration of our lives. These people are usually our family and a small handful of friends. While this offers little comfort when you've just broken up, it can help you to understand that not all relationships are meant to last forever.

Reasons for Breaking Up

There is always a reason for a breakup. Whether it's revealed or not is another thing. The reasons can be completely logical or not make any sense at all. Maybe a relationship has lost its passion or one of the two people has stopped loving the other. Sometimes the relationship has just run its course and both people know it's time to end it. In these cases, no one is at fault; the relationship is just over. Some reasons are shallow and some are profound. The breakup might be because of something big like a Fatal Flaw. Here are a few reasons why couples decide to breakup:

- Lost respect for the other person (You get on each other's nerves a lot).
- Unable to trust the other person (You feel jealous or check up on them).
- Unable to resolve conflict (You fight constantly).
- Someone is cheating or being unfaithful.

- Outgrown each other emotionally (You don't have much to talk about or share).
- Abuse—either physical, verbal or emotional.
- Chemical dependence, such as drugs or alcohol.
- You have different goals for the relationship (One of you wants to date seriously and exclusively, while the other wants to date casually).
- Incompatible values (You try to get each other to change your views or opinions).
- One of you stopped being a 'challenge' or is no longer interesting (One of you gave up your life for the relationship).

Fatal Flaws

So what is a Fatal Flaw? Sounds like a movie, huh? Actually, a *Fatal Flaw* is a character issue. It is a deep-rooted belief or behavior that is, intentionally or unintentionally, destructive or hurtful and affects both parties of the relationship. Some people will try to help their Significant Other overcome their Fatal Flaw. Trying to change someone is usually unproductive. People only make big changes in their characters or lives because they are ready to. Fatal Flaws don't suddenly stop or change just because you told the person about your feelings. Some examples of Fatal Flaws include:

- Uses or abuses alcohol or drugs
- Is verbally, emotionally or physically abusive
- Cheats on you, is unfaithful
- Can't be responsible for themselves; can't hold a job, flunking out of school, always in trouble, etc.
- Drama Queen (change is long and hard, usually takes years)

Quirks

A Fatal Flaw is a profound reason to breakup with someone, and a quirk is kind of a shallow reason. A *Quirk* is something each of us has, although we may not be aware of it. A quirk is a minor habit or behavior that can get on your nerves over time, but isn't destructive. Most people have multiple quirks. You can point out a quirk to someone, but they may not want (or be able) to change that aspect of their behavior. *You* get to decide if you can live with it. What quirks do you have? Because good relationships are hard to find, it might be worth-while to overlook quirks in an otherwise great person, such as:

- Knuckle-cracking
- Nail biting
- Stuttering
- Loud, or other breathing sounds
- Bizarre or ridiculous laugh
- Peculiarities, such as always wanting to sit on the right side (or left side), etc.
- Odd facial expressions or tics*
- Habits, such as leaving doors open or the TV on
- Talking too loud or too quiet, mumbling, etc.
- Overuse of particular word(s) or phrases, such as always saying, "Ya know whadda I mean?"

✦――――――――✦

There is hardly any activity, any enterprise, which is started out with such tremendous hopes and expectations, and yet which fails so regularly, as love.

—Erich Fromm (1900-1980), American psychoanalyst

✦――――――――✦

I've Been Dumped

Being dumped sucks. I've been on both sides of the coin: I've been dumped and I've dumped. You know the old saying that it's just as hard to breakup with someone as it is to be broken up with? It's not entirely true. It's always easier to be on the dishing side of being dumped. You have no sense of control when someone breaks up with you. You feel a terrible sting when you hear the news, especially if you didn't see it coming or didn't want the relationship to end. You're not sure whether to be sad or mad.

It's human nature to take this devastating rejection as a critique of our worthiness. A breakup can deeply affect our self-esteem. We can rehash

---

Any involuntary, regularly repeated spasmodic muscle contraction.

in our minds what went wrong. We wonder if we had just done something else, or didn't do something, maybe we could've avoided the breakup. You may never know or completely understand why your Significant Other broke up with you. Everyone has one relationship memory where they never fully understood why their Significant Other broke up with them. Not knowing *why* the relationship ended can be hard to come to peace with, but it's a reality of relationships. But, if you are mature enough to be in a relationship, then you'll need to be mature enough to risk feeling hurt, disappointment and uncertainty. It's part of the package.

How Did This Happen?

It can be hard to believe it when someone who once said that they would love us forever breaks up with us. Some breakups can seem to come out of nowhere and blindside us. The person who hears that their beloved no longer loves them can be thrown for a loop. Of course, most relationships *don't* end overnight. It's usually a process of 'undoing' where many telltale signs are sent that the relationship is crumbling. However, some people are asleep at the relationship wheel as they drive their love mobile down the road of bliss. They don't see those signs until the breakup hits them like a Mack truck! What are those telltale signs that let you know your Significant Other is unhappy? They include less affection (hugs, kisses, kind words), increased arguments, being distracted or unavailable, spending less time together. If *you* notice these things happening in your relationship, talk to your Significant Other. Ask them what's working and what isn't working in the relationship to see if you can head off potential problems.

If the breakup takes you by surprise, you might want to carefully evaluate whether you ignored some of the telltale signs. If you did, why weren't you more attentive? Maybe your lack of attention is one of the reasons your relationship is over! This information may not help repair this relationship, but it can help you to be more aware in the next relationship.

What Do I Do Now?

When you get the news that your relationship is over, the normal response is to take action! You want to regain some control in the situation. If you do something, you will feel more in control. You want to find out why the breakup happened; you might want to get back together with your Ex* and want to think of a way to make that happen; you might be angry and want your Ex to hurt as much as you do. So, what *can* you do? Nothing. That's right. Nothing.

Resist the urge to contact your Ex. Resist the urge to talk to his/her friends to find out what you did wrong or why the breakup happened. Their friends may inadvertently give you misinformation, which can make you feel worse. Right now, you need to let time go by. Give yourself space to heal your heart before contacting your Ex. A breakup hurts like crazy in the beginning. You can feel like your heart and head will dissolve from the weight of the grief. Read the next chapter on *Grieving* for ways to work through these feelings.

A breakup will not appear on your "permanent record." It's not a statement about your worth as a person. Breakups happen. Love is a risk and you took a risk when you started dating. Breakups are part of relationships. It's a cliché but I swear to you time does heal all wounds. The relationship and the breakup will become like a movie; you will remember scenes. It'll be a story that you can tell in the future without feeling the level of hurt that you do right now. So, let a little time pass to get some emotional distance. There is more in this chapter about being friends and those couples who get back together.

Daniel's Breakup Story

Daniel and Natalie had been dating for 8 months. Daniel was a senior and Natalie was a junior. He had dated other girls, but Natalie was the first one he loved. Their relationship had been great. No fights, no conflicts. He couldn't believe how easy it was.

As a senior, Daniel's school schedule was a little different than Natalie's, especially at the end of the school year, as he was getting ready for graduation while she was focused on finals. In fact, for two weeks Natalie was so busy that they didn't have much time to spend together. Daniel missed Natalie, but they still had phone calls. However, during the last few phone calls Natalie had been talking a lot about a guy named Kenny who

(Continued)

---

*"Ex" is a reference for your former Significant Other, as in ex-boyfriend, or ex-girlfriend.

lived in her neighborhood, but went to a different school. Daniel didn't know Kenny, but he sure heard more about him than he wanted to know from Natalie. It started to grate on Daniel's nerves. He told her that he wasn't jealous, but she had been talking about Kenny so much that it was starting to bother him. He asked if their relationship was okay. Natalie said she didn't realize the conversation involved Kenny so much and apologized.

Just a few days later Natalie and Daniel were sitting with a small group of friends enjoying a post-graduation dinner at Daniel's house. As it cooled off in the evening, Natalie put on an oversized sweater. Someone asked about it and she said it was Kenny's. Daniel couldn't believe it. Why was she wearing this guy's sweater? Why did she *have* his sweater? Daniel said to Natalie, "It's a good thing I'm so confident. Most guys would be going through the roof with this mysterious Kenny." Natalie didn't say a thing. They were both silent as Daniel drove Natalie home later that night. It was a long drive. He kept waiting for Natalie to tell him not to worry and that everything was good between them, but she said nothing. It was a short 'goodnight.'

The next few weeks were as busy as the past few and again Daniel and Natalie didn't see each other. When they finally got together, Daniel knew something was wrong because Natalie was acting strange and distant. He asked her what was up. Natalie said she wasn't sure, that maybe she was outgrowing the relationship and just needed some time. About 6 weeks later, Daniel called Natalie to check in. She said she still needed more time.

Daniel was frustrated that Natalie wouldn't just come right out and tell him that she was breaking up with him. Instead, she kept stalling. Daniel really loved Natalie and felt like he deserved to be told what was happening instead of having to 'get the hint.' If the relationship was over, he wanted her to say so and he wanted to know why she was breaking up with him. So, that's how their relationship ended—without a real close. Six months later, Daniel still misses Natalie. She was his first love.

Breakup 101

You're at the breakup stage. The relationship has serious problems, your attempts to work through them have been unsuccessful and you've decided that now it's time to call it quits. What is the best way to tell someone it's over? Well, as you might have guessed, there is a technique to this. There are a few ways to approach a breakup. You can run in willy-nilly without thinking through the details and just breakup. Like Natalie, you can even take the coward's way out by acting distant and stop calling them in hopes that they get the message. This is a mean way to breakup with someone. Sure, you don't have to feel bad about dropping the ax, but the other person is left hurting for much longer than if you had just been up front about it.

The other breakup option is that you can handle yourself like a class act all the way to the end. Remember, there is always a chance that you will see your Ex around school, town, etc. To make those moments easier, you want to be as gracious as possible under the painful current circumstances. You want your last action to be remembered as classy, not trashy. Let's walk through this process together and I'll point out a few things.

By now you know that a good relationship is hard to find. Because they are rare you want to *be certain* that your motive for ending the relationship is founded in a substantial reason. If you change your mind two weeks after you've broken up, your Significant Other may not be eager to have you back. To threaten a breakup in hopes of shocking your Significant Other into change is manipulative. Testing the water to see how they feel about a breakup can seriously undermine trust if you aren't serious. It can also backfire on you if they tell you that they'd like to breakup. I'll say it again: Breakup only and *after* you are certain this is what you want, and you've really tried to work out the differences.

Exception: This entire section on how to breakup does not apply to people who are leaving an abusive relationship. That needs to be handled with adults who can support you through that process.

Timing

If you are waiting for *the exact right time*, it may never come, but timing does has a place in a breakup. Timing is important because you want to be considerate of the other person's emotions and what's happening for them. You don't want to breakup the day before they have a big event, so they sob their way through it. You aren't heartless, so take a moment to think about big events that are going to happen or have just happened. How will the breakup affect them considering that event? For example, breaking up two days before the Senior Prom is bad timing. Breaking up the day before his brother's wedding is bad timing. Breaking up the day of finals is bad timing. Breaking up the day after his dog died is bad timing. Breaking up the week after her parents have separated is bad timing.

What is the best time to breakup with someone? Sometime when they'll have a day or two to recover. Breaking up in second-period class on a Tuesday is mean and thoughtless. Friday night or Saturday mornings are good because they'll have the entire weekend to compose themselves. Again, you might never have the exact right time, but some times *are better* than others. Use your good judgment as you plan when to tell them that the relationship is over.

Clean Break Check List

Once you have decided to breakup, it's best done clean and quick. This is known as a **clean break**. First, you are clear about why the relationship is over for you. Second, you've thought about your timing and know you have a good window of time where there are no big events happening. Third, you know you are not testing the waters or hoping to get a certain reaction from them: this is the real deal. Once you have these things thought through, then you're ready to start the Clean Break Check List.

Step One

Decide where you'll tell them. Breaking up face-to-face is the most honorable way. It's also really hard. *Don't* have a friend break the news. You need to do this job yourself. *Don't* send a letter or email. It's tempting to take the coward's way out, because breaking up is painful and most people don't enjoy hurting others. However, your soon-to-be-Ex deserves the basic courtesy and respect of hearing it from you face-to-face.

Pick the time and place where you'll make the clean break. How you think they'll take the news will dictate where you should tell them. It might be best to find a neutral and public place, but don't choose a crowded place where people can overhear your conversation. If you think they might react badly (if they have a temper or sometimes behave unpredictably), you should let a friend or your parents know you are planning to breakup and where you'll be just in case the situation gets heavy. However, if you're both emotionally mature and you both have known on some level that this day was coming, you can do it privately. In this situation it's likely that you'll both be sad and the privacy will afford you a chance to cry together.

The only exception to the face-to-face is with long distance relationships where it's difficult to see each other (a 30-minute drive is not difficult). If you're doing a long distance breakup, a phone call is appropriate. The phone call allows you to have a two-way conversation. A "Dear John* Letter" is cowardly.

Step Two

Call your significant other and arrange to meet them. If they are normally with friends, you need to arrange to be alone. It's likely that there will be tears and other emotions when you break the news, so don't make it harder by breaking up in front of their friends or family. When you tell them you want to meet, don't be dramatic or make a big deal. It will make them worry.

Step Three

Say it fast. Once you and your soon-to-be-Ex are together, don't beat around the bush. Just like Kristi did with Paul, get to the point. Be respectful when you break the news. Don't raise your voice. This isn't a fight. You are just delivering bad news. Be clear so they understand that you are breaking up. If you are vague or indirect, they may not understand. You can say, "I've done a lot of thinking, and I don't want to be in this relationship anymore. It's over." It's also a good idea to let them know that you are sorry. You should stay long enough to make sure they understand what's happening and offer a little support**. You

---

*"Dear John Letter": A letter, usually from a woman, ending a romantic relationship. John being a common male name.

**Sometime it's appropriate to give them hugs, reassure them that they'll be all right, or make sure they get home safely.

both might cry. Ending a relationship is very sad, even if you want to end it.

They may ask why you're ending the relationship. This is a fair question. State the facts, but don't point fingers or call names. Be prepared for the possibility that they may become defensive. It's human nature to be defensive when someone points out our faults. Also, remember that you need to be clear in your own mind whether the relationship is really over. What if they're suddenly willing to make changes in order to stay in the relationship? Are you willing to give them another chance? Don't tell them you want to breakup in hopes that they will change. You may not get the reaction you hope for with this deceptive technique.

Step Four

Get support. Once you are alone, call your friends to get support*. Try to meet with a good friend right after you deliver the news. Even if you think you're happy about the relationship ending, you'll have emotions that need to be processed or sorted out. Talking is a good way to work through your feelings and get clear in your own mind.

Backlash

If you've been honestly working on the relationship and have shared your feelings, hurts and frustrations as you've gone along, the breakup probably won't be a total surprise to your Significant Other. If the breakup appears to come out of the blue or if they are a Drama Queen, here are some responses you might hear during a breakup:

- "I don't understand this."
- "I'll change this time, I promise."
- "Why?"
- "But, I love you."
- "You never really loved me."
- "I'm devastated!"
- "You said you'd love me forever."
- "I'll die without you."

Someone to listen to you, offer encouragement and words of solidarity.

- "You bitch/bastard!"
- "You owe me an explanation."
- "I'm going to kill myself!"

Plan ahead for the possible backlash and prepare how you will respond. Again, if you think they might react badly (if they have a temper or sometimes behave unpredictably), you should let a friend or your parents know you are planning to breakup and where you'll be just in case the situation gets heavy. If they get very angry, it is best for you to leave immediately. They are responsible for themselves and will need to go to their friends and family for support after the breakup. You don't have any responsibility to sooth their anger around the breakup. They need to work through this on their own.

The backlash of "I'm going to kill myself" throws most people off balance. Many people feel that they have to stay with the Significant Other who threatens suicide to keep them alive. This is not your responsibility. Feeling that you're going to die is not completely uncommon after a breakup. However, that impending doom feeling usually goes away in about a day. If you think someone is serious about suicide, you have many options: Tell your parents, call their parents, tell a school counselor or call the police. You are not responsible for their happiness.

The Code

The Code is an unspoken code of conduct one follows after a breakup. How you conduct yourself or behave *after* the breakup is just as important as your behavior on the first date. Your friends and potential future Significant Others will see how you act after the breakup. Here is the code: Tell No Secrets and Share No Details.

Tell No Secrets. Be discreet after a breakup. This means don't share your Ex's deepest secrets or fears with other people. When you share your Ex's secrets or faults with others you will look bad, not them. When you tell secrets, it becomes gossip. In a breakup, people will observe you "bad mouthing" your Ex. You will look less attractive, and others will wonder if their secrets would be exposed if they ever dated or confided in you.

Share No Details. You will want to talk about the relationship and your feelings after a breakup. However, you should only talk about the details of your relationship with your absolute closest and most trusted friend. Even then, only share those details that will help you heal. You run the risk of your stories getting around when you talk to someone who has loose lips. If you can, talk with a trusted adult who won't blab to people in school.

What about those people in passing who ask why you and your Ex aren't together? The best response is simple: "We broke up." If they are nosey and push for details say, "Out of respect for the relationship, I don't want to talk about it." If the nosey person is rude and still pushes you for details, then you can be rude back and say, "It's none of your business. Don't ask." They'll get the picture and stop asking.

Cooling Off

Right after a breakup, it's hard to imagine that you'll ever love someone again. However, it's most likely that you **will** love again. Depending on how long your relationship lasted, it may take several weeks or several months to recover from the breakup. You want to cool off before you dive into your next relationship.

Starting another relationship immediately after a breakup is called a "Rebound Romance." While a rebound romance will distract you from your immediate feelings of hurt around the breakup, it will mess you up. Rebounding can mess you up because you haven't dealt with the hurts from the last relationship. Rebound romances tend to be short-lived, as those leftover feelings often get tangled up in the new relationship. Be sure to give yourself enough time to recover from the breakup so you don't rebound. Not just for your sake, but for the new love in your life.

Still Friends

Can you still be friends with your Ex? Yes, it's possible to be friends with an Ex. But it depends on two things: Time and Respect. It usually takes a bit of time to pass before either person has recovered enough to spend time together without a lot of hurt. The other factor depends upon how the relationship ended; was it respectful and agreeable, or dirty and mean? Don't rush a friendship in an effort to smooth things over or avoid hurt feelings. Once you've broken up, don't keep seeing each other to rehash the issues, as it will slow down the healing process for both of you. You might be able to be friends when enough time has passed that the hurts have been healed. Be patient.

Together Again

Some couples have an on-again/off-again relationship. These couples breakup for a period of time and then get back together. Sometimes they just take a break from the relationship; sometimes when they're apart, they realize that they care about each other more than they knew and get back together. Can everyone do this? Just like being friends after a breakup, it depends on how the relationship ended the first time.

The together-again couples present an interesting situation for their friends. If friends trash-talked the Ex after the original breakup, it can be pretty embarrassing a month or two later when they've gotten back together. Since couples don't know ahead of time that they might be on-again/off-again, it's a good idea to be *neutral* when supporting a friend who is recovering from a breakup.

Dating Ex's Friends

There's an old saying that goes, "A bird doesn't poop in his own nest." Applied to humans, you don't want to create a bad situation in your day-to-day life. Dating either your friend's Ex, or your Ex's friend can be an awkward situation. Your friend might get angry when they learn that you're going out with their old boyfriend or girl-friend. You can risk losing that friend. If you are dating a friend of your Ex's, this can be uncomfortable for both you and your Ex. So, don't make a mess in your own nest: Avoid dating friends Ex's if you can. However, in small towns or communities this situation is more common. If you really want to date a friend's Ex, take the high road! Have an open conversation with your friend *before* you pursue their Ex. Make sure they are okay with it. An awkward conversation is better than losing a friend.

Check Point

Let's review where we are. This is a hard topic, but you've hung in there. You're now practically a master at managing a breakup. You understand why couples might breakup. You know the difference between a fatal flaw and a quirk. You know what to do after a breakup: Don't contact your Ex! You know how important timing is when you're going to breakup with someone. I told you about the Clean Break Check List and the four steps to take. You've also thought about the possible backlash at hearing the news. Finally, you understand about the Cooling Off period and why rebound romances can be messy.

I hope that you are among the lucky few who never experience the pain of a breakup. However, if you are among the 99% of the rest of us, you have the basic tools to get you through the process. The very last part of the breakup is grieving. You might be surprised by how sad/hurt you feel about the breakup of your relationship. Grieving is a natural stage. Don't try to avoid it. The next chapter goes into detail about how to recover from a broken heart.

Suppressed grief suffocates, it rages within the breast,
and is forced to multiply its strength.

—Ovid (born in 43 B.C.), Roman poet

Grieving

Grief is typically associated with someone dying, so it's kind of funny to think about it for a breakup. When we grieve for someone who has died, we are grieving for our loss; the loss of our relationship with that person. Well, a breakup is the loss of an important relationship. You are grieving a loss.

The end of a relationship is usually sad and painful. Whether you initiated the breakup or you've been broken up with, you'll have a process of hurting and healing. You may need to lean on your friends and family for the next few weeks. Be sure to tell them what is happening and how they can help you. If you need to be left alone, let them know. If they just see you sulking around or crying or acting angry, they'll be confused. They might take it personally. If they know you're grieving they will understand your behavior and can be patient as you go through your process.

> *Shared joy is double joy. Shared sorrow is half sorrow.*
>
> —Swedish proverb

Beth & Miguel

Beth

Her eyes blinked slowly, not wanting to wake up. Her bedroom was dark, but she wished it could be darker. *What time is it?* she wondered, as she fumbled for the clock radio on her nightstand.

Three o'clock. Beth knew it was 3:00 in the afternoon. She had been sleeping in three-hour increments since 9:00 p.m., the night before. That was when she fell into bed crying. She wished she could sleep for the rest of her life. Except without the exhausting dreams she'd been having. Her eyes felt dry, heavy and swollen so she closed them again. Ugh.

Miguel broke up with her last night. Seven months. Seven months. She couldn't get that out of her head. How do you just break up after seven months? Her thoughts were interrupted by the phone ringing next to her on the nightstand. *I'm never answering the phone again*, she thought. A minute later her younger sister yelled, "Beth, it's for you! It's Aiesha!"

"Hi," Beth croaked into the phone.

"Hey, woman, what's up? I thought you were going to call me this morning," said Beth's best friend on the other end of the phone.

"Oh, God. It was horrible," said Beth, "Miguel broke up with me last night," Beth's voice cracked on the words. She wondered if this was how the rest of her life would be.

"No way!" said Aiesha, "Oh, my God. I can't believe it." Beth and Miguel were like *the perfect* couple. Sure, they had disagreements and stuff, but if *they* broke up then anything is possible.

(Continued)

"I want to die. Or at least just be absorbed by my bed, so my mom can file a missing persons report," Beth's voice was slow and thick. Every word felt like an effort.

Aiesha had broken up with her boyfriend a few months ago, and she knew exactly where Beth's head was. Aiesha knew the best way to support Beth.

"I'm coming over," said Aiesha, "We'll make a plan and you're gonna get through this."

"No plan. I can't plan. I can't think. I'm going to die."

Tears were streaming across Beth's face and onto her pillow as she laid there. She wondered if she could drown in her own tears.

"Don't move. I'll be there in 10 minutes," Aiesha hung up the phone with the last word. Beth laid there in the same position, still holding the phone when Aiesha opened the door to her bedroom.

Beth cried and cried, recounting every horrible, painful detail of the night before. Aiesha stood ready with a box of tissues she had retrieved from the bathroom, and listened quietly as everything poured out of Beth. Aiesha made Beth take a shower while she fixed her a bowl of cereal.

As they ate, Aiesha and Beth made a list of all their friends for Beth to call when she felt like she was going down the slide of despair. They also made plans to get together with another friend for the next day. Tonight they would have a Saturday-night-sleep-over-extravaganza together. They raided Blockbuster for videos and stockpiled all their favorite treats. They also took down all the "Miguel Memorabilia"—the pictures of them together and the cards he had given her—from Beth's room so he wasn't in her face at every turn.

Miguel

Miguel was up at 7:03 a.m. on Saturday. He immediately got into the shower.

(Continued)

It felt strange to know that he wasn't going to see Beth tonight. He felt sad, and even kind of lonely. He loved Beth. They were just always fighting about something and it had started to wear on him. He couldn't live with all the unresolved issues. It was kind of like an ongoing power play between them. Sure they had fun, and everyone thought they were Mr.-and-Mrs.-Perfect. That wasn't enough to keep him in the relationship. It had begun to cost more than he could pay emotionally.

Miguel went for a run—not far, just a little more than a mile. He felt drained, but at the same time he needed to be moving. After the mile, he walked the rest of the way back home. He thought it was strange the way his emotions hit him every few minutes. Like waves on the beach. Once he felt sad, like he could cry right there. Just as suddenly, he'd feel okay. Then the wave would come and he felt glad that he wasn't going to be dealing with all that relationship stuff. He wondered if this was normal. Beth was his first girlfriend, so he'd never had a breakup before. Somehow, he figured the person who did the breaking up wouldn't hurt. But he was hurting. How long was this thing going to last?

As he rounded the corner of his own street, coming towards him on a bike, was one of his best friends, Chuck.

"Amigo! Hola, mi compadre!" shouted Chuck in his worst Spanish effort.

"Hey, Buddy," said Miguel laughing as his friend practically knocked him over, stopping his bike just an inch from Miguel's foot.

"What's new?" Chuck asked.

"Oh, everything and nothing. I broke up with Beth last night."

"No waaay! I don't believe it." Chuck thought Miguel was playing with him.

"No, no, seriously man," Miguel looked him square in the eye, "It's over."

(Continued)

"No way! That's big. What happened?" Chuck wanted to know the details.

"Nah, nothing to share. Time to move on," said Miguel. "Hey, let's go shoot some hoops. I have to be to work at noon today." Miguel changed the subject quickly as they headed towards his house in search of a basketball.

Recovery Time

There is no magic number for the days, weeks or months it takes to recover from a breakup. The first two weeks are typically the worst. After that, the hurt will subside gradually over time. The time needed to recover from the breakup will depend upon how emotionally involved you were. If you dated casually for a month, then a week or so might be fine. If you were sexual, it will take you longer to recover as your emotions were involved at a deeper level.

As a general guideline, it takes about one week for each month you were together to recover from a breakup. For example, if you were together for one year, you might be fully recovered in about 12 weeks. If you were together for a year and a half, it might take about 18 weeks. It may take a little longer, or it may take a little shorter depending upon the relationship. This is just a guideline.

Four Key Things to Do after a Breakup

Right after a breakup, your emotions will be up and down. This is normal so don't worry. You will react to these emotions if you don't anticipate them. Here are four things to do to help you move through the rollercoaster of post-breakup emotions.

1 Don't contact your Ex

The urge to contact your Ex, or hang out at the places you think you'll 'accidentally' run into them can be very strong right after a breakup. This is a mistake. You both need physical and emotional distance from each other. Ongoing contact right after a breakup can be confusing. Seeing each other now will slow down your recovery process. Change your routine if you have to in order to create some distance; at least right after a breakup. You and your Ex might be able to be friends later in time, but until you have healed completely, you are too vulnerable to risk the possible hurt.

What if you need to return things to them? Don't worry about returning gifts. Unless you were given something of personal or emotional value, such as his grandmother's heirloom bracelet, the gifts you received are yours to do with as you please. If there are personal items, such as a jacket, books, photos or music to be returned, wait until enough time has gone by that you have recovered. Better: Arrange for your parents or a friend to return the items for you.

2 Don't be afraid to feel sadness and hurt when it comes up.

Like Miguel, you'll probably experience waves of pain, sadness and even anger. In the beginning, the feelings will be very strong. In fact, you might feel overwhelmed by them. One of the reactions to strong emotions is to ignore them. Don't! These feelings will subside and eventually go away. But while you have them, don't fight it. We can control our action, what we think, our temper, the language we use and the volume of our voices. We can even control the temperature in a room. However, controlling or suppressing hurt and sadness is difficult and usually leads to long-term problems. Stifled grief can show up later in health or emotional problems. Your feelings will eventually get the better of you.

So, let the feelings come up. Let yourself be sad. Cry. Scream into a pillow. Cry some more. The more you allow yourself to feel ALL of your feelings, the quicker the feelings will go away. Writing is a highly effective tool to let your feelings out. The best way to face emotions is the same way to face a fear or an enemy: Head on.

3 Create a To-Do list every morning to give yourself direction.

It's easy to lie in bed all day and be sad or depressed for weeks on end. This is dangerous because it's hard to dig yourself out of that hole. You don't want to get in too deep. You want to get into *action*. If you are struggling to get through the day after a breakup, create a To-Do list every morning. This will keep you moving ahead.

Put everything, including the small things, on your list: Take a shower; take vitamins; meet a friend for coffee; return videos; do science project; mow lawn. Cross them off as you go through the day. Your To-Do list will give you a sense of accomplishment as well as keeping you focused on the next thing you need to tackle. Even if you don't want to do anything, a To-Do list can help to jump-start you out of a depression and get you moving again.

4 *Make plans to meet friends and have fun – in other words: Stay busy.*

I know that I just said to not avoid your feelings. I'm not suggesting that. But you do need to have a balance between processing your emotions and staying in action. You don't want to fall into the depression pit anymore than you want to ignore the reality of your hurt. Total isolation can make you dwell on the negative aspects of the recent breakup. I know you can stay busy *and* deal with your emotions.

The first few weeks after a breakup are the hardest. The weekends and typically Sundays are often the worst days of the week for the newly single because they're slow days without lots of things to do. Make plans with your friends *ahead of time* — don't wait until the last minute when everyone is out of the house or already has plans. Feeling rejected by your friends is not what you want right now.

♦————————♦

Those who weep recover more quickly than those who smile.

—Jean Giraudoux (1882-1944), French playwright, novelist and diplomat

♦————————♦

20 Ways to Heal a Broken Heart

Here are 20 ways to help get over the pain of a breakup. This is the quick list. The how-and-why of each item is explained in detail later. The items with a pointer (↤) next to it are good ways to help you work through your feelings faster.

1) Movie Blast
2.) Sugar Coma
3) Deep Crying ↤
4) Scream into your pillow ↤

5) Journal Writing (pen and paper) ◄
6) Take long walks
7) Exercise ◄
8) Observe how it feels to be alone
9) Create a new routine and schedule, especially for Sundays
10) Self-Help Reading
11) Fiction Reading
12) Talk to friends on your Support System Call List ◄
13) Stay Hydrated: Drink plenty of water and eat good food
14) Group Therapy ◄
15) Clean your room/house/closets
16) Video Games
17) Listen to music or don't listen to music
18) Start a new hobby
19) Treat yourself
20) Be patient with yourself

1 Movie Blast

Set aside an entire day or afternoon/evening to watch several movies back-to-back. Go to your local video store and rent 2 or 3 action films or comedies (preferably not romantic comedies). This is best done with at least one good friend and combined with the Sugar Coma.

2 Sugar Coma

The Sugar Coma is only for non-diabetics. Because of the high-sugar factor, you should only do this once or twice. The Sugar Coma is best done with a Movie Blast! Basically, it's a movie with candy. So, load up on your favorite treats. My personal favorites for a Sugar Coma are Wonka Nerds, Cotton Candy and SnowCaps. Do the Sugar Coma late in the afternoon or evening, so you can go to sleep after the sugar-high wears off☺

Warning: Doing this more than once or twice can make you feel worse than you already do. Be careful to not use food as a way to handle your feelings. If you think you're using food or if someone says that you're eating too much, then talk to a counselor about it.

3 Deep Crying ◄

Lie across your bed, face down on your pillow and cry. Sob as hard as you can. Let your body rack. You know you are having a deep cry when you have snot running down your chin. Not very attractive, but highly therapeutic. Be sure you have lots of tissues on hand. Also, be sure to drink lots of water, as deep crying can be dehydrating (see #13 below). You might need to take some Advil or Tylenol afterwards, as deep crying usually produces a headache.

4 Scream into your pillow ◄◄

This is a great emotional release and no one can hear you. However, if you do it too long, you will get hoarse.

5 Journal Writing (pen and paper) ◄◄

A journal isn't a diary and it isn't just for women. There's an incredible benefit in writing out your feelings. It's best if you write by hand and not use a computer. Writing by hand allows for a connection between the subconscious and the hand to open up as you write about your feelings. Once the flow gets started, the hand kind of writes on its own. It's amazing to learn the surprising things about your feelings when you write by hand. Be sure to write about what worked *and* what didn't work in the relationship. This will help you in your next relationship.

A journal doesn't have to be a special book. Get a soft cover spiral-bound notebook. These are very inexpensive and can be found at any office supply, grocery or drug store. Your journal is where you'll write absolutely anything you want. No one is supposed to read this but you. Keep your journal somewhere private, like in a locked drawer or between your mattress and box springs so it's not accidentally found and read by someone.

Don't worry about it sounding good. Don't worry about how neat your handwriting is or the spelling and grammar. (Remember, no one is going to read this.) Just get it **out**! Be honest. Use swear words if you feel like it. Some days you will write only 2 words and other days you'll write 20 pages. You may find yourself stuck and unable to get started. When I'm staring at the blank page, a good journal ice-breaker is to write: "Life sucks. I hate this." That usually gets my pen in motion, because it's an honest statement at the moment.

6 Take long walks

Walking can be very meditative and reflective. Be careful that you don't obsess over the relationship while reflecting.

7 Exercise ◄◄

Working out is a great way to channel pain, frustration and anger. The endorphins that your body releases during the workout will also help you to feel better long after you stop exercising.

8 Observe how it feels to be alone

This exercise is really effective, because it will put you back in control. First, observe yourself in a detached way, as though you're watching someone else in a movie or reading about a character in a novel. Make internal comments as you observe yourself. "My stomach hurts." "My heart is beating fast." "My hand is shaking." "I feel so embarrassed, like everyone is looking at me and knows I just broke up." "I feel like I might trip over my own feet." The exercise is to be an observer. You don't have to *do anything* about how you feel. Let the observations float away like a helium balloon.

It's common to feel very awkward and even lonely the first time you do routine things after a breakup. Going to school or work can feel surrealistic*. Instead of rushing through the activity or feeling overwhelmed by your feelings, observe what you are thinking and feeling. By acknowledging how you feel, it will diminish the strength and power of the feelings. Next, become aware that no one knows what you are feeling or thinking. Do you see that they are busy with their own internal agenda? They are worried about what other people are thinking about them.

9 Make Plans

The weekends and typically Sundays are often the worst days of the week for the newly single. Sundays can be slow days without a lot of structure. Identify the days that you will be most vulnerable, and make plans to go out with friends from your support call list *ahead of time*. Don't wait until the last minute when everyone is out of the house or already has plans!

10 Self-Help Reading

Read books about self-development, self-improvement or relationships. A few good books are listed in the reference section at the end of this book.

---

*Bizarre or unreal; distorted. Surrealism was an art movement in the early 1900s that tried to represent the unconscious mind with elements that seemed fanciful or contradictory.

11 Fiction Reading

Fiction is a wonderful way to get your mind off yourself and your situation. A good fiction book is like taking a mental vacation.

12 Support System Call List ◄◄

Write out a list of all of your friends who you can call. Call them when you feel overwhelmed or if you get the urge to call your Ex. Start with calling the first name on the list, and go down until someone answers the phone. These are also the people you will make plans to have fun with.

13 Stay hydrated and eat good food

It's easy to lose your appetite when you're grieving. On the other hand, it's also easy to overeat and stuff your feelings with food. Be sure to drink plenty of water and eat healthy food—not just fast food and junk. Food can affect your mood significantly.

14 Counseling or Group Therapy ◄◄

Talking to a counselor doesn't mean you are crazy or "broken." Sometimes it can be helpful to unload your feelings to someone who isn't too close to you. They can be more objective. If you feel that talking to a counselor would help, ask your parents or the counselor at school about getting therapy. They may know of a low-cost/no-cost program just for teens.

If you were in an abusive relationship, or a long-term relationship with a Drama Queen, you may be co-dependent* and would benefit from therapy. You can meet individually with a therapist or in a group. Group Therapy is where you sit in a circle with several people and a therapist. Each person in the circle takes a turn to talk about what is happening for them and how they are feeling. The therapist or other group members might offer you feedback or suggestions. You also get to offer feedback and suggestions to others if you want.

15 Clean your room/house or Organize your closets

Cleaning out your room, organizing your closets, sweeping the garage and cleaning out the bathroom cupboards can be incredibly therapeu-

---

Relationship of mutual need: a situation in which one person feels a need to be needed by another person.

tic when grieving. It's also productive. It can help you to feel more in-control because your personal environment now has a sense of order.

16 Play Video Games

Like movies and reading, this creates a temporary escape. Be careful that you don't spend 24/7 in front of video games. A temporary escape is fine, but avoiding your feelings can backfire.

17 Listen to music/don't listen to music

You may find that you are hypersensitive to music right after a break-up. Sounds and smells can trigger memories. You may feel like crying if you're walking in a store and hear a song playing that reminds you of your Ex. This is normal. You can adjust your listening habits as you need to. My all-time favorite grieving songs are REM's "Everybody Hurts" and "It's the End of the World as We Know It."

18 Start a new hobby

Get involved in a new activity or hobby. It's a great way to give you a new focus in your life. It can turn out to be fun in ways you didn't realize.

19 Treat yourself well

When you're grieving, you need to take extra care of yourself. Be sure you get lots of sleep. Good ways to pamper or treat yourself with extra care are taking vitamins, getting a haircut, working out, or doing whatever you consider special.

20 Be patient with yourself

Don't get discouraged. Everyone grieves differently and at different rates. It's easy to get mad at yourself if you think you aren't recovering fast enough. Be patient. Getting over a breakup takes time. The more you try to rush yourself, the longer it will take.

Check Point

The end of a relationship needs to be grieved. You now have some good tools for working through that grief. You know the four main things to do after a breakup: Don't contact the ex; make a list to stay focused; make plans with friends; and most important—feel your feelings. You also have a list of 20 possible ways to deal with grief. We know that working through feelings is better than stuffing them and ultimately faster. Time is your best friend. The suggestions outlined in this chapter will help to make the time move faster.

The next chapter is the last one! We're on the last leg of our relationship trip.

The Last Mile

The last four chapters were pretty heavy. We dealt with abuse, drama, breaking up and grieving. Those first 14 chapters that dealt with the positive aspects of relationships seem so far away. Before you decide to never have a relationship, I want to be clear: Not every relationship is doomed to fail. Not every relationship is abusive or destructive or negative. Being realistic, we know that there's no guarantee that a relationship will be successful over the long term. We know that relationships are a gamble—it's a risk you take when you get involved. But the benefits of relationships far outweigh the risks, or people would never get involved. Plus, you've been smart! You've stacked the odds of having a successful relationship in your favor by reading this book.

You now have valuable tools that will serve you well in your relationships. Think about it: You know how to fight fair, communicate, know what trust and respect are, and have realistic expectations for what a relationship can and cannot do for you. You are *miles* ahead of the average person. But don't rest on your laurels*. Just because you read this book, it's not a magic pill. It will be up to you to use the relationship tools that were laid out for you. You might refer back to this book to refresh your memory from time to time. My hope is that you will read other books (some of which I've listed in the *Reference Section*) about relationships. This book isn't the last word on relationships. There is a lot more to learn. Knowledge will not hurt you.

When you finish this book, I want you to know that relationships are good and can be very successful. They can be positive, nurturing and supportive. It's wonderful to be in a healthy relationship where you have a partner, someone to face both the good and bad times with together. It feels good to be hugged and held, and to know that someone loves you. Being in a relationship isn't a requirement for your happiness, but a good relationship can enhance your happiness.

Snapshots

Well, it's been one heck of a road trip! We've gone through every possible state of relationships. Kind of like looking at pictures from our trip, let's take a quick peek back at all the places we've been.

Chapter 2—Learning Curve

We saw that love is one of the strongest desires we'll feel in our lives. We also saw that we have to manage our expectations about the relationship and remember that it won't automatically fix every problem in our lives. We saw that relationships teach us a lot about ourselves. We learned that not everyone is ready to date. Hopefully you took the test to see how ready you are. We also talked about making decisions and the steps to take when faced with a big decision.

Chapter 3—Attraction

In this chapter we learned all about the chemistry of attraction and about the imago. We saw the differences between type and beauty and that true

---

Success, glory, fame.

beauty is intangible because it's what people have on the inside. We know that we want to be authentic and let someone be attracted to us based on who we *really* are. We know that all people are concerned about being accepted. We saw the difference between interests and values, and that common *values* are more important than common *interests*.

Chapter 4—Flirting

Here we learned all the basics of flirting and have a good idea of what works and what doesn't work. We saw how confidence plays a big role in attraction. We also learned how to spot the signals when someone is flirting with us!

Chapter 5—Action Plan

In this chapter, we saw how planning is important to a successful first date. You picked up some ideas to get started planning your date. You know that the best first dates are low-key and it's best to save elaborate plans for date #2.

Chapter 6—Asking Someone Out

We saw how to ask someone out on a date. We also learned not to get freaked out if they don't say yes right away. We know to ask if a change of activity or date would make a difference in their answer. We saw that it's best to not beat around the bush, but to just come out and ask. You also know it's better to ask in person and have a plan in mind before you ask.

Chapter 7—The Big Chill

In this chapter we saw that the best way to deal with rejection is to develop coping strategies before it happens. We also learned not to take "no" personally. We saw that it's okay to ask for more information when you're rejected. We even saw that how you reject someone is important. We learned that rejection needs to be accepted graciously and that to threaten, beg or harass someone in hopes that they will go out with you never works and will only cause big problems. Finally, we saw that our last rejection has nothing to do with the next person you ask out.

Chapter 8—Meet the Parents

Here we saw that honoring parents' curfews and rules will most likely get you a longer leash. Also, the simple things that show respect towards adults, such as calling them *Mr. and Mrs.,* and shaking their hands when meeting them goes a long way in making a good impression. We also saw that it's best to keep physical contact and touching to an absolute minimum when you are with parents. Another important thing we saw was that parents of your Significant Other may not like you for one of two reasons: controllable or uncontrollable.

Chapter 9—Smooth Moves

This chapter showed us the manners that gain points. We saw that good manners are on the *Top 10 Turn-ons List* so we paid attention to the details, including how to make introductions, opening doors, eating out and the smooth move of helping a woman with her coat. This chapter also walked us through how to handle a restaurant setting, from getting good service to leaving a tip.

Chapter 10—Showtime

Here we saw each step of going through a date. We covered everything from the pick up to the good-bye kiss, and the important day-after call. We also saw how to end a date that was a disaster. The theme of 'Light and Easy, Fun and Breezy' was suggested for keeping dates from becoming a drag.

Chapter 11—Relationships

This chapter was really important because it showed us that successful relationships take time and work. We looked at the difference between casual dating and exclusive dating. We saw the two ingredients to a strong foundation: Trust and Respect. We also learned about emotional intimacy. We looked at the Ambiguous Relationship and talked about how to get out of the Friend Zone.

Chapter 12—Making a Relationship Work

Here we covered a lot of the things that make a relationship work. We looked at the three pillars of relationship doom: Balance, Neediness and Mind Reading. We learned how to communicate clearly. You also saw how important it is to not take each other for granted. We looked at long distance relationships, jealousy, being a doormat and the finer points of gift-giving.

Chapter 13—Fight Club

Here we looked at conflict as a natural event in relationships. We also saw that how the conflict is handled determines whether the result is constructive or destructive. We learned about the main types of fights and the solutions, as well as active listening and 'I' statements. Most important is that we looked at the 10 Rules to Fair Fighting. Finally, we saw the right way to apologize and why forgiveness is important.

Chapter 14—Sex in the Big City

This was the biggest chapter of all. Here we saw quite a bit about sex; the emotional, physiological and psychological aspects of it. We learned about the 3 Big Realities/Responsibilities of sex and covered the basics on STD's, pregnancy and protection. We looked at how sex can have a different meaning for people and the importance of being clear about where you and your partner stand. We also looked at the Killer Kiss, orgasms, masturbation, oral and anal sex, and date rape.

Chapter 15—Trouble in Paradise

This chapter was all about bad relationships and abuse. It was interesting to see how many teens deal with abuse in their relationships. We saw the value of listening to family and friends, and not being blinded by love. We looked at why we shouldn't rationalize bad behavior and how to recognize the signs of various types of abuse (verbal, psychological, etc). We saw that abuse has **no** place in a love relationship and that it's not smart to give up our personal power to anyone else. Most important, we saw that it's critical to get others involved to help us when we're in an abusive relationship.

Chapter 16—The Drama Syndrome

Here we saw how a high-drama relationship is different from an abusive relationship. We looked at the Anatomy of a Drama Syndrome and how it creates a cycle. We also learned about the physiology of an Episode and how some people can get hooked on the feelings it produces. Most important, we saw that the Drama Queen is emotionally *immature*. We looked at what causes the Queens to be dramatic. We also looked at why someone would stay in this kind of a relationship. We talked about breaking the Syndrome and the Three-Step Solution. Finally, we briefly looked at the important role of setting emotional boundaries.

Chapter 17—Breaking up

In this chapter we saw the different reasons why couples break up. You learned about fatal flaws and quirks. You know how important timing is when you're going to break up with someone. I told you about the Clean Break Check List and the four steps to take. You've also thought about the possible backlash at hearing the news. You saw what to do after a breakup. Finally, you understand about the Cooling Off period and why rebound romances can be messy.

Chapter 18—Grieving

Here we looked at the fact that the end of a relationship needs to be grieved. You picked up some good tools for working through that grief. You know the four main things to do after a breakup: Don't contact the Ex; make a list to stay focused; make plans with friends; and, most important, feel your feelings. You have a list of 20 possible ways to deal with grief. We also saw that working through our emotions and feelings is better than stuffing them and ultimately helps us heal faster.

Chapter 19—Final Check Point

This is where we are now. This is my stop. I get out here. It was a great ride. Thanks for taking me along. I hope you learned one or two things that will help you on your next road trip. The last thing I want you to know is that love and relationships don't always follow a straight line. It usually takes lots of turns and curves along the way. Love is not a destination. It's a series of days strung together, which becomes a journey. As the driver of your life, you will learn when to hang on tight, when to speed up, when to take in the scenery, when to slow down and when to pull over.

Remember to enjoy the journey!

More Smart Teenagers

If you enjoyed this book and want to read more Real Life stories, or share your own, visit the Smart Teens website. You can also look for other upcoming titles in the "Smart Teenagers" series. Check it out at *www.4smarteenagers.com!*

A Note to Parents

It was hard to see my son with a girl for the first time. I stopped seeing him as a little boy at that point, and I felt a significant loss. Jason is my only child, my 'baby,' and I wasn't entirely prepared for my feelings. I wondered how much influence I would have with him in this new phase of his life. We'd always been close, but suddenly I didn't know if he'd listen to me anymore. He seemed more independent now.

After three or four months of dating, I became concerned that he was taking on more than he needed to be dealing with at age 16. Thankfully, I didn't let my fears get the better of me, which allowed me to stay level-headed and connected to him as the relationship progressed. For all of his newfound independence, he needed direction.

I've always been up front with Jason about sex. We've never had one big, single, definitive 'Sex Talk' because it's been an ongoing conversation since he was very young. Jason was quite knowledgeable about the birds-and-the-bees, anatomy, reproduction, sexually transmitted diseases and how to protect against infections and pregnancy. I also told him that I hoped he would wait for sex. I explained all of the emotional aspects of sex, and told him that he had a responsibility to protect both his own and his girlfriend's heart. Having had sex at a very young age myself, I could testify that it was not worth rushing into. I wish I had waited, but you can never take that back.

So I gave him the facts and shared my hopes for him. However, I'm not naive. I know the statistics about teens and sexual behavior. I know that more than 60% of all high school students will become sexually active before graduation.[47] I know that 3 million teenagers will contract sexually transmitted diseases (STD) this year.[48] While I'm glad that teen pregnancy rates are down, I'm still unsettled by the fact that 800,000 teenage girls will become pregnant this year.[49] I'm also aware that in spite of the decrease in teen pregnancy, the numbers for teens infected with STD's have increased every year since the Center for Disease Control (CDC) began tracking it in 1997.[50]

For many teens, there seems to be a fuzzy line between virginity and sexual behavior. I was surprised when several sources cited the trend of teens engaging in oral and anal sex because they don't consider it 'sex,' which they believe lets them remain virgins[51] because it isn't intercourse. Okay, I was shocked. The CDC has said that, "the data clearly show that young people are sexually active ... and they must be provided the skills and support to protect themselves."[52]

I'm a realist and I know it's impossible for me to be with Jason every minute of every day. At some point, our teenagers make decisions for themselves without us there to monitor their every move. So, I had to rest on all the years of training and rearing I had put into my son. And I had to stay available, just in case he needed me.

Because I treated my son with respect, we were able to keep the lines of communication open between us and I was able to influence him without 'dictating' to him. His relationship became more complicated as it developed. He and his girlfriend were having problems and I could see the pressure weighing on him (you can read Jason's story in Chapter 16, *The Drama Syndrome).* He would talk to me about his situation, and I'd casually make suggestions that might help.

Of course I *wanted* to tell him to break up with the girl, but I remembered from my own days as a teenager that I tended to do the opposite of what my parents wanted, or I resented them for making proclamations about how I 'should' live my life. So, I refrained. Instead, I engaged him in a dialogue where I'd ask questions and get him talking about what was going on. We'd brainstorm ideas. I shared my own teen dating war stories. We bonded over the very issue I was afraid would divide us.

During our talks, Jason asked me to write some of my suggestions down on Post-it® notes for him, and soon his computer was covered with those yellow notes. One day, he brought all the notes to me and asked if I would type and organize them onto a single page so he could simply refer a 'crib sheet.' It ended up being about five pages long. He read them and said, "This is great! You should write a book … and put the stuff you told me about taking her out on our first dates in there too – that was good information." So, I started writing a 'love letter' to my son about how to navigate the finer points of dating, relationships and sex.

I didn't intend to write a book for teens about dating, but word got out to his friends that I was writing a book for teenagers. I suddenly had teenagers from all over talking to me, asking me questions, telling me things and sharing their stories. Sure enough, they confirmed the statistics, including the one about the oral and anal sex trend. Well, two years later, after endless hours of research, many interviews with teenagers, and multiple focus group meetings with parents, the book was done.

Now, what surprised me the most is this: Most parents don't talk to their kids about sex … or dating, or relationships or love. 90% of all the parents I interviewed said they had never talked to their teens about sex. 100% of the teens I interviewed said their parents had never mentioned sex beyond short one-liners such as, "Don't be stupid," or "Be safe," or "You're waiting until marriage." In my research, I even found sociologists who had studied this "reluctance" phenomenon. Their findings matched my own, in that this parental reluctance to discuss sex is caused by either generational attitudes about sex (it's dirty, shameful, nice girls don't *do* that, etc.), embarrassment due to their own lack of knowledge about the topic, or the fact that they waited so long to have 'the talk' that their teenagers were already street-educated and wouldn't listen to their parents.[53]

The reality is, while parents don't *want* to talk to their teen about dating and sex, the teens *are* talking to each other about it. By parents withholding information, their teenagers are actually more vulnerable. Many parents think if they talk about sex, their teens will be more likely to have sex. The opposite is true: Knowledge is power. Without information teens are at significant risk for pregnancy and infection. Misinformation creates confusion, and ultimately leads teens to disrespect their parents.

One teenager told me of a girl from his sixth grade class whose parents wouldn't let her participate in the 'sex education' class. The next year, she was pregnant at age 13 in the seventh grade. No, this didn't happen in a big crime-infested city; it was a regular town, in a nice neighborhood. It was a girl without the information she needed. One 20 year old girl I interviewed came from a family who told her she was to remain a virgin until marriage. At age 20, she is very angry with her parents for not giving her any information other than "Don't do it." She's away at college now and feels overwhelmed by her lack of knowledge of dating relationships in general, as well as her lack of sexual knowledge. Even within strong church families, there are incidents of pregnancies and STD transmissions outside of marriage. People are human, including teenagers.

Now my book had a purpose beyond giving teenagers the inside scoop about dating, relationships and sex; it became a valuable tool for parents to start that difficult conversation about sex. There's only one chapter in the book devoted to sex, but it's a big chapter. I let the teens know that while sex is important, it's a relatively small portion of a relationship. The book starts with flirting and asking someone out, and goes through the various stages of relationships. As we know, people mature at different rates, and not everyone who dates will have sex. However, the book covers all of the relationship stages, so as your teenager matures, they have all the information they need.

In Chapter 14, *Sex in the Big City*, there's a small section about the dangers of anal sex. This section has upset about 10% of the parents, who've told me that I'm irresponsible to include it, because it will "put ideas in the teen's minds." The World Health Organization found there is no evidence that comprehensive sex education programs (where condoms, facts and details are discussed) encourage sexual activity.[54] Also, 37 percent of teens described oral sex and 24 percent described anal sex as **abstinent** behaviors.[55] They don't consider these behaviors 'risky' and are more likely to engage in them while not using condoms. Sure, condoms are only 95% effective, but when used properly, they're the best protection available. Not all teens will remain abstinent, and they deserve to know how to protect their health.

While parents are upset that there is "too much information," people who work with teens and in public health (such as physicians, nurses, social workers, health researchers, and even high school guidance counselors) have asked me to include even *more* information. The people who are in the trenches, dealing with the realities of teen behaviors wanted *more*, not *less* information. Many parents don't understand the serious health risks teen face because of the lack of information. I'd experience less conflict if I omitted the section on anal sex, but I realize I would be irresponsible if I *didn't* include it. I'm **not** promoting the idea of anal sex to teens: In fact, I point out the pitfalls and dangers so teens will recognize it as a high-risk behavior.

You'll notice that I don't deliver a heavy, 'Abstinence Only' message in this book. I point out that sex is a big deal, that it comes with lots of responsibilities, and that the only way to 100% avoid pregnancy and infection from an STD is through abstinence. Parents can then share their personal views, values and beliefs with their own teenager.

Why didn't I make this book a crusade for the 'Just Say No' campaign? Well, first and foremost at this point, I know teenagers; they'll tell you what you want to hear, with a smile, just to get you off their backs. Then, they'll do whatever they want. A report released in 2003 showed that three out of five teens think that remaining abstinent until marriage is "a nice idea, but nobody really does."[56] The World Health Organization has concluded that abstinence-only programs are actually less effective than comprehensive classes that include safe-sex practices such as contraception and condom use.[57] The problem with the abstinence-only approach is that it doesn't provide a back-up plan in the event the teen does become sexually active. If teens don't know how to use a condom, and their abstinence plan fails, they are at tremendous risk.[58]

Teenagers don't respond well to manipulation, threats or scare tactics ("I'll kill you if you get pregnant," "You'll go to hell if you have sex," "No man will want you,"). Teenagers today are surprisingly sophisticated. Don't let the 4% of the teen idiots bias your opinion of all teenagers. Teens are, by and large, pretty smart. They respond very well to facts and information. They appreciate being treated with respect. So, that's just what I did with this book. I laid out the facts, all very carefully researched, and I gave them information they can use in a manner that doesn't talk down to them. The facts and information can stand alone, or be enhanced with guidance from their parents.

Parents best influence their teens through casual conversations, not big lectures. This book is a great tool to facilitate those conversations about relationships and sex! If both the parent and teen read this book, they have a common language. The parents can simply say,

"Hey, I didn't realize ..." and begin a conversation with their teenager! The parents who've used this book that way reported that they were able to offer their own opinions or values on the subjects without the conversation becoming a one-sided authoritarian lecture. And, they told their teen if they disagreed with the book, and why.

Parents have said that using the book changed the dynamic of the discussion because the book was a neutral third-party that they referenced to bring up a particular subject. It wasn't an *emotional* conversation about the teen; it was an *intellectual* conversation about a book! Even better, sex is only *one* of many issues included that teens deal with commonly. Of the many topics that affect teens in this book, one in particular is the growing problem of abuse among teenage couples (see Chapter 15, *Trouble in Paradise)*. Sadly, Dating Domestic Abuse has become as common as traditional spousal Domestic Abuse.[59] Also covered is grieving after a breakup. Many teens experience depression after a breakup which can affect their school performance, as well as the family (see Chapter 18, *Grieving)*.

So, the parents were relieved to have a tool that prompted these important conversations; the teens were happy that the book is focused heavily on the *relationship aspect*, which is the most important facet to them in their dating experiences. Even if you aren't ready to begin talking to your teen about relationships and sex, you can give them this book so they have the facts and information they need to stay safe.

To respond to the overwhelming need to support parents as they talk to their teens, I founded The Teen Dating Project, a nonprofit organization committed to supporting parents as they discuss the many aspects of dating, relationships and sex with their teenager. On our website, you'll find resources, get tips for talking to your teenager, and a list of Do's and Don'ts just for parents! Please visit our website for more information on how you can begin talking with your teenager. My hope is that you can share with your teenager on a deeper level and hopefully, become closer in the process.

www.theteendatingproject.com.

About Deborah Hatchell

Deborah Hatchell wrote What Smart Teenagers Know … About Dating, Relationships and Sex® while attending college as a full-time re-entry student. She's also the single mother of a teenager.

What Smart Teenagers Know … About Dating, Relationships and Sex® is the result of her 16 year old son asking for advice about dating and his relationship with his girlfriend.

She is the founder and director of The Teen Dating Project, a nonprofit organization dedicated to helping parents talk to their teenagers about relationships and sex.

Deborah worked for several years as Executive Assistant to Jack Canfield, the nation's leading self-esteem expert. She was also the Vice President of Operations for Chicken Soup for the Soul® Enterprises, Inc.

Deborah lives with her teenage son, Jason, in Santa Barbara, California.

You can contact Deborah at *deb@4smarteenagers.com*.

For more information about Smart Teenagers, go to *www.4smarteenagers.com*

273

Resources

The items listed in this section will show you just a tiny bit of the information available on dating, relationships and sex. I don't agree with all of the things that are in all of these books, but they are listed because there was some value to their content. Remember, not everyone offers great information/advice 100% of the time. Just because it's in print, doesn't mean it's true! Be sure to use judgment and decision-making skills when reading materials. Also, be sure to talk to your parents or other adults you trust for direction and guidance.

BOOKS

Flirting and Dating

1. *How to Make Anyone Fall In Love With You* and *How To Talk To Anybody About Anything* by Leil Lowndes *(www.lowndes.com)*
2. *The Fine Art Of Flirting* by Joyce Jillson
3. *Dating for Dummies* by Dr. Joy Browne
4. *The Shy Man's Guide to Success With Women* by Terry A. Heggy
5. *The Shy Man's Guide to Dating* by Barry Dutter
6. *Flirt Coach* by Peta Heskell
7. *Dating: A Singles Guide to a Fun, Flirtatious and Possibly Meaningful Social Life* by Amy Cohen and Hedda Muskat
8. *Emily Post's Teen Etiquette* by Elizabeth L. Post
9. *The Sound of Your Voice: The Essential Program for Communicating Confidently and Clearly* by Carol Fleming (To help you with changing your voice)
10. *Change Your Voice: Change Your Life: A Quick, Simple Plan for Finding & Using Your Natural Dynamic Voice* by Morton Cooper (To help you improve your voice)

Love and Relationships

11. *Getting Dumped & Getting Over It* by Cylin Busby (A great book on recovering from a broken heart)
12. *Red Flags!: How to Know When You're Dating a Loser* by Gary S. Aumiller & Daniel A. Goldfarb (I loved this book—great advice on how to end bad relationships)

13. *The Gift of Fear: Survival Signals That Protect Us from Violence* by Gavin De Becker (Hollywood's A-List security expert gives good insight)
14. *Who Moved My Cheese* by Spencer Johnson (About managing change)
15. *Co-dependent No More* by Melody Beattie (An early classic on breaking your own co-dependent behavior)
16. *Women Who Love Too Much* by Robin Norwood
17. *If Love is a Game, These are the Rules* by Cherie Carter-Scott
18. *Love is Letting Go of Fear* by Gerald Jampolsky

Sex

19. *Changing Bodies, Changing Lives: A Book for Teens on Sex and Relationships* by Ruth Bell Alexander, Ruth Bell (excellent and extensive information about puberty, reproduction, anatomy and health; an excellent reference for anyone.)
20. *The Underground Guide to Teenage Sexuality* by Michael J. Basso (Another comprehensive book on puberty, reproduction and anatomy, written by a high school sex-ed/health teacher)
21. *The G Spot and Other Discoveries about Human Sexuality* by Alice Kahn Ladas, Beverly Whipple and John D. Perry (This is the best book I've read on the subject of G Spot orgasms and orgasms, in general. Written by the researchers who named the G Spot and presented their findings about the G Spot to a medical conference. It is very medically oriented and has lots of scientific background to get through, but well worth the time! Has lots of stories from couples about their experience with G Spot orgasms).
22. *Everything You Always Wanted To Know About SEX, but were afraid to ask* by David Reuben, M.D. (The original classic 'sex book'. This is an older book and contains some outdated information, but still a good read)
23. *Sex Smart: 501 Reasons to Hold off on Sex* by Susan Browning Pogany. (Offers common sense and non-religious support for those who want to be celibate until adulthood or marriage.)
24. *The Guide to Getting It On!—The Universe's Coolest and Most Informative Book About Sex* by Paul Joannides (I didn't read all of this 700-page book, but it offers some good information. This book is pretty explicit in details and drawings.)

25. *Tao of Love and Sex* by Jolan Chang (This is a beginner's book on the 2,000 year old Chinese practice of ejaculation control. Not an easy read, as it deals with history, medicine and psychology, but informative.)

General Self-Development

1. *Teens Can Make It Happen: Nine Steps for Success* by Stedman Graham
2. *Life Strategies for Teens* by Jay McGraw (I really liked this one)
3. *The Seven Habits of Highly Effective Teenagers* by Sean Covey (This is the teen version of his father, Stephen Covey's classic *7 Habits of Highly Effective People,* which offers good self-management skills)
4. *Dr. Drew & Adam Book: A Survival Guide to Life & Love* by Dr. Drew Pinsky and Adam Corolla (For both teens and adults. The Q&A format covers a wide variety of topics from sex to substance abuse and general health, etc.)
5. *How Rude!: The Teenagers' Guide to Good Manners, Proper Behavior, and Not Grossing People Out* by Alex J. Packer, PhD. (a great 'smooth moves', book that you can really use.)
6. *Tiffany's Table Manners for Teenagers* by Walter Hoving (Written by the CEO of the famed Tiffany & Co. jewelry store, lots of people like this book.)

VIDEOS

1. **Movie:** *When Harry Met Sally* (Has the classic scene about faking an orgasm)
2. **Movie:** *The Tao of Steve* (Shares a fictional dating philosophy to attract women using the principle of "We pursue that which retreats from us.")
3. **Movie:** *Shallow Hal* (A great movie to see how we let people's physical appearances keep us from seeing the 'real' person.)
4. **Movie:** *Annie Hall* (A classic relationship movie. Shows people's insecurities—very funny)
5. **Movie:** *Kate & Leopold* (Shows how women really appreciate good manners)

TELEVISION SHOW

"Blind Date" is a syndicated television show, which is a great socio-logical study of how *not* to behave on a date. The episodes are gener-ally funny, although some of the dates are a little contrived. Roger Lodge is the show's host who provides some biting and obvious com-mentary on the date's events.

WEBSITES AND OTHER RESOURCES

1. **American Social Health Association: http://www.ashastd.org/** (Good information about sex, STD's, condom use, etc.)
2. **Teen site by ASHA http://www.iwannaknow.org/** (Good informa-tion about sex)
3. **CDC—Center for Disease Control** Website on Sexually Transmitted Diseases. **http://www.cdc.gov/nchstp/dstd/dstdp.html** (Government site that has interesting statistics on STD's.)
4. **Sex, Etc.** (The Network for Family Life Education) **http://www.sxetc. com.** A cool site with lots of good information for teens (okay, and adults too) by Rutgers University.
5. **HPV and cervical cancer hotline;** The American Social Health Foundation; call **(919) 361-4848** from 2-7 p.m. EST, Monday to Friday. They'll give you information about the virus and about diagnosis and treatment, but the call is NOT toll-free (ASHF is in North Carolina).
6. **HIV/AIDS Hotline 1-800-367-AIDS (2437)** Get information about how to protect yourself from HIV infection.
7. **Teen Wire www.teenwire.com** (Great website from Planned Parenthood. Has advice on dating, relationships, health, sex and more!)
8. **The Center for Domestic Violence Prevention: Teen Site! http://www.cdvp.org/teens/.** Good information and resources about dating/domestic violence. Hotline numbers are listed for help.
9. **The National Sexual Assault Hotline** Free, confidential, 24/7. **1-800-656-HOPE**

10. **Befrienders International** (Worldwide organization headquartered in London. Provides information and hotline for suicide prevention) **http://www.befrienders.org/suicide/warning.htm**
11. **Suicide Letter** (Great one-page site for anyone contemplating suicide) **http://www.metanoia.org/suicide/**
12. **Table Manners: http://www.westernsilver.com/etiquette.html**
13. **Tipping information: www.tipping.org** (Guidelines on appropriate gratuities)
14. **Radio Show: Love Line** with Dr. Drew Pinsky and Adam Corolla (To find what station they are on go to: **http://www.adamanddrew.com/stat.htm**)
15. **Manners by Michele http://www.mannersbymichele.com/Tips.html.** (Michele is an 'etiquette trainer', and offers books and videos, and holds workshops. She posts a free tip on her website every now and then.)

Glossary of Terms

Anal Intercourse—The penetration of the penis into the rectum (anus).

Chivalry—Medieval knighthood. The qualities of an ideal knight; courteous, gallant, courageous. It is considered Chivalrous for a man to open the door for a woman.

Date Rape—A rape that occurs during a date or with an intimate partner.

Digital Stimulation—Using hands or fingers (i.e. digits) to provide sexual stimulation.

Drama Queen—Someone who is in constant crisis and acts overly dramatic to get attention.

Dutch Treat—Everyone pays for him or herself. Sometime separate checks at restaurants are requested to make this easier. Sometimes the bill is split 50/50.

Ejaculate—Male release of sperm, during an orgasm.

Feeling Up—Another term for petting. Usually refers to feeling of breasts.

French Kiss—Kissing with open mouths and tongues. Also called Soul Kiss.

Heavy Petting—This is petting that borders on intercourse, includes oral sex, digital stimulation.

Intercourse—An act carried out for reproduction or pleasure involving penetration, in which a man inserts his erect penis into a woman's vagina.

Infantile Love—The love we perceive as infants, that the entire world revolves around us and that we are one with our parents/caretakers.

Imago—Term coined by Psychologist Carl Jung (Pronounced "A-Ma-Go") to mean the "inner representation of the opposite sex". Imago is also the Latin word for "image".

Make out—Kissing on the lips for more than a few seconds. Often includes French Kissing and touching/caressing the hair, face, shoulders, arms.

Make-out point—This is a local park or remote, unpopulated area that young couples drive to and park their car so that they can make out without interruption. Make Out Point is often a location that has a view of the city.

Oral Sex—Sexual activity that uses the mouth or tongue to stimulate a partner's genitals.

Orgasm—The climax of stimulation to the genitals, which is experienced as a release of muscle tension and fluids.

Petting—Touching that causes sexual pleasure, but does not include intercourse.

Peck—Quick kiss, with mouth closed.

Pine away—To yearn for someone that you can't see or have; unrequited love.

Psychological Abuse—Words or actions that cause confusion, emotional pain or mental anguish to a person.

Provocative—To stir up or excite to some action or feeling.

Rape—The crime of forcing someone to have sex.

Soul Kiss—See French Kiss

Quickie—Term to describe sex without foreplay or after-play. The sex is done quickly for the sole purpose of an orgasm, because there isn't time for tenderness that usually goes with lovemaking.

End Notes/References

[1]Hendricks, Harville, *Getting the Love You Want*© 1988 Harper & Row, p.284/Jung, C.G. *Collected Works,* vol. 9, pp. 60ff.

[2]Professor Helen Fisher, Department of Anthropology Rutgers University *Discovery Health Channel—The Science of Love: Falling in Love, 2002*

[3]Professor Helen Fisher, Department of Anthropology Rutgers University *Discovery Health Channel—The Science of Love: Falling in Love, 2002*

[4]Professor Arthur Aron State University of New York at Stony Brook *Discover Health Channel—The Science of Love: Falling in Love, 2002*

[5]Professor Helen Fisher, Department of Anthropology Rutgers University *Discovery Health Channel—The Science of Love: Falling in Love, 2002*

[6]Microsoft Network MSN, Personals—Match.com article, 2002

[7]Peta Haskell, *The Flirt Coach http://www.flirtcoach.com/*

[8]Research summarized by J.K. Burgoon, "Nonverbal Signals" in M.L. Knapp and G.R. Miller, eds., *Handbook of Interpersonal Communication* (Newbury Park, Calif.: Sage, 1994), p.235

[9]Hocker and Wilmon, *Interpersonal Conflict, pp.20-28.*

[10]Dr. John Gottman, The Gottman Institute *John Gottman's Marriage Tips 101* , (2002) http://www.gottman.com/marriage/self_help/

[11]Solin Wells, Sabrina, author, *We Are Not Monsters,* editor, Cosmo Girl Magazine poll (2001)

[12]Insight on the News, Feb 22, 1999, Article: Love Gets Lab Tests by Joyce Howard Price

[13]Professor Robert Friar Department Biological Sciences Ferris State University *Discovery Health Channel—The Science of Love: Falling in Love.*

[14]Cane, William, author of The Art of Kissing, Discovery Health Channel—The Science of Love: Falling in Love.

[15]Berman & Berman. *Discovery Health Channel* (2002)

[16]Newsweek June 3, 2002 Article: *Meet the Gamma Girls* by Meadows, Susannah

[17]Dr. Laura Berman on Berman & Berman. *Discovery Health Channel*

[18]*The G Spot Orgasm* by Alice Kahn, Beverly Whipple and John D. Perry, pp 20 & 33.

[19]CDC Healthy People 2010 Campaign. http://www.cdc.gov/nchstp/dstd/dstdp.html

[20]Time Magazine Feb 18, 2002—Kaiser Family Foundation

[21]American Social Health Association: http://www.ashastd.org/stdfaqs/statistics.html (2002)

[22]American Social Health Association: www.ashastd.org/stdfaqs/condom_nopics.html

[23]Singh S and Darroch JE, Trends in sexual activity among adolescent American women: 1982-1995, *Family Planning Perspectives,* 1999, 31(5): 211-219; special tabulations by The Alan Guttmacher Institute (AGI) of data from the 1995 National Survey of Family Growth; and Sonenstein FL et al., *Involving Males in Preventing Teen Pregnancy: A Guide for Program Planners,* Washington, DC: The Urban Institute, 1997, p. 12

[24]Harlap S, Kost K and Forrest JD, *Preventing Pregnancy, Protecting Health: A New Look at Birth Control Choices in the United States,* New York: AGI, 1991, Figure 5.4, p. 36

[25]Special tabulations by The Alan Guttmacher Institute of Ibid, Table 5 and of data from the 1995 National Survey of Family Growth

[26]AGI, Teenage pregnancy: overall trends and state-by-state information, New York: AGI, 1999, Table 1; and Henshaw SK, U.S. Teenage pregnancy statistics with comparative statistics for women aged 20-24, New York: AGI, 1999, p. 5

[27]AGI, Teenage pregnancy: overall trends and state-by-state information, New York: AGI, 1999, Table 1; and Henshaw SK, U.S. Teenage pregnancy statistics with comparative statistics for women aged 20-24, New York: AGI, 1999, p. 5.

[28]Henshaw SK, Unintended pregnancy in the United States, *Family Planning Perspectives,* 1998, 30(1):24-29 & 46, Table 1

[29]AGI, *Sex and America's Teenagers,* New York: AGI, 1994, p. 38

[30]Donovan P, *Testing Positive: Sexually Transmitted Disease and the Public Health Response,* New York: AGI, 1993, pp. 24-25

[31]Glei DA, Measuring contraceptive use patterns among teenage and adult women, *Family Planning Perspectives,* 1999, 31(2):73-80, Tables 1 and 2.

[32]Befrienders International, non-profit organization http://www.befrienders.org/myths/false7.htm

[33]"Domestic Violence," Microsoft® Encarta® Online Encyclopedia 2002

http://encarta.msn.com © 1997-2002 Microsoft Corporation. All Rights Reserved.

[34]Time Magazine September, 2001—University of North Carolina at Chapel Hill.

[35]"Domestic Violence," Microsoft® Encarta® Online Encyclopedia 2002

http://encarta.msn.com © 1997-2002 Microsoft Corporation. All Rights Reserved.

[36]Education Wife Assault Toronto, Ontario, Canada http://www.womanabuseprevention.com

[37]Education Wife Assault Toronto, Ontario, Canada http://www.womanabuseprevention.com

[38]*The Brain Game* abc news July 31, 2002

http://abcnews.go.com/onair/DailyNews/braingame020731.html

[39]AGI, *Sex and America's Teenagers,* New York: AGI, 1994, pp. 19-20.

[40]AGI, *Sex and America's Teenagers,* New York: AGI, 1994, pp. 38

[41]AGI, Teenage pregnancy: overall trends and state-by-state information, New York: AGI, 1999, Table 1; and Henshaw SK, U.S. Teenage pregnancy statistics with comparative statistics for women aged 20- 24, New York: AGI, 1999, p. 5.

[42]CDC Healthy People 2010 Campaign Data Result: http://www.cdc.gov/std/stats/2000 AppHealthy2010.htm

[43]Cosmo Girl Magazine. Sabrina Solin Wells, author of *"We Are Not Monsters"*

[44]Centers for Disease Control & Prevention. *CDC Update,* January 1997.

[45]Simanski, Julia Weeks Reprinted from *Adolescence Magazine* Spring, 1998

[46]Center for Domestic Violence Prevention http://www.cdvp.org/teens/

[47]AGI, *Sex and America's Teenagers,* New York: AGI, 1994, pp. 19-20.

[48]AGI, *Sex and America's Teenagers,* New York: AGI, 1994, pp. 38

[49]AGI, *Teenage pregnancy: overall trends and state-by-state information,* New York: AGI, 1999, Table 1; and Henshaw SK, U.S. *Teenage pregnancy statistics with comparative statistics for women aged 20- 24,* New York: AGI, 1999, p. 5.

[50]CDC Healthy People 2010 Campaign Data Result: http://www.cdc.gov/std/stats/2000AppHealthy2010.htm

[51]Berman & Berman For Women Only, *Discovery Health Channel,* May 28, 2002, "Virginity"

[52]Centers for Disease Control & Prevention. CDC Update, January 1997

[53]Simanski, Julia Weeks Reprinted from *Adolescence Magazine* Spring, 1998

[54]Maslund, Molly, MSNBC article, *'Beyond the Bird & the Bees'* March 20, 2001, http://www.msnbc.com/news/535245.asp

[55]Remez L. *Oral sex among adolescents: is it sex or is it abstinence?* Fam Plann Perspect 2000; 32:298-304.

[56]Kaiser Family Foundation, *Nat'l Survey of Adolescents and Young Adults: Sexual Health Knowledge, Attitudes and Experiences.* May, 2003

[57]Maslund, Molly, MSNBC article, *'Beyond the Bird & the Bees'* March 20, 2001, http://www.msnbc.com/news/535245.asp

[58]Pinkerton, Steven D. (2001). *A relative risk-based, disease-specific definition of sexual abstinence failure rates.* Health Education & Behavior, Vol.28 (1): 10-20 (February 2001).

[59]Center for Domestic Violence Prevention http://www.cdvp.org/teens/

[60]Kaiser Family Foundation, Nat'l Survey of Adolescents and Young Adults: Sexual Health Knowledge, Attitudes and Experiences. May, 2003, and, Remez L. Oral sex among adolescents: is it sex or is it abstinence? *Fam Plann Perspect 2000;* 32:298-304

Index

Sexual Revolution, 2–3, 165
sexually transmitted disease (STD)
    and alcohol consumption, 191
    and anal sex, 182
    and casual sex, 165
    having regular checkups, 191
    herpes, 190
    hotline, information about, 277
    list of (table), 192–193
    and oral sex, 180–181
    protecting against, 193
    statistics/facts about, 164, 193, 268
    transmitting during kissing, 177
Shallow Hal (movie), 30, 276
silences, handling when flirting, 50–51
sincerity, 48
slapping, as abuse, 152
sleep habits, effects of abuse on, 206
small talk, ideas for, 49
smell, role of, in attraction, 24
smiling, 46,100
solitude, appreciating, 254
soul kiss, 280
specifics, focusing on during fights, 156
speech, flirting using, 46
spit, and kissing, 176
sponge birth control, 194
stalemates, 159
stalking, 83
STD. *See* sexually transmitted disease
stereotypes, 29–30. *See also* imago
sterility, and sexually transmitted disease, 190
Strike Out dates, 117
style, personal, communicating, 33–34
substance abuse, 129, 206, 232
successful relationships, 13, 124
sugar, for post-break-up therapy, 252
suicide
    hotlines, information about, 278
    threats of following break up, 241
    warning signals, 200–201
support
    from family/friends, 116, 203, 240–242, 252, 255
    mutual, in healthy relationships, 129
    need for, to get out of abusive relationships, 210–211
syphilis, 193

T
table manners, 107–108, 278
talking during sex, 180
Tao of Steve, The (movie), 52–53, 276
technical knowledge of sex, limits of, 7
Teen Dating Project, 272
teen love, 230–231
teen pregnancy. *See* pregnancy risks
teen suicide. *See* suicide
telephones
    for asking someone out, 69–70
    for breaking up, 239
    cell phones on dates, 92, 113, 118, 172
    long-distance relationships, 142
tenderness, 16, 280
time. *See also* dating; manners; punctuality
    with families, 64, 88–89, 94
    for getting to know someone, 12–13, 82, 88, 116, 125

for grieving, 249, 256
    personal, 129, 134–137, 254
    for sex, 187, 280
timeouts
    during arguments, 157
    for Drama Queens, 224–225
timing
    and anal sex, 182
    of kissing, 176
tipping, 105–106, 278
to-do lists, 250–251, 254
tone of voice, 139–140
torture, playful, 207–208
touch
    flirting using, 46
    sensitivity of breasts and nipples, 178
towels, using during sex, 178, 186
trash-talking, 241–242
Trichomoniasis, 193
trust, 124–125, 129
    implied versus earned, 125
    and openness to intimacy, 127
type (imago), 25–27

U
urethra, 178

V
vagina
    dental dams, 181
    G-spot, 185
    lubrication during foreplay, 178
    slang names for, 189
vaginitis, 193
values, shared, as component of attraction, 38–39
verbal abuse, 204–205
victimhood, and high-drama relationships, 223
violence, 156, 203–204. *See also* abusive relationships
virginity, definitions of, 164
voice, tone of, 34, 139–140
vulnerability, and intimacy, 126–127

W
walk/gait, and attractiveness, 34
walks, long, as post-breakup therapy, 253–254
wants, communicating, 140–141
washing hands, 183. *See also* cleanliness
watches, wearing on dates, 113
When Harry Met Sally (movie), 186, 276
wimpy behavior
    versus assertiveness, 36–37
    avoiding when flirting, 54
withdrawal, on dates, handling, 116
women
    asking men out, 70
    attraction to older men, 81
    as Drama Queens, 213
    flirting behaviors, 46–47
    importance of foreplay to, 178
    manners for, 100–101
    and oral sex, 181
    orgasms, 183–187
    paying for dates, 59–61, 101–102
    responses to flirting, 51–52
    worries about breast size, 188
"wooing," versus stalking, 83
word choice, and communication, 139